Charles
AZNAVOUR
Memories of My Life

Charles AZNAVOUR
Memories of My Life

SCHIRMER
TRADE
BOOKS

Exclusive Distributors
Music Sales Limited,
8/9 Frith Street,
London W1D 3JB, UK.

Music Sales Corporation,
257 Park Avenue South,
New York, NY 10010, USA.

Macmillan Distribution Services,
53 Park West Drive,
Derrimut, Vic 3030,
Australia.

To the Music Trade only:
Music Sales Limited,
8/9 Frith Street,
London W1D 3JB, UK.

PHOTO CREDITS
All photographs from the Charles Aznavour Collection, except: section 2/page 8: © BIPNA;
2/9 © Lévon Sayan; 2/10 & 11: © Présidence de la République Française/service photographique;
2/12: © L. Castel; 2/15: © L. Castel; 2/16: © M. Pelletier.

Every effort has been made to trace the copyright holders of the photographs in this book but one or
two were unreachable. We would be grateful if the photographers concerned would contact us.

Typeset by Phoenix Photosetting, Chatham, Kent
Printed by Creative Print & Design, Ebbw Vale, Wales

A catalogue record for this book is available from the British Library.

Visit Omnibus Press on the web at www.omnibuspress.com

To my parents, and in order of appearance:

To Aïda, Seda, Ulla, Katia, Mischa, Nicolas, Lyra, Jacob, Leïla,

With special thanks to Stéphanie Chevrier for the confidence that she had in me and her help in putting my thoughts in order,

And also to Gérard Davoust who for years has encouraged me to believe in myself whenever I doubted my ability to write anything else besides verse,
And thanks, once again, to both of you for correcting my spelling mistakes.

Contents

PART 2

Contents

Preface to UK Edition

Not expressing myself sufficiently well in English I am unable to make a correct translation in this language. I am nevertheless particularly attached to the fact that my songs in a language other than mine are the exact reflection of what I intended to express in my texts, I have therefore translated them myself. This translation will seem a little strange to you, but in fact it is aimed at helping authors who translate or adapt my texts to do so satisfactorily. Moreover, my collaborators such as Herbert Kretzmer or Dee Shipman, to name only those two, do not speak French. My translations might amuse you, but more importantly you will see at the end of the book (while reading the versions I had the pleasure of interpreting) the surprising result and astonishing work arising from my collaborators talent, which I would once more like to thank.

Foreword

Telling your life story is no easy task: how do you avoid sounding pretentious, wearying the reader, or even offending those whose names you have mentioned or left out? You often hear: tell us about your life, your misfortunes, your success, the people you have met, and, most of all, your love affairs. And why not the way I make love?

I am a discreet man, even if I am unafraid of words. A certain sense of reserve, a secretive side, prevents me from baring my soul easily, from shining the spotlight too brightly on myself, from using words such as "triumph" and other superlatives associated with successful careers.

PART 1

PART 1

CHAPTER 1

On With The Show!

These days, organic is all the rage, or bio, as we call it in French; what we eat, drink, and produce has to be organic. I, in turn, resolved to go with the flow and produce my memoirs organically, as a stream of reminiscences. Oh, the idea didn't suddenly jump up and bite me on the nose; no, with biographies being in vogue, a number of publishers, and highly prestigious ones at that, had intimated that they would be interested in publishing my story. I went away and thought about it long and hard. I wouldn't say that I am slow, but it took me fifteen years to come to a decision. I had already produced an autobiography, in 1974, but for this first effort I had enlisted the help of journalist Jean Nolli who rewrote the pages of prose that I gave him. It was something akin to my life, but the voice was not mine.

After much thought – fifteen years, which should give you some idea of just how unconvinced I had been of the interest of the exercise – I got down to the task in earnest, recalling best-selling American author Harold Robbins' words to me: "People love a success story, especially when it's been a fight and things were tough in the beginning." When it comes to tough beginnings, I have had a lion's share, and as for putting up a fight, I owe nothing to anyone. I've had plenty of kicks in the teeth – I still have a few bruises in my soul and on my chin – and a few artistic kicks in the pants! So here we are. I have taken the plunge and immersed myself in the past. Curiously, I have no idea if my life and journey are of any interest to anyone other than myself, but we shall see; nothing ventured, nothing gained. I have had enough setbacks in my life to have forged a certain philosophy of my own. If what I am about to relate succeeds in interesting you, and you enjoy it, I will be delighted. Otherwise? Heavens above, it won't be the first time, and I'm sure that, once more, I will survive.

I wanted to sing. I was told that I would do better to give it up, that I stood no earthly chance of getting anywhere, that no one with a voice like mine or who looked the way I did could seriously hope to make it as an entertainer. I wanted to write lyrics and songs; I was discouraged at every turn. Here again, there could be no future for a simpleton like me in this field. Those who listened to my lyrics assured me of the contrary, and none more so than the audience; I am writing my memoirs today knowing full well that I am neither a writer, nor a literary person. However, I have lived a life that is perhaps, and I mean *perhaps*, worth the telling. What kind of reaction should I expect? Having reached an age where I have few illusions about myself, I still have my doubts. What is more important, the style, the way of writing, or what I have to say? Should I renounce the pen, as I was advised to renounce singing. Ah, but then after everything I've been through, what matter, to hell with it! So, once, twice, thrice and many times upon a time, there was a boy who went by the unpronounceable name of Charles Aznavourian.

CHAPTER 2

Hapless Beginnings

I look at the sun through the tinted lenses of my glasses; I am not bored in these rare moments of inactivity. I confess that I am never bored. I sometimes think about the fact that I am the son of stateless parents, what Americans would call a *survivor*. If I have everything I want now, I have not forgotten where I came from, no, I keep it safe in a corner of my mind, and these days, having reached the unexpected age of seventy-nine summers, or should I say autumns, when I have nothing in particular to do, I lose myself in reverie. Young people dream of their future; since my life is mostly behind me now, I plunge into my past to recharge my batteries – I should say *our* past, for the past is never purely personal; on the contrary, it is a collective experience, especially when you come from an Armenian family. I lose myself in reverie, and think to myself that I might never have opened my eyes and seen this fiery globe at all. I might have remained locked in my father's seed as he suffered, sweating and struggling to stay alive, on that long walk, that cursed march across the desert, from Istanbul to Damas. The Ottoman state police and the Kurdish hordes – who were later subjected to the same fate – hounded and harried those unfortunate souls for the few riches that they were carrying with them, like their gold teeth. Kill an intellectual, impale a priest, have a hanging and cut off their heads, rape a young girl, an old woman, and smash a baby's head against a tree just to hear the noise it makes… Perhaps I might have been miscarried at birth on the desert sand, while my wretched mother continued her slow, agonizing march towards death, legs bathed in the blood that she would have shed when she released me into this world, a world from which the Young Turk government fiercely hoped to rid them all. Eliminated, annihilated; to hell with the Armenians and on with the final solution! Such a delightful turn of phrase!

Der el Zor: a cemetery for close to one and a half million of my people, my family, my ancestors; robbed, raped and murdered in the name of race, in the name of religion, in the name of what, in truth, I ask you? In the name of the Envers, the Talaats[1], those murderous pashas, faithless, lawless assassins, who interpreted the Koran to suit their own purposes, and still, the Koran does not absolve these bloody deeds. Talaat is the only infamous criminal whose statue is still standing; right in the centre of a square in Turkey.

Final Solution? You failed, you bastards, you didn't get me. And I'm still here, like it or not; a man of memory. But I have not become a sworn enemy of the Turkish people, and I would love to visit the country of my mother's birth, but, but, but …

They Fell (Ils Sont Tombés)[2]

They fell not knowing why
Men women children who only wanted to live
With heavy gestures, like drunken men
Mutilated, massacred, eyes wide open with fear
They fell invoking the name of their God
In the front of their churches, or the steps of their doors
Herded into the desert, staggering in cohort
Stricken low with thirst, hunger, iron and fire

---

[1] Turkish politicians, members of the Young Turk party, who, together with Djemel Pasha, instigated the 1908 and 1909 coups d'etat in Turkey, and formed the triumvirate with him in 1913.
[2] From *Ils Sont Tombés / They Fell* by Charles Azanvour.

CHAPTER 3

Here I Come

I was born at the end of a journey from hell, at the gates of the paradise that we call emigration. Those who had escaped the genocide, like my parents, had known so much adversity that most of them avoided talking about their families and forefathers, or indeed spoke so little of them that, in the course of our lives, my kindred companion – my sister Aïda – and I have only been able to piece together small fragments of our family's past: very little, if the truth be told. "Look where we came from, look how far we have come," they used to say.

Whether they were being overly protective or whether the memories were simply too painful to recall, our parents seldom brought up the subject of the hundreds of thousands of Armenians now scattered across the globe, the flight of these people to escape the horror until they were able to find refuge in a host country. Rare snatches of conversations between those who had witnessed and survived the same events have left us with only a vague idea of the exodus. What is certain is that they did not travel first class carrying a few bare essentials and a surplus of luxuries in Vuitton cases, with the requisite credit cards in their wallets. Today, when I see immigrants from all corners of the globe holding the shabby bags that they have bundled up as best they can and that contain all their worldly possessions – a miserable collection of odds and ends, a few paltry belongings that they hold precious but which would cause even the lowest of second-hand dealers to turn up his nose – at the sight of these heartrending figures, I feel ashamed and guilty even though I have had no part in their misfortune.

When I see hapless illegal workers who have come from heavens knows where to seek out a better life in our country, which they believe to be a land of plenty, I always feel a pang of sorrow, imagining the journey of my uncles, aunts, and grandparents who never returned from the "Club Med of Horror".

How did others manage to make it out alive? God alone knows. And, besides, where was He anyway, He who is so often absent at such times; God, Allah, Jehovah, where were You? In Turkey, in Germany, and in Cambodia, where were You when we needed You? Try and figure that one out.

I Would Like To Know

I should like to see any power in the world
destroy this race,
this small tribe of unimportant people,
whose wars have been fought and lost,
whose structures have crumbled,
whose literature is unread, music is unheard
and prayers are no longer answered.
Go ahead, destroy Armenia.
See if you can do it.
Send them into the desert
without bread and water.
Burn their homes and churches.
Then see if they will not laugh,
sing and pray again.
For when any two of them meet
anywhere in the world,
see if they will not create
a New Armenia.[1]

[1] William Saroyan, extract from *My Name Is Aram* (1940).

Today, France has officially recognised the Armenian genocide. It has taken eighty-five years for her to consent to do this. For reasons of State, it was said. So it is done, at last, but while I am proud of my country's decision and pleased by it, I have no desire to crow victory. In fact I have never been virulent on the subject. For my parents, the simple fact of recognition was the key; the reparations, the restitution of land and homes were not the most important aspects; they had no intention of returning to the old country, too many memories lay buried there, some wonderful, some unbearably painful. There is no doubt that this official recognition constitutes an important initial step forward, but until Turkey has recognised the genocide, it remains disproportionately one-sided.

I feel that these few lines about the tragic past of the Armenian people are fundamental in explaining who we are and where we come from.

Autobiography (Autobiographie)[2]

I opened my eyes on a sad furnished room
Rue Monsieur le prince in the Latin Quarter
In the midst of singers and actors
Who had a past, but no tomorrow
Marvelous people somehow a little unconventional
Who spoke Russian and also Armenian

Nevertheless, whatever certain Turkish or Azeri journalists may have said or written in the past, I have never – and I mean never – marched in Paris or anywhere else, on April 24th, to commemorate the massacre; nor have I had weapons sent to Karabakh, or even organised the collection of funds to buy weapons during the war between the Azeris and the Karabakh Armenians. I have too much respect for human life to dirty my hands by doing something that would result in the death or injury of women and children. I prefer to believe – naively, perhaps – in diplomacy, in the goodness, intelligence and honesty of men, even if diplomacy, which is swimming in petrol, has failed on all counts thus far.

[2] From *Autobiographie / Autobiography* by Charles Aznavour.

My mother, Knar Bagdassarian, had a knack for creating family ties – she was probably driven by a sense of loss and longing for a family that she had not known. Whenever she ran into someone from the town where she was born, upon hearing their family name she would recall the grandfather or the grandmother. And even if they had only been neighbours, they were suddenly practically family. I used to call them "my mortar cousins[3]": "Oh, yes, he was a baker, or a dairy-man…" My mother was Turkish, since she was born in Turkey, in the same way that I am French. So she was a Turk of Armenian origin, born in Adapazari of a father who was a tobacco expert. She had two brothers and a sister; they all went missing during the genocide, God alone knows what happened to them. My Father, Mischa Aznavourian, was a Georgian of Armenian origin, and born in Akhaltzkha. The Georgian Armenians were not subjected to the genocide. My parents were both performing artists; my mother was an actress, my father a singer blessed with a voice that prompted Louiguy – the hit composer of *Cerisier Rose et Pommier Blanc*[4] among others – who heard him sing one day, to say: "It seems to me that the voice in this family has skipped a generation!" How my parents met, where and when they were married, we do not know. This was back when marriage registers were kept by the church, which served as the public records office. Our churches, alas, were pillaged and destroyed … One thing I can be certain of: I never heard my parents vilify modern Turkey, they never raised us to hate the Turkish people. On the contrary, I always heard them say what a beautiful country it was, that the women were striking, that the cuisine was the best in all the Middle East, and that, when it came down to it, we had much in common with these people. If there had been no genocide – or if it had at least been recognised – this bone of contention would not be so deeply buried in the memories of the second and third generations of our peoples today.

[3] "Mes cousins de murs" – literally my *wall* cousins.
[4] *Cherry Pink And Apple Blossom White.*

10

Letter To A Turkish Friend (Lettre A Un Ami Turque)[5]

You have a thorn in your foot
My brother
As I have one in my heart
For you
As for me
It makes things difficult
Uneasy

The rose has thorns
If we are heedless
It may draw a drop of blood
At your finger tip, but
If you are careful
It will offer its beauty
Embellishing and perfuming your days
Even flattering your palates
With its sweetness

I love the rose
But her thorns exist
There is no changing that
My brother
If you should choose to remove
The thorn in my heart
The one in your foot
Would disappear of its own accord
And you and I would be
Free
And brothers

Pursued and harried despite my father's Georgian passport, my parents managed to find passage on an Italian boat, in Istanbul. My mother was already on board when a zealous soldier, dismissing the

[5] Charles Aznavour, 1997.

passport, barred my father's way upon hearing the hated language. The captain came to his aid, declaring the boat to be international territory and shouting that no one had the right to stop a passenger from boarding. A rich American woman of Armenian origin had offered to pay the passage of every survivor who managed to crawl on board. The boat headed out to sea and disembarked the Armenians and Greeks in Salonica, where my sister was born. In a gesture of thanks to Italy, she was given the name of an Italian opera – Aïda – which is actually an Egyptian first name. A year passed, time enough to learn Greek, their sights set on the mirage of America, my parents and sister arrived in Paris, via Marseilles I believe, where they were issued with a Nansen visa, a kind of residence permit that had to be frequently renewed. Then came the waiting at the American Embassy, in the hope of obtaining a visa, the famous visa that led to the promise land, the land of opportunity where anyone could try their luck and maybe become rich and powerful.

CHAPTER 4

Stateless

The Emigrant (L'Emigrant)[1]

All stations look about the same
All the ports die of boredom
Every road comes together
To lead to infinity
In the crush of life
There is always a passer-by
Who never had a lucky line of destiny in hand
And who became an emigrant

"You want to emigrate to the United States? Do you have friends there, family, money? What is your religion? Do you speak English? You will have to wait, this year's Armenian quota is complete. Fill in this form, someone will let you know when you can leave, assuming, *of course,* that your application is accepted."

Twelve months of hope in a cramped lodging on the boulevard Brune, twelve months of hope and privation, of queuing up at the

---

[1] From *L'Emigrant / The Emigrant* by Charles Aznavour.

Prefecture[2], twelve months of trying to make yourself understood – no one speaks Armenian in inner city Paris.

"Anyway, what exactly is Armenian? Are you Russian, Jewish, Arab? What then? A stateless person with a Nansen passport? You are stateless then, foreigners, that we have had the good grace to take in! Fine, but don't come up here and bother us, just wait your turn, go and sit down on that bench with the others and keep it shut, someone will call you. We have more important things to do here at the Prefecture than dealing with indigents. Your wife is pregnant? Well, she's not the only one in the world ..." And bang, the counter window is slammed shut in your face. Come back tomorrow, and the day after, and the day after that, and so it goes on for weeks on end, because there is always some document or certificate missing, or some stamp that has expired.

But Paris is beautiful, especially in the spring. There are others besides the Prefecture officials, like the neighbours who are kinder and more understanding, and the other emigrants, the Jews, the Poles, the Italians, the Russians, and, of course, the Armenians. Everyone supports each other, they understand each other, they tip each other off and help each other out. After all, we're all stuck in the same sorry boat, aren't we?

The long-awaited visa finally arrived; but my parents no longer wished to leave. My mother was about to give birth, and they liked this country. My father earned a living singing at dances and evening parties organised by emigrants of all nationalities – he sang well, in Russian and Armenian. They now had to find an affordable place to have the baby, at a hospital for the poor. On May 22nd, 1924, at the Tarnier Clinic in the Rue d'Assas, a few weeks late – it's just like show business, you have to play hard to get – I made my entrance into the world. Eight pounds – that takes some doing!

"What are you going to call him? Shâhnourh? What was that, Shâhnourh?" It was too much for the nurse who was already running round in circles. "Right, how about Charles? It's really more civilised. Well, all right then, Charles it is ..." What a stroke of luck! If she only

---

[2] The Préfecture issues official documents such as residency permits and driving licences in France.

14

knew today, that nurse would be claiming royalties for the use of my name – yet more costs! Whew! That was a close call.

Mischa waited three days – well he had to celebrate my arrival, didn't he – before going along to the 6th arrondissement[3] town hall and registering the birth of Charles. I'm lucky he remembered at all. For when it came to filling out the residence permit, my father could not remember my mother's maiden name – Bagdassarian – and he gave them the first name that popped into his head: Papazian. Which prompted my poor mother to say: "Thanks, you've managed to bury my parents a second time!"

Some expressions just stick in your mind . . .

Who?[4]

He will take your mouth
He will take your bed
And will bury me
For a second time

Boosted by my arrival, the family was then made up of my father, my mother, my sister, my mother's grandmother, the only surviving member of that branch of the family, and myself. We moved into a room of about two-hundred-and-fifteen square feet on the second floor of a furnished flat, at 36, Rue Monsieur-le-Prince, in the heart of the Latin Quarter, in a building owned by Monsieur and Madame Mathieu. It was a dark room with a washing area composed of a kind of rickety dresser that held a washbowl and a pitcher for water; next to that, there was a sort of alcove where my parent's bed stood, with a curtain that they would draw at bedtime "like in the theatre". Talk about privacy! My great grandmother slept on a sagging divan, and my sister, Aïda, and I, head to foot, on a small, folding iron bed that had to be set up every evening. The room was furbished – and what fine furbishing it was – with a Godin stove that served for heating and cooking. Water had to be fetched from the landing, and the toilets

---

[3] The city of Paris is divided into 20 arrondissements.
[4] From *Qui / Who* by Charles Aznavour.

were located the floor above us; the height of luxury and comfort! The room was so small that, on one occasion, Aïda actually sat down on the stove; luckily, she was not too badly burnt! We used to play on the landing where an old dilapidated moleskin bistro bench stood. I remember that my father and I would often sit there as if in our living room, chewing away happily on what we called "sam sam gum".

Hey! Let's not get ahead of ourselves. This is about me. Now let me see, where was I? Oh, yes! So there I was, howling and hollering, giving it my all, and for free at this point, in this 6th arrondissement establishment. My voice went unnoticed, except by my mother; it was my first flop – there were many more to come but that's another story, and one that I will have plenty of time to tell later.

It was at this time that our paternal grandfather – whom my sister, Aïda, had nicknamed "Aznavor Baba", a nickname he kept for the rest of his life – arrived in Paris with his mistress in tow, a buxom Prussian woman who had lured him away from his family and children. Why did he come? It's easy to guess: to get away from his wife and the unwelcome attention of others in view of his enviable position as head cook to the Governor of Tiflis, the Georgian capital, and to avoid having to divorce – both difficult and frowned upon in those days. It probably also had something to do with the fact that communist revolutionaries had taken to forcing employees of the rich and powerful to sweep the streets while enduring insults and jeering. The couple had declared themselves to be married upon their arrival in France. It made things much simpler! But how had they managed to turn up here and find us? Nobody knows. Since they were not Turkish Armenians they were among the fortunate who had been spared the murderous furor of the Young Turks' henchmen. Aznavor Baba must have had nice little nest egg hidden away, for no sooner had he found somewhere to live in Paris than he put in a bid for a restaurant, which he later baptised *Restaurant Caucase.* One of the first Russian restaurants in Paris, it was located at 3 Rue Champollion, a stone's throw from the Sorbonne. The opening night coincided exactly with the date of my arrival into the world. So you might say that I was born into the restaurant trade.

Our grandfather was an irascible man: "Must be the cook's piano playing that makes him edgy". His Teutonic consort bore the brunt of it; perhaps, deep down, he resented her for having driven him to abandon his family at what was proving to be such a distressing time in the history of that part of the globe. Whenever he felt a pressing need to vent his frustration, pointing to the restaurant floor, he would say in a controlled voice: "Batval", which is Russian for cellar. She, like the obedient German she was, would lift the trapdoor that led below and make her way down there with her head hung low, to be followed by her husband who would then administer a good, solid hiding. After which, pacified, he would return to his ovens; the rest of us would be delighted. She deserved it. Elisabeth Christopher was her real name. She had been born in Russia, into one of the Prussian families who had followed Catherine the Great there; she could manage a few words of Armenian and get by in Russian, but she spoke flawless German. I was the only one she liked in the family and she always spoke to me in German. When the Wehrmacht invaded France, she went and offered her services to the German Embassy, where they employed her to do the Kommandantur's housework. *Heil Hitler!* With a wipe wipe here. *Heil Hitler!* And a sweep sweep there. *Deutschland über alles ...* Oh, the shame of my parents who were actively involved in the Communist cause. When my grandfather died, she set off to find her roots in Berlin. Roots run underground, and that is where she must have ended up, under the Allied bombings, poor woman, for we never heard hide nor hair of her after that.

A Curious, Curious Cousin

Not everyone is lucky enough to have a fakir in the family. One of my mother's cousins, the fakir, Tahra Bey, had his hour of glory in the years which preceded and followed the war. During his performance he would lay on a bed of nails, piercing his cheek and his body with a long needle, and claimed to be able to bleed at will. He used to persuade the audience that the sea would engulf the room, thus creating a moment of panic. When some members of the audience attempted to flee, he would use his powers of persuasion to allay all fears; the sea would retract and calm would be restored in the room. Cataleptic trance was the highlight of his act: he would lay in a coffin filled with sand, the lid would be nailed down, it was then submerged in a lake

17

or the sea for forty-five minutes, after which time, it would be brought back on to land. He used to hypnotise people, too. My mother told me that when he was a child he had tried to hypnotise her, but that it was he who fell asleep. Tahra was quite a celebrity, and a womaniser to boot, the archetypal ladies man. He is supposed to have enjoyed numerous affairs with the stars of his time. To supplement his income he read horoscopes and sold small phials of a liquid with supposedly magical properties.

As a very young man, Tahra had travelled to India to study his art, notably that of hypnosis. He made use of his deep, disturbing, black eyes, while the beard that he had grown lent him the air of a wise man, quite belying the life of revelry in which he indulged every night. My parents had met up with him again in Salonica not long after the Armenian genocide. My jobless father found himself employed as cousin Tahra's secretary. His job was to prepare the envelopes that contained the mysterious talismans, which would guarantee fame and fortune. In Salonica, Tahra had found the perfect dupe: a local commissioner. He had convinced the man that treasure was buried somewhere in the vicinity of his birthplace and that excavations would have to be carried out to discover where it lay. Thanks to the bogus digs, he was able to supplement his weekly income and make ends meet. He managed to live off the official's gullability for a good six months before he was forced to leave town to avoid being thrown into prison. One day, my father pointed out to him that the magical fluid for the phials had been exhausted. "Go and pee in it, that'll do the trick," was Tahra's reply.

Tahra was neither a wise man nor a holy one. He was an artist and liked to have a good time. A journalist – whose first name escapes me, but whose surname was Heuzé – wrote a book about him called *Fakir, Fumiste et Compagnie*[5]. But it didn't diminish Tahra; the purveyor of dreams, whether fakir, phoney, artist or poet, is always welcome.

But let's get back, if you will, to my parents, to my own life, and what happened next! Although he continued to sing and was very well paid for his appearances at events organised by associations of nostalgic Russian and Armenian exiles, my father essentially started

---

[5] *"Fakirs and Phoneys Et Al."*

18

working for himself, which allowed us to move to a more comfortable furnished apartment at 73 Rue Saint-Jacques; the people who ran it were adorable. The owner, Madame Petit, who came from the Limousin region, her dog Toto – who used to have a large bowl of milky coffee with bread soldiers for breakfast – the sister, Liliane – Madam Petit's, not the dog's – and her husband, Monsieur Rigolo, basically adopted us. We children were more likely to be found in the lodge than up on our own floor, and the local kids and I used to play together, riding pell-mell down the streets on boards that were mounted on ball bearings, which had the passers-by jumping out of their skins.

My mother was also working, sewing and doing embroidery for some of the local stores or those in the Faubourg Saint Honoré district. My parents managed to put aside enough money to allow my father to start up his own business and open a Caucasian restaurant on the Rue de la Huchette, where the Huchette theatre stands today. Fate is strange indeed; my parents, both artists, were obliged, since they had not yet sufficiently mastered the language of their adoptive country, to work in the restaurant trade and the sewing trade in order to make ends meet, and years later, after it had closed its doors, the restaurant was transformed into a theatre, while Aïda and I took up the profession that should have been that of our parents. And so we had come full circle.

CHAPTER 5

Childhood Pastures

The Armenian Theatre

The wings of the stage were my childhood pastures
The streets of Paris my schooling
And life itself my teacher

In New York, The Yiddish Theater on 2nd Avenue was well-established. It was here that many film actors learned their craft. No equivalent existed in France, for either the Jewish or the Armenian community. However, there were a great many gifted actors and singers among the stateless, who did not speak French and who had been forced to accept whatever work they could find to keep their families fed. But they were itching, all the while, to get back on stage and twice a month, one of these actors would assume the role of show producer. It was always the same process; the temporary director of the troupe would pick a scenario and do the rounds of the frustrated actors to cast the roles in the upcoming production – if you could call it a production. Between 1935 and 1939, many new plays were put on, primarily comedies. The most interesting playwright was called Krikor Vahan, and I often wonder what became of the manuscripts of his work; his plays could be revived today in Armenia, and perhaps, once they had been translated, even performed in Parisian theatres.

A meeting would be held at one of the actor's homes to cast the play, discuss the costumes, which the wives would create, and set dates for the rehearsals that would be held after work, once again, at the home of one of these actor-come-tailors, -packers or -linotypists. The choice of the theatre depended on the available funds of the entrepreneur in question; if the budget were a meagre one, then it would be the Scientific Society Hall, near Odéon. The stage at this venue came with a choice of two fixed backdrops consisting of small metal panels that could be rotated to show an insipid interior on one side, or a garden scene of completely washed-out greens, on the other. When they had a little more money in the kitty, performances were held at the Salle de la Mutualité, near the Place Maubert; and if it were a classic French play translated into Armenian prose or verse, then it would be held at the Salle de l'Iéna, not far from the metro station of the same name. Rehearsals were always tumultuous affairs, as each protagonist would invariably recall some detail or other of the original production. On the day of the performance, curtain up would be scheduled for nine p.m. The audience would trickle in and take their seats; if the auditorium was not full by half past nine, then the performance would not start until a quarter to ten. No one was in any hurry for this was a chance to catch up with one another. Only the actors, waiting in the wings, were nervous, and when the curtain was finally raised, everything would be ready: the women would have prepared the food that the actors were supposed to eat during the course of the performance – most Armenian plays include a scene that involves eating and drinking. And while the actors were putting on their faces – it wasn't called getting made up in those days – the men would pick at the food as they passed the table, a dolma here and a baklava there, which provoked no end of protestation from their wives who had gone to so much trouble and who had scrimped and saved like mad to be able to provide a sumptuous, generous, spread. So, during the meal scene, the plates having already been picked clean, so to speak, and the actors would have to pretend to eat and drink after all!

Once the performance was over, backstage, the takings would be counted. But since the tickets had been sold by the actors themselves and some of their friends, the result was often disastrous, in spite of a full house. Actors who had to provide for their family's needs and who were struggling to stay in the black each week would borrow from the funds they had raised from selling tickets, with the genuine intention of replacing the borrowed sum before the day of the performance. Unfortunately, this was often easier said than done. And so the time would come for vigorous debate and explanations, for shouting and wailing; pockets would be turned out to scrape together enough to pay the venue's hire fee, and they would take leave of each other swearing that this time was definitely the very last time. Until someone suggested a new play, and everyone threw themselves back into rehearsals with renewed passion and delight, and the whole comedy would start all over again.

I have always had a very special place in my heart for those actors and singers who, though frustrated, were passionate, and hungry for applause and contact with the audience. It was probably those actors, singers and musicians who made me want to take to the stage. They had a special light in their eyes, a mixture of joy and pride. It was doubtless when I learned of all that they had endured, their pain and their anguish, before they found refuge here in France, where they were finally able to rediscover the joys of performing together again in their native language, that the child that I was then came to realise that their destiny, on the stage, would also be his own.

A Sneak Preview

My debut performance in front of an audience was an impromptu one and my own initiative entirely. My parents were not able to stay away from the stage for any great length of time, any more than the other Armenian actors could; so they had formed a troupe of sorts and did their best to put on Armenian operettas. On performance nights, my parents, who could not afford to provide us with English or Swedish nannies, would leave Aïda and myself to run around freely backstage. One night – I must have been three years old – the show had not yet begun, I parted the front stage curtain and found myself face to face with the audience, whereupon I had the bright idea of launching into a recitation of Armenian poetry. Hearing the sound of applause, the artists backstage assumed that the audience were growing impatient and started to panic until someone came to reassure them. It was just a surprise support act, which, by Jove, seemed to be going over rather well. This was the only time in my life that I have ever performed on stage in Armenian; it was also the first time that I took pleasure in receiving applause. I suspect that it was that night, on stage at the Scientific Society Hall in front of an audience of immigrants, that I was first bitten by the bug that has never left me.

The Stage (Ce Métier)[1]

This trade
Is the worst, also the best
You can fight it but it owns you and haunts you
You can be an actor, dancer or singer
This trade is always in your heart

My First School

My first school was on the Rue Gît-le-Coeur, and I never went in without first paying a visit to the small greengrocers on the corner opposite, to stock up on liquorice whirls and licking toffee. They also sold transparent, multicoloured marbles with which my pals and I used to play epic tournaments. I was six years old at the time and used to have to cross the Place Saint-Michel to reach school. A small black lad, seven years older than I, who attended the same school, would accompany me. My father always gave him a banana. He may have believed that that was what all small coloured boys used to eat. I suspect that Banania's advertisement, which showed a beaming Somali infantryman eating a banana on its tins of drinking chocolate, may have had something to do with this. We subsequently lost sight of each other; Aïda and I often wondered what might have become of him, and then, in 1997, when I was appearing at the Palais du

---

[1] From *Ce Métier / The Entertainer* by Charles Aznavour

Congrès, in Paris, I was told that a Monsieur Alexandre Coloneaux had presented himself at the artists' entrance and that he wished to see me, if possible. Aïda was standing right next to me and suddenly the penny dropped. I saw a smiling man of around eighty approach. I was so surprised that I didn't know what to say, but having recovered from the shock, I sent someone out into the audience during the interval to find Alexandre and invited him to join me backstage at the end of the show. He may not have been my first classmate due the difference in our ages, but he was my first schoolmate.

My first mistress, as they were called then, was named Mademoiselle Jeanne and she lived on the top floor of the building. She had a soft spot for me and would often invite me into her small home to munch on biscuits. The other classes were taught by Monsieur and Madame Guette. He liked the way I recited La Fontaine's fables and had told my parents that I was surely destined to become an actor. The school was an independent Roman Catholic school, near the church of Saint Séverin. Seduced by the muffled, theatrical atmosphere of the place, and although I was not of the Catholic faith, I would serve mass every morning before going to school. The altar boy: my first costume, my first classic, an ageless production; it was admittedly only a minor supporting role, but even so!

La Huchette

My father had a real passion for gypsy music and particularly that of the Hungarian Tzigane. So he had a twelve-piece orchestra of musicians and singers brought over specially from Budapest, which took up a large part of the restaurant. The dining area was of a moderate size, the price of the meals modest, and my father used to feed a small number of students of Armenian origin, who came from all over, many from Abyssinia, to study medicine and whose parents used to forget or were simply not always able to provide for their needs. For all these reasons, even when all the tables were taken, while the atmosphere was extraordinary, the takings remained poor and insufficient. We made just enough to keep the business going without ever saving a penny. Then the inevitable happened. The depression of the 1930s forced my father to shut up shop.

Nevertheless, with unrelenting optimism he took over the management of a café in the Rue du Cardinal-Lemoine and moved us to a flat nearby, in the Rue des Fossés-Saint-Bernard. I had just turned nine and was sad to leave the school on the Rue Gît-le-Coeur; but as luck would have it, right opposite the café was a stage school for boys and girls. Our parents enrolled us there. When fate really wants to, it finds a way of pointing you in the right direction, whether you realise it or not. If you'll pardon the cliché: every cloud has a silver lining. We had lost the restaurant, we barely had two pennies to rub together, but we had ended up opposite the school that would change my whole life, and as a result, that of my whole family.

CHAPTER 6

The Days of Knee Pants

My First Audition

One September day, in 1933, I have no idea how I got the idea into my head, but I decided with nary a word to my parents to put pen to paper and offer my services to Monsieur Pierre Humble, the director and host of the Petit Monde theatre, which put on children's shows on Thursdays and national holidays. The letter was riddled with spelling mistakes, but then I wasn't trying to get into the French Academy. I waited impatiently for an answer; it soon arrived, confirming an audition date. I selected one of the piano pieces that were lying around at home and asked my mother to accompany me. Nothing compares to the horror of a children's audition; especially for my mother who had suddenly found herself presented with a fait accompli.

When we arrived, confronted by a horde of jabbering mothers busily telling anyone who was interested – and anyone who was not, for that matter – in loud, unintelligent voices, how talented and gifted their offspring were, my mother didn't know where to put herself; as for me, I got my first real taste of stage fright. When my turn came, I handed the sheet music to the pianist, explained to him what I intended to do and, using my foot, indicated the requisite tempo for the execution of my Caucasian dance. Silence, introduction, then, without glancing at the others, I launched into the "Russian Dance" to give it its French name. My *tchitchotka* came off without a hitch. When I had finished my number, I heard them say: "Thank you, please leave your address, we'll get in touch with you", and, heads bowed, my mother and I set off on our way home without much hope.

Two weeks later, I received a typed letter signed in red ink by Pierre Humble himself, which began: "Dear little Caucasian," and informed me of the date of my first appearance as well as the sum I was to receive as my fee. Back home, it was all hands on deck; I needed a costume, a *tcherkesska* (a Cossack coat with cartridge pockets), a silver belt, a *khantchal* (a curved dagger set with mock precious stones that was worn to one side), and, of course, supple soleless boots that allowed the dancer to stand on tiptoe as if barefoot. My mother set about making the outfit, and my father dug out the necessary accessories for my performance from a trunk. And so it was that, on the last Thursday before Christmas, 1933, I made my first appearance as a dancer, on stage at the old Trocadero. As far as my career is concerned, this day in 1933 marks the beginning, for it was the first time that I was paid for my services. After this, I often performed at the Petit Monde theatre in other troupes, Roland Pilain's and Madame Doriel's, always as a dancer in the light entertainment segment. But my dream was to appear in the theatrical segment.

Not Just School, But Stage School

So there we were in our new neighbourhood and as soon as Monday came around, Aïda and I crossed the street to go to school. What was special about this school, how was it different from other schools? Well, it wasn't really very different, except that children who had set their sights on becoming professional actors, dancers or musicians could continue with their schooling while learning their future profession. If a child had an evening theatre performance – the laws protecting child performers had not yet been introduced – he was allowed to take the following morning off school. In the same way, if a pupil had rehearsals in the afternoon, she only attended classed in the morning. A whole host of child actors, who went on to make names for themselves in theatre and cinema in the 1930s attended this stage school, which was directed by Raymond Rognoni, a member of the Comédie-Francaise. Rognoni was assisted by Madame Maréchale and the teaching staff included Madame Essertier, Madame Chabaud, and Mademoiselle Velutini. Twice a week, in the covered part of the school playground, Monsieur Guy Lainé taught classical dance. We had decent school meals there, and even now, if I close my eyes, I can sometimes smell the bread soup that was a staple on the menu.

It was during my time at this school that my heart skipped a beat for the very first time. She had blond hair and blue eyes – a sign of things to come! – she was Brazilian and her name was Graziella Fursman. I was twelve, she must have been sixteen or seventeen. Any glances we might have exchanged were purely accidental. Then she returned home to her country of origin. I didn't suffer in the slightest, I suppose that unspoken or platonic love is not made to last at that tender age . . .

Directors often came to the school to cast children's roles in plays, revue shows, or even films. We boys and girls would line up along the wall at the far end of the playground and the man would inspect us, asking questions. One day, a director got as far as me and asked:

"Can you do accents?"

"I can do any accent you want, or learn to do it."

"I need an African accent."

I reeled off a few words, dropping all my r's.

"Right," he said to me, "Be at the Champs Elysées studio on Monday morning. I may have a small role for you."

He spoke to me as if he were quite convinced that I had already worked in theatre, seeing that I was attending the stage school. I certainly wasn't going to put him right, and this was how I got my first job after the Caucasian dancing gig, in a thespian theatre. Blacked up, I played the part of Siki in a German play that had been successful across the Rhine, in Germany, Erick

29

Kastener's *Emile and The Detectives.* Unfortunately, in France, the production was taken off after only thirty performances. The play was dying on its feet and my father's café wasn't making us rich either, far from it. Once again, we upped and left. The new lodging at 2 Rue Béarn, not far from the Place des Vosges, was a small, dark flat with a low ceiling. Almost all the young friends I played with in the street were Jewish. What's Jewish? My father explained to us that it was a religion. So that's what it is! Invited into the family homes, I gradually became acquainted with their way of life, which was not so unlike that of our own, and picked up another accent.

At stage school I learned the tricks of the trade, where to go, how to find parts. We used to tip each other off. One day, when there was an audition at the Marigny theatre and one at the Madeleine, I attended both. At the Marigny, Pierre Fresnay had plans to direct a play by Edouard Bourdet, *Margot,* featuring a dazzling cast including Yvonne Printemps, Jacques Dusmesnil, Maddy Berry, and Sylvie, all in all fifty-four actors and actresses, something which today's directors can only dream of! I auditioned and landed the role of Henry of Navarre as a child, the future Henry IV. Jeanne Albret, Henry's mother, was played by the great Sylvie. At the Madeleine I had a less prestigious role: I played an altar boy in Shakespeare's *Much Ado About Nothing* – and that couldn't be closer to the truth! From Henri IV, in the first act, at the Marigny, to altar boy, at the Madeleine, in the second – the higher you fly, the farther you fall – the latter was more of a walk-on part than an actual role, but since the two theatres were located close to each other, I accepted both parts, which allowed me to bring enough home to help us through our latest financial crisis. I went everywhere on foot, even when I returned home in the evenings. Taking a taxi would have cost too much, and the Parisian streets were safe. I was so happy to be working and earning enough to help the family that, even when the weather was bad, I used to walk home with a spring in my step. It was 1935 – I was all of eleven years old, but I felt responsible. I would keep a few francs from my earnings and give the rest to my mother, who held the family purse strings.

Prior and the Cigalounettes[1]

My sister, Aïda, who must have been about twelve or thirteen years old, I think, had found work with a Marseilles singer, a regional star by the name of Prior, who organised tours of France and Belgium, singing songs in a Southern French accent.

In Provence, around the stoops
Chickens peck and scratch the dust
Followed by their skittish broods
Of chattering chicks in the Southern sun

In Belgium, he used to tell Belgian stories in his strong Meridional accent, following each one with this little refrain:

Oh, Godfordek, the stories they tell
You'll split your sides in Brussels, hell
From the Rue Royale down to Ixelles
You'll laugh so hard you'll cry

Together with his wife, Mina, a former belly dancer, he had put together a small troupe of child artists who all played musical instruments. Aïda played piano. She has always been a gifted pianist and has a keen sense of music that has always been of great help to me. The little troupe were the opening act of the show, and accompanied the star for the main show; it was all great fun. Besides being a singer, Prior owned a small publishing company whose offices were located in the apartment beneath his own, at 61 Rue du Faubourg Saint-Martin, in the publishing quarter, and that served as a kind of labour exchange. Artists who had no regular work and who were looking for bit parts would sit in the café Batifol for hours on end in the hope of catching an impresario or a promoter. We were dressed all in white with a red belt, like the tambourine players down South. The posters announced "Prior and the Cigalounettes". Compared to these kids I passed for a classicist, I was moving in higher circles. After my two

---

[1] Cigale is French for cicada.

engagements at the Marigny and the Madeleine, I obtained another role after auditioning at the Odéon theatre, in a play by Victor Margeurite, *L'Enfant*.[2]

Then, one fine day, I found myself out of work. Aïda let Prior know that I was available to join the troupe. I had to come up with an act: I did reasonable impressions of Mayol, Charlie Chaplin and a few others. I would have liked to have added Maurice Chevalier, but that number was reserved for Mina Prior's little pet, whose father, an English clown, had abandoned his French family to return to his homeland and start a new life. Harry Scanlon was his name and his impersonation made him the highlight of the opening act. After the interval we used to accompany the star of the show; I played metallophone, with Harry on drums, Kiss Nascimbeni on violin, Bruno, the eldest among us, on accordion, and Tony Ovio on guitar. Then there was Palmyre, who was Bruno's sister, Guiguiche, and Jackie Luciani, who had had a part in the film *Zouzou*, with Josephine Baker, but I don't remember which instruments the girls used to play. Bruno's father gave us music lessons. He had a very strong Piedmontese accent: *"Doh rrray me fah shoh lah tchee doh."*

The atmosphere was fantastic; we would arrive in the morning to get everything ready for the show, and on the days when we didn't have a show, we'd help send out the sheet music to band leaders, and sort out the costumes and props. Then we'd set off on tour in a big car, a Renault, with Prior at the wheel; and every time he topped twenty-five miles an hour there would be shrieks of: "Pierrot, you're crazy, you'll get us all killed, you're driving like a maniac! Think of the children!" from Mina. The children in the back would be feeling queasy, throwing up, complaining. So we'd stop, have a picnic, and have a little sing; we were happy ... It was like being part of a second family. The Priors used to pay our parents and give us pocket money for sweets and other small things we hankered for. In summer, Prior used to hire the Quinson Town Hall, in the Basse-Alpes[3], and we spent some wonderful holidays in this charming little village. Some

---

[2] *The Child.*
[3] Basses-Alpes is the old name for the Alpes-de-Haute-Provence; the name of the *département* was changed in 1970.

years ago, I wanted to see Quinson again; the village was surprisingly unchanged, the lady who ran the grocery-come-haberdashery was much older, of course – as was I – but I recognised her immediately, and the parish priest had retired but was still living there.

Come On, Marseilles (Allez, Vaï, Marseille)[4]

Go on Marseilles
In the shade or the sun
Drink your pastis and sing
Those tunes of Scotto
That suit you so well
Go on and give some advice
To the pétanque players
Talk out loud and talk out strong
And contest the score
But at the hour for love
When like a wind of Provence
Half light half wild
Some to disturb your days
Go on Marseilles
Go on to court Mireille
She waits and burns for you
And give her children
Whose accent will be yours
Marseilles

Provence. I began to fall in love with it as a result of touring and holidaying with the Priors. I loved the climate, the often excessive but extraordinarily warm and friendly ways of the local people, the potatoes that we used to go and dig up, mass when Bruno played accordion – as he didn't know any liturgical music, he just used to play popular tunes of the time at a much slower tempo. It worked and no one had any complaints. I loved, too, the smell of the lavender that we plaited together with coloured ribbons to make little baskets that our

[4] From *Allez Vaï Marseille / Marseilles* by Charles Aznavour.

parents put in the wardrobe to scent the linen; the spicy local cuisine that was similar to our own, and *chichi fregi,* which looked like a sausage and was sold by the yard[5] ... We were always sorry to leave the South, although we were glad to get back on the road, back on stage, knowing that we would return the following summer.

Those were the summers of yore, when holidays in the country, often only a few miles from Paris, in Saint-Brice or Meudon, thrilled us. We were more than happy with the small things in life.

The Small Things In Life (Heureux Avec Des Riens)[6]

Our little trip is scattered with fantasy
Of childish laughter flying up to the morning light
There's no reason to complicate life
We are happy with little things
While we are walking if suddenly I am humming
And for the chorus your voice is harmonizing with mine
Rhythmed by the tip tap of our feet
We are happy with little things

In The Days of Before

1936. The Communist Party used to organise picnics where Waldeck Rochet[7] would bang out his speech; Russian films were all the rage. There were Soviet productions on every Sunday morning at the Pigalle theatre. We used to go to two showings – armed for the occasion with shopping bags full of victuals and drinks – to see films like *Maxim, The Youth of Maxim, The Battleship Potemkin, Lenin In October, Strike* and heaven knows how many others, all propaganda films of course. But we weren't concerned with that, it was the acting itself that we enjoyed above all. We also went to see *Beppo*, the first Armenian film. These were the days when we still believed in the

---

[5] *Aune* in the text, an old French unit of measurement: 1.18 or 1.20 metres.
[6] From *Heureux Avec Des Riens / The Small Things In Life* by Charles Aznavour.
[7] French politician (1905–1983), a communist member of parliament from 1936 to 1939, he succeeded Maurice Thorez as the Communist Party Secretary in 1964.

Soviet paradise that gave us hope for a new world, the days when we'd break into revolutionary song, and gather at the JAF (The Armenian Youth of France), whose secretary was Méliné, the future Madame Manouchian, and which counted Missac Manouchian among its active members.

We hung out at dances organised by the Armenians at which my father had been asked to sing – he had a knack for making the women in the audience cry. Aïda and I would get up and do our own act, too. While the band that was hired for the evening was not always an Armenian outfit, wherever they came from, their repertoire had to include numbers that would allow couples to dance the national folk dances. Someone or other would always film part of the evening, and, miraculously, make it back before the end of the night to project his silent, grey and white film onto a sheet that served as a screen.

The Armenian community was still not completely integrated at this time. It was something new; the moments of reunion, times of laughter and tears. It might seem childish today, but there was great solace to be found in getting together with other survivors. It was wonderful, it was Before with a capital B. What we mean when we say, "those were the days": the days before it all went bad, the days before the storm clouds gathered, the days before the flight, before the civilian exodus[8], before the privations, the betrayals, the hatred and the settling of debts; they were carefree days, the blessed days before the war.

Before The War (Avant La Guerre)[9]

I was twenty, my soul was tender
You were sixteen with a hunger to learn
I used to write you poems
Where everyline was a rhyme for I love you
You were still a schoolgirl
It was just a little while before the war

---

[8] *The flight of French citizens from Paris and Northern France to the South when the Germans broke through the Allied lines.*
[9] *From Avant La Guerre / To Be A Soldier by Charles Aznavour.*

1936. Paris rises up. Paris takes to the streets, Paris marches in protest, Paris demands paid holidays for workers, talks politics, becomes still more unionized. Paris dreams of taking vacations and finally gets the right. The city forms a united front, a populist front, sings the *Internationale*, moves to the left, and all of France follows suit.

CHAPTER 7

Free At Last

We had wonderful parents, who trusted us; they gave us room to grow. They were creative artists but responsible parents nonetheless – our father liked to have a good time and was perpetually optimistic; both parents were always ready to help those less fortunate than ourselves. Goodness knows how many times Aïda and I slept with our mattresses on the floor so that a friend of the family who was going through a bad patch, or fugitives during the Occupation, could make use of the bed frames! Aïda and I accepted this small sacrifice without a second thought, it was simply part of our family's way of life. My mother was a very funny woman, my father something of a madcap. Aïda takes after them; I am more restrained, more distant perhaps, less demonstrative. I often wonder how I have managed to pursue a career that, in manner of speaking, requires baring one's soul to an audience every night. Aïda has a habit of asking me in the morning, before starting the day: "Did you wake up as Charles or as Aznavour?"

I didn't surprise or impress anyone in my family, they were proud of me, naturally, they just never mentioned it; they were proud and that was that. Their attitude kept me from becoming bigheaded. Since then, my wife Ulla and all of my children have treated me in just the same way, which sometimes prompts me to say in a tone of feigned umbrage: "Really! I say! You do realise that you are dealing with an international star!" Now, now! This never fails to send them into fits of laughter that I am delighted to to incite.

When Aïda and I were still living with our parents, my father would sometimes come home at rather late hour, after an evening of merrymaking and drinking. He never snuck in the door soundlessly on tiptoe to disguise the fact, oh no, on the contrary, he'd make enough noise to wake the whole household. He would return with sheet music, purchased from one of the musicians in the nightclub where he'd been living it up. Then Aïda would go and sit at the piano and sight-read the songs that my father had found so irresistible back at the club, and we'd all sing them together. We weren't exactly fresh as daisies in class the following morning. But we were happy in the knowledge that our family was different to the other families we knew. People used to think: "Those poor kids, what will become of them?" Well, we didn't turn out so badly, did we?

Though our father was something of a spendthrift, he was nevertheless shrewd enough to turn the purse strings over to my mother; she was more economical, more responsible and always managed to put a little something away for a rainy day. We knew full well how she went about making ends meet at the end of the month. She would pretend to borrow the missing sum from some lady with a name ending in *-ian*[1]; the *dear friend* in question supposedly lending her the money, but insisting – so our mother would explain – that it was imperative she be paid back by a fixed date. That friend only ever existed in the form of a large chest for which my mother alone had the key, and which was, in fact, filled with small lengths of fabric and clothing. No one fell for it, and when I think about it now, I'm sure she must have known that we knew. It was a kind of open secret.

This is why Aïda and I did everything in our power to help our parents when we were children. All the members of a displaced family are in the same proverbial skiff: everyone helps with the housework, the washing up, and takes the rubbish out. Once a week, we'd take care of the wooden floors, using our feet to rub them down hard

---

[1] Common ending for Armenian family names.

with steel wool, before sweeping and waxing them. Woe betide anyone who dared set a muddy foot down before our work of art was
dry! Often, while Aïda was peeling vegetables, I would roller-skate
across two Paris neighbourhoods to go shopping at the Rue de Buci
market, one of the cheapest in the whole capital at the time, where
eggs were sold by the baker's dozen. An extra egg for nothing and
fuel-free transport; you couldn't argue with that.

In spite of all this, we never wanted for entertainment: there were
the Armenian plays, of course, the dances and the picnics. But what
we really loved more than anything else was the silver screen. We had
harboured this passion since my father took us to the cinema, back in
the silent days; we were enthralled by Harold Lloyd, Charles Chaplin,
Ivan Mousjoukine and Gloria Swanson. Years later, in addition to the
films we saw on the days that we skipped school and the Soviet films
at Sunday matinees, we used to camp out in the local cinemas three
times a week, where it was common practice to show two or three
films in one sitting. We gorged ourselves on nine or ten films a week
on average, films of all kinds: love stories, adventure movies, musicals,
horror films, French and American dramas. We witnessed the arrival
of the talkies and the first musicals; the advent of colour was really
something. Danielle Darrieux, Charles Boyer and Harry Baur were
Aïda's favourite actors; as for myself, I admired Jean Gabin, Michèle
Morgan, and Raimu, Jules Berry, Gary Cooper, James Cagney, Bette
Davis, Pierre Fresnay, Fred Astaire and Ginger Rogers. We also
enjoyed wonderful supporting actors like Aimos, Carette, Jean Tissier,
Marguerite Moreno and Saturnin Fabre; we knew the casts, the composers, the directors – you couldn't catch us out when it came to cinema, and, I have to admit, Aïda was even more unbeatable than I was.
My sister has the ability to recall our past in phenomenal detail. She
remembers it all: the Saint-Michel, the Odéon, the Cluny, the Delta,
the assorted Rochechouarts, the Gaumont, the Moulin-Rouge, the
Berlitz, and the Paramount – our favourite venues … After I met
Micheline, my first wife, whose mother was a cashier at the Marivaux
and whose stepfather was a projectionist, we were able to get in for
free. We never missed a film, and often, our parents would accompany
us. We got so much joy from the big screen, how happy we were sitting there in the dark thanks to the talent of those I have already

mentioned and many more beloved, long-departed actors besides; not to mention authors and directors like Carné, Duvivier, Prévert, Janson, Spaak and Companeez, who gave us a taste for great cinema, for beautiful poetic, sensitive and intelligent cinema; and let's not forget the music! My father used to buy records that we would listen to on a large gramophone: tangos, paso dobles, jazz, and Hungarian music, as well as Tino Rossi and Édith Piaf's first recordings, Jean Tranchant, Damia, Fréhel, Maurice Chevalier, Charles Trénet and so many others. The theatre already had its classics, the film industry was on its way to creating its own, just like the world of French chanson that was soon to become a phenomenon.

Aïda and I had access to all kinds of entertainment, even radio! As a small boy, I had built a Galena radio set all by myself after purchasing the key components at a specialist shop in the Rue Montmartre. Galena is a kind of charcoal-coloured mineral that, when touched with a needle, allowed it to detect the signal. My set had no speaker, so I would use a pair of headphones to listen to radio shows.

Today, our artistic heritage is readily available to the younger generation thanks to new technologies that keep memories alive. The memories of my generation, of cinema buffs, song lovers, theatre, film, and music enthusiasts, the memories of the activists who battle against the colorisation of classic black and white films... Happy are they, at last, those singers and songstresses, actors and actresses, gone but immortalised by modern technology; they are reborn, their looks and youth unblemished, and their place in history intact.

CHAPTER 8

Charles of All Trades

After being regular readers of *La Semaine de Suzette*[1] (Aïda), *Bicot et Le Club Des Ran-Tan-Plan*[2] and *Bibi Fricotin*[3] (yours truly), and once we were old enough to seek out reading material more in tune with our interests, we used to frequent theatre bookshops where we would buy *La Petite Illustration*[4], which published unabridged manuscripts of the plays we wanted to read and learn. We would each choose a role that allowed us to enter auditions: *L'Ane de Buridan*[5], *On Purge Bébé*[6], and, for me, *Le Carosse du Saint-Sacrement*[7] as well. We

---

[1] *La Semaine de Suzette* – a weekly periodical for young girls in France (1905–1960). The magazine was filled with games, crafts, recipes and stories, as well as dressmaking patterns for a doll named Bleuette.

[2] *Bicot* - a French comic strip.

[3] *Bibi Fricotin* – a French sci-fi comic; the adventures of Bibi Fricotin and his companion, Razibus Zouzou.

[4] *La Petite Illustration* – weekly magazine that published new plays that were being put on in Paris as well as unpublished novels.

[5] *Buridan's Ass* by Robert de Flers and Gaston-Arman de Caillavet.

[6] *For Better or Worse: Purging The Baby* by Georges Feydeau.

[7] *The Coach of The Blessed Sacrament* - Jean Renoir's 1953 film *The Golden Coach* was an adaptation of this one act play by Prosper Merimée.

took it all extremely seriously, conscious that we were already professionals.

In 1936–1937, I was hired to perform in the Marseilles revue show *Ça C'est Marseille*[8], directed by Henri Varna at the Alcazar theatre on the Rue du Faubourg Montmartre, in Paris. The star of the show, Paul Berval, had made his name as a film actor. As for me, I appeared in the sketches and, curiously, I was also a member of the young girls dance line, in a tutu, if you please, a budding drag queen before my time. Truth be known, Monsieur Varna was not fond of spending money: for example, when it came to the subsequent revue, *Vive Marseille*[9], he reckoned that Berval was too expensive and confidently appropriated the role for himself!

It was during rehearsals for *Ça C'est Marseille* that I ran into a fair-haired young man in uniform who was there to present a couple of his songs – *Ma Ville*[10] and *Bâteau d'Amour*[11] – to the star of the show. His name was Charles Trénet. A few months later, the young poet's songs were all over the radio; they rocked the foundations of French chanson, sweeping everything aside that we had heard up until then like a tidal wave. I recognised the compositions of the young military man who had shyly presented his work at the Alcazar, and instantly became not a fan – the term did not exist at the time – but an unconditional admirer. He was my idol, my master – albeit unwittingly – and later, a dear friend.

If the Germans have a reputation for being disciplined, the French for being the best lovers, the Americans for being addicted to money, and the Scottish for being tightfisted, they say of Armenians: "They have a strong head for business," before adding, "It takes two Jews to get the better of one Armenian." I have no idea if there is any truth in that; perhaps we are the exception that proves the rule. I am not a good business man, and my dear father was even less of one than I am. Having declared himself bankrupt at Rue de la Huchette and having closed the bistro in the Rue Cardinal Lemoine, my father

---

[8] *That's Marseille.*
[9] *Long Live Marseille!*
[10] *My Town.*
[11] *The Love Boat.*

found a good position at La Méditerranée, a restaurant on the Place de l'Odéon. It was early 1937, the year of the International Exhibition. With the opening of the exhibition, the entire restaurant staff were packed off to work at the Méditerranée's pavilion. Aïda and I used to eat lunch there for free. Two things made an impression on me: the immense and imposing Russian and German pavilions that stood facing one another as though they were squaring off; and the new, fascinating invention on show in the German pavilion that would later come to be known as television. A cinema near the Madeleine church, the Cinéac, subsequently set up a small studio, equipped with a camera and microphone, in its basement: a screen at the entrance to the cinema allowed passersby to discover this new technology. Aïda and I, our faces painted green, as the image required, would often drop by there to sing popular songs. We were among the very first French people to ever sing – albeit anonymously and unpaid – on private television.

CHAPTER 9

Nostalgia

Yesterday (Hier Encore)[1]

Still yesterday I was twenty
Caressing the time
And gambling with life
As one plays with love
I was living by nights
Not counting on my days
That were flying with the hours
I have made so many plans
That ended in the air
And built so much hope that flew away
That I feel so lost, not knowing where to go
My eyes searching the skies
My heart buried in the ground

If you'll forgive me, I am going to allow myself – like the cinema – a brief moment of nostalgia. It doesn't matter how old we are, the day

---

[1] From *Hier Encore / Yesterday When I Was Young* by Charles Aznavour.

45

we lose our parents we become orphans. I became half an orphan when my mother died, then completely orphaned with the death of my father. Not a week goes by since their passing that I don't dream or think of my parents. I get a lump in my throat and tears well up in the corners of my eyes. The images that assail me are like photographs that I have framed anew, removing superfluous detail so that only my parents are in focus.

I can still see my mother sitting under the paraffin lamp, pedalling away relentlessly at her old Singer sewing machine, hurrying to finish the piece of work that was due the next day, so she could reap the reward for her sleepless night, the franc that she needed to keep her small family going. Francs for bread, francs for meat, francs for the rent, francs for children's clothes – they grow so fast – francs for shoes that wear out too quickly, for the dentist, and the doctors – back then no one had ever heard of Social Security. And a few francs, too, if possible, for sweets, not to mention francs for the cinema. That magic lamp whose pale glowing light intensified the atmosphere, while the purring of the machine finally carried us off to the land of nod... It was only much later in life that I realised what sacrifices my parents had made in order to give their children a decent upbringing. Sick or healthy, tired or not, Maman would tackle the task at hand. Chalk in hand, running back and forth between sewing table and tailor's dummy, measuring, cutting, sewing, ironing, sacrificing her sleep, this is how my mother managed to raise us.

During the rare moments of calm she enjoyed, my mother would give herself over to playing piano or writing. As a young woman, she had been a member of the editorial team of an Armenian newspaper in Turkey and the urge to write had never left her. Her dream was to find a typewriter with an Armenian keyboard. Many years later, when I was touring in America, I managed to track one down. Alas, Maman never had the chance to use it. She left us before that, and the new machine stayed in its box until the day that my sister Aïda and I donated it to an Armenian association. Seeing the machine there, unused, was too much for us to bear.

She had had another dream: she wanted to drive. By the time I had the means to buy her the car of her dreams, it was too late; this dream was never to be fulfilled. For this and more there is much sadness in me. When I think about those people who still have their parents, who fail to spoil them in their old age, and who, if they can afford it, rid themselves of them by sending them away to retirement homes, I pity them for forgetting the most tender moments, the hardest moments, the ones that we carry in our hearts for as long as we live.

CHAPTER 10

Living, Surviving, Learning

In the 1930s, a family lacking the means to send its offspring to school had only one solution open to it: sponsorship had to be found. The preferred course of action was to approach a generous member of the family's own community. Which is what happened. A well-off Armenian agreed to sponsor me under the condition that I study a serious profession. Now what exactly constitutes a serious profession? Not an artistic one, such as I dreamed of, that's for sure. It was out of the question that a child of the community be allowed to enter a disreputable milieu so lacking in prospects. An uncle of mine who was a tailor had explained to me in great depth how his profession allowed him to work anywhere in the world – he didn't even need to speak the language. But I could not see myself plying the needle; I can sew on a button, but that's as far as it goes. And so, in order to make the most of the this sponsorship, because nothing we ever learn is wasted, a few months before war was declared I decided to enrol in the Merchant Navy Radio Studies Department at the Central School of Wireless Telegraphy[1], on the Rue de la Lune; *dot-dash, dot-dash-dot, dash-dash-dot-dot*, and so on.

[1] The T.S.F in Paris.

There was something musical about it, and since I had a good ear, it was unlikely to present too much of a problem. I needed some basic mathematics, a subject that was not included in the primary school certificate programme – the only diploma I had. The problem was solved when a staunchly communist couple – who were later tortured and finally shot by the Gestapo for Resistance crimes – the Aslanians, who lived in Belleville and to whom we were introduced by Missac Manouchian, agreed to give me a free crash course in the basics. After several weeks of lessons, I sat the entry examination and was accepted at the school.

It was hardly enthralling stuff, but I did my best. Mathematics has never been my strong point. Fortunately, Professor Bloch was a young man whose kindness and humour helped us get through the examinations. Then there was the school headmaster, Monsieur Poireaux, who was rarely seen. And the hare-lipped deputy head, a really nasty piece of work, who was always quick to box our ears and many a pupil bore the imprint of his hand across their face! In the lecture theatre I always hoped that he would one day raise his hand to me, so that I could push him and send him tumbling down the stairs, head over heels, to the sound of humiliating laughter from the avenged class. But it never happened and it's something I have always regretted.

I don't know what obscure reason led to my being expelled from the school. I remember saying at the time to Georges Bacri, a classmate I used to walk home with – he lived in the building opposite ours on Rue LaFayette: "You'll see. Given what they charge for the course, they can't afford to go losing pupils." Four days later, bingo! My parents were informed that the headmaster in his great leniency had reconsidered the School Committee's decision and agreed to allow me to rejoin my class.

I often used to go across the street to Georges' parents' place. He had a brother whom I believe I never saw until many years later, in the business, when I discovered that Eddy Marnay, a hit songwriter of beautiful, poetic songs, was Georges' brother. As for Georges, he had had a change of vocation and entered the world of music publishing. I was delighted to run into this old classmate again at the Palais des Congrès, in 2000.

As for me, I know for a fact that the Merchant Navy were better off without me … So what next? *Dot-dot-dot dash-dash-dash dot-dot-dot*[2]. I needed to get my teeth into something, I needed an outlet. I'm very fond of the ocean, but for swimming in, not for dot–dot–dashing about on. And so, to shed the rigour of the Rue de la Lune college, I started going along to the Variety Theatre with Aïda, where she was taking Jean Tissier's acting classes. Here, everyone shared a common passion for theatre and dreamt of a future with more pizzazz than *dot-dot-dash*.

My head was filled with *L'Ane de Buridan, Les Vignes du Seigneur*[3], *Le Carosse du Saint-Sacrement, Seul*[4] as well as other more classical plays; I was itching to start auditioning and get back on stage. But it was a tense time; the theatre was going through a rough patch, I was going to have to look elsewhere. Dot–dot–dot dash … Great, school's out.

---

[2] S.O.S.

[3] *The Lord's Vines* by Robert De Flers and Francis Wiener, aka Francis de Croisset (1923).

[4] *Alone.*

CHAPTER 11

A Phoney War,
One Hell of a War

1939. Germany had just invaded Poland. My father, who sensed that there was trouble in the offing and thought that basic necessities might soon become scarce, decided that we needed to stock up. So off we went to buy oil, sugar and cracked wheat – *boulrouth*[1]. Back then, the average French consumer had no idea that this even existed; people were not yet accustomed to eating Middle Eastern cuisine. Sugar, oil and bulghur can be kept safely for a very long time; while we were able to find what we needed in the shops, they would remain stored in readiness for any bad times ahead. And then the "phoney war[2]" started. We were convinced that if Germany was not on the attack in France, it was because she had done her homework. The "Fifth Column" was bound to have sent back reports. The "Fifth Column", the "Fifth Column", it was on everyone's lips. They're here, they're there! Be on guard! Walls have ears! The "Fifth Column", people said, had long infiltrated the workings of the French state.

[1] Bulghur or bulgur.
[2] *Drôle de Guerre* in French , also known as the *Twilight War*.

Keep quiet, watch what you say, enemy ears are listening! The invisible, hypothetical "Fifth Column" was not a product of French military propaganda, it did actually exist. Its members had been in France for many years, they were an integral part of the population, they spoke perfect, accentless French, they led lives similar to our own, they ate and drank as we did, and had made friends with people living on their street or across the landing. During the Occupation, they came crawling out of the woodwork once they had shed their civilian clothes for a uniform – preferably Gestapo – during the "Phoney War."

The French thought: "Thank heavens we have such advanced weaponry, we'll be able to make short work of these *Boche*, these *Hun*, these *Blockheads,* these *Schleus*, these *Krauts* ..." as we liked to disdainfully refer to them. Then, one morning, we learned of the attack – the war had begun, the seemingly unstoppable German troops were advancing, parachutists were dropping from the skies ... It was the kind of celestial providence we would have rather done without. The impregnable Maginot line – overrun, humiliated. Field grey uniforms were advancing, on forced march, in the direction of *die Grosse Paris*[3]. "We'll hang our washing out to dry on the Siegfried Line!" Dream on. My father decided to enlist in the French army; we accompanied him to Austerlitz railway station; once the train had pulled out, Maman, Aïda and I remained standing for a while on the platform as if in a daze, crying.

Paris is gripped by terror. Panic sets in. The city empties: there is a mad rush to reach the railway stations, especially Austerlitz. People leave everything behind so they can flee as fast as possible. We had been duly warned by the propaganda in our newspapers: the Germans were all bloodthirsty brutes who hacked off the hands of adults, slaughtered children, and raped women. People took flight without stopping to think. Those who had come by bicycle abandoned them in front of the stations. There were hundreds of them: old ones, new ones, children's, men's and women's bicycles. A bunch of friends from Montholon Square and I made several return trips to

---

[3] In German in the text.

pick up as many as we could, with the intention of selling them once we had repainted them and things had calmed down again. You have to make a living somehow!

Before leaving to join his regiment, my father was most insistent: whatever we did, come what may, we were not to leave Paris. This was judicious advice in retrospect, when you know how much those who took immediate flight suffered. Before he went up to the front, my father was stationed in Septfonds, in the south-west of France, together with six-thousand other voluntary conscripts, all of whom were Russian, Armenian, or Jewish. He had taken his *tar*[4] with him, and, having been assigned to the kitchens, he prepared Russian and Armenian dishes for the troops instead of the traditional army grub. In the evenings, when they gathered after dinner, he used to give short performances in several languages, much to everyone's delight.

Then, the immaculate and formidable German army invaded northern France before descending like a wake of predatory birds upon Paris and a large part of the rest of the country soon thereafter.

They came, stiff legged and arms outstretched, clad in leather, wearing helmets and boots, in field grey uniforms, imposing and cold like robots, heroic gods, to administer the new order. They came from the cold lands of the east, arrogant men in their modern war machines, to occupy our land, to force us to submit, to Germanise us, to discipline us, we, the Latins, with our carefree attitude to life, art lovers rather than warmongers. They came to occupy us, civilise us, lighten the colour of our hair and our eyes so that we might meet the ideals of racial purity that they professed. We were there to watch when the elite troops marched up the Rue Lafayette. Everyone was rooted to the spot, men and women stood crying on the pavements at the sight of this alien column as it trod and sullied the soil of our capital. Everyone returned home with their heads bowed, grumbling about the mendacity of governments. We were worried sick, we had no news of our father, but we hoped he was alive, in good health, and ready to come home.

---

[4] Armenian lute-shape stringed instrument.

Small Trade

Well, life is what it is, the point was we were going to have to adapt. My father was absent, and, as everyone knows, if you plan on staying alive, eating regularly is a good idea. But what do you do when you have no experience in business and you are jobless? I started by getting my hands on a batch of 4 oz chocolate bars whose packaging alone must have weighed a whole ounce! When my supply was exhausted, I bought some rayon stockings, the kind that laddered and ran like crazy as soon as you put your hand inside, and with saddlebags jam-packed, I set off astride my bicycle, to take up position on the main roads into Paris, where the Occupation army trucks used to set up camp before driving through the capital. I was able to earn a few occupation Marks in this way and then I would run, faster even than the stockings, for if our charming field grey chums had ever been curious enough to unwrap their merchandise, I would have found myself locked up in a concentration camp in no time!

When I failed to come up with any more goods that were liable to interest our occupiers, I looked for some other essential commodity in short supply. Fortunately, bartering was an option: I'll swap you a bicycle tyre for half a pound of butter, a quarter gallon of oil for two yards of fabric. But you could also trade in shoes, a runaway success. Whenever my friend and impresario, Jean-Louis Marquet, managed to get his hands on one or two pairs at a good price, he would call me and tell me that he had seen Monsieur Gaûchik who wanted to set up a meeting. Gaûchik means shoe in Armenian; we used words of our mother tongue as code! Oh yes, it was all black market, but those were black years, people understand that today and at our small level we were hardly mercenary profiteers, we were just young men using our heads to survive.

One night, there was a knock at the door. It was my father, heavily bearded and in need of a haircut, standing there smiling. He had managed to give the slip to the victors who were planning to take the soldiers in his contingent prisoner and pack them off to the stalags or set them to work in Germany on farms and in factories. Once again, we packed up and moved: our new home was at 22 Rue de Navarin, still in the 9th arrondissement in Paris.

Then came the Germano-Soviet pact that divided the ranks of the communists. There was no question of anyone in our community siding with the enemy. Little by little, resistance groups formed. Missac Manouchian, one of the leaders, and my parents, too, used to help out by hiding Jews, resistance members on the run, or Russians and Armenians who had been press-ganged into the Wehrmacht and whom the communists had helped desert. They entered Rue Navarin in uniform, but walked out as common civilians in clothes that we had acquired for them. My job was to dispose of the uniforms. Once night had fallen, I would go and dispose of them in the sewers of districts far away from ours, but I once hid a pair of occupation army leather boots in our cellar. Put it down to the folly of youth: if we'd have been searched, we'd have been staring deportation in the face.

In fact, the French police, sent by the Gestapo, did come knocking at our door one day. Luckily for us, we had received prior warning of the visit, and my father and I took refuge in a small hotel opposite the building where we lived. We knew that these gentlemen only called at the break of dawn, before the curfew was lifted. They came back again two or three times, then, one morning, the Gestapo turned up. My father fled then to Lyon to stay with some cousins. A month later, when things had calmed down, he returned to Rue Navarin.

What became of those Armenians, Russians, Azeris and other citizens of the Soviet Republics? We never received any news of a single one. It's said that soldiers who were captured ended their days in the gulags. The Little Father of the People had a curious way of rewarding his children.

Odd Jobs

The war had put most artists out of work. I started selling newspapers on the street to keep my head above water. I used to pick them up on the Rue Croissant and sell them as I walked – without a licence, I was not allowed to have a stand – until I reached the Champs-Élysées, at which point I would set off again with a new bundle of papers. My only fear was the potential embarrassment of running into one of my confreres. Luckily, the situation never arose, except for when Ray Ventura bought a paper and left me the change, but he didn't know me.

When my father was issued with a new stallholders licence, we went back to being market traders. There was no time for taking it easy, on the contrary, we had to be up at the crack of dawn. This wasn't so bad during the summer, but getting out of bed in the winter was a struggle. We would drop by Olida's the evening before and purchase our wares: garlic sausage that, in times of shortage like those, sold like hot cakes. Don't forget that you needed ration coupons to buy anything at all then. By 5 a.m., after devouring breakfast, my father would mount his bicycle, which had a small trailer attached to transport our meagre merchandise. I would sit on the cross bar and we'd ride as fast as we could to join the ranks of one of the Seine-et-Marne or Seine-et-Oise open-air public markets. Since our licence did not permit us to trade at any of the Parisian markets, we set off in a different direction each day. We had to arrive sufficiently early on as all the good spots were quickly snapped up. Most of the time we used to bribe the person in charge; we often got away with slipping him a sausage or two.

Once we had set up the stall, we would sit tight and await our customers. My father had a cunning ploy to get things moving: sacrificing a few sausages, he'd cry out: "Try a taste, try a taste!" and, wielding a long knife, he would offer slices to the passing customers looking for something to fill their pantries. "Try a taste!" People were delighted, no other traders gave away their produce in this way, for things were too hard to come by and too expensive. "Try a taste, try a taste!" We did a roaring trade, well, when I say roaring, we weren't making a fortune, just enough to live on, while we waited, hoping and dreaming of better days to come. Already a scarce commodity, sausage became a spoil of war booty and impossible to come by. After that, we tried selling socks, but were forced to abandon this, too, and fast, as they sold considerably less well than charcuterie. Our "Try a taste, try a taste!" ruse was no longer an option, and customers were in no hurry to buy. So, my father and I had to look for work, he in the restaurant trade and I in the entertainment business.

The Things You Have To Do To Earn Your Bread and Butter

Having made themselves at home, the Germans had visions of "Grosse Parissse, moosseek, champagne, pretty mattmazzelles", in short, all the thrills and frills for which our capital had long been renowned. Little by little cabarets started opening again for business. I was hired by the Jockey Club in Montparnasse and travelled there on roller skates; I would use this singular means of transportation – rare in those days – to return home to the Rue Navarin at night. To begin with, the German patrols, who would stop and check anyone found in the streets for their *Ausweis*[5], used to stop me for my papers. But they learned to recognise the sound of my skates and, since they knew that my papers were in order, finally let me be.

I had a proboscis in those days that got me into no end of trouble and that could have been my downfall. On more than one occasion, I was obliged to present myself at the Kommandatur of cities in the provinces armed with my baptism certificate that had been issued by the Armenian Church in Paris. More often than not I had to show my credentials, well, you know what I mean by credentials ... I'd walk out the door a free man, but a humiliated one.

I finally joined a troupe that put on a revue featuring a host of pretty young girls and we set off on tour across France. Once again, my work consisted of appearing in sketches, performing an Apache dance routine, and singing. My partner was the star of the troupe, Sandra Dolza. I met Christiane here, a gorgeous dancer, and, right from the first night, to save money – the perfect excuse! – we found ourselves sharing the same hotel room. This tour was supposed to earn me quite a lot of money, but I needed a wardrobe. My parents had no hesitation in selling their furniture. Alas, a few days later, the small cabin trunk containing all my things packed *its* proverbial trunk, so to speak, and I ended up with a curious selection of costumes purchased at the local charity shop.

Once this tour was over, I joined a company that was run by Jean Dasté. Aïda played piano since our repertoire also included folk songs.

[5] Special work permit.

After a few rehearsals, I was off on the road again playing in Molières's *Les Facheux*[6] and Jacques Copeau's *Arlequin Magicien*[7]. Dressed as Harlequin, I made my entrance hanging from a rope – Tarzan eat your heart out! – and my vaudeville touch worked wonders.

[6] *The Bores.*
[7] *Harlequin the Magician.*

CHAPTER 12

Loulou Gasté

Ino longer remember where nor under what circumstances I first met Jacques Jim. It was during the Occupation years; I remember that he was working as an usher at the Olympia, and that he needed a musician to put his lyrics to music. So I came up with a highly rhythmic number, and Jacques and I called the song: *Y' Des Hiboux Dans Le Beffroi*[1]. Beyond the title, I cannot recollect a single word or note of this dated ditty of my salad days. But, proud of my first small opus, I was already singing it every night at the Jockey cabaret, to universal indifference, and decided to overcome my shyness and take my song – on roller skates – to a publisher.

Since I had undertaken to launch my career, I figured that I may as well approach one of the most sought-after men of the moment, and I set my sights on hit songwriter, Loulou Gasté. He received me most cordially, not in the least taken aback by my unusual garb, the same I wore for my evening performances: a pair of black trousers, a sweatshirt of the same colour, and open-toed beach sandals. It was the best I could do. It gave me a "Saint-Germain-des-Prés" look before its time. Loulou showed me to an upright piano, sat down on my left and

[1] *Owls In The Belfry.*

61

indicated that I should begin playing. I struck the first three chords of the introduction – the only three I knew: C minor, F minor, and G major – and immediately set about torturing the piano, belting out the lyrics as I played and tapping out the beat with my foot to emphasise the rhythm, like some lunatic trying to smash a hole through the floor. Most of the chords sounded off-key. It made no difference to me, I was firing on all cylinders; the more I sang, the harder I played and pounded the floor with my feet, the more the tempo accelerated. The song, which should have lasted about three and a half minutes long, was wrapped up in two minutes and fifteen seconds flat.

Once I had finished, confronted with the look of surprise, not to say stupefaction, on Loulou's face and the long silence that ensued, I offered to play a second equally rhythmic song, that I had written with Jacques Jim, *Père Noel Swing*[2]. Without letting his half smile slip for a moment, Loulou congratulated me but made it clear that this was not the kind of song that his publishing company was looking for. He kindly and politely saw me to the door.

Many years later, somewhat calmer and a little better established in the business, I ran into Loulou Gasté again, who had married Line Renaud. She filled me in on the conclusion of the story, already a notorious anecdote amongst their friends: the person living in the flat below had rushed upstairs to find out what kind of catastrophe had befallen Loulou, for my manic assault on the floor had almost shaken his crystal chandelier loose and had succeeded in sending flakes of plaster showering down onto his dining room table. My chord playing has much improved since then, and I am a more reasonable man these days, at least I hope so.

[2] *Swinging Santa.*

CHAPTER 13

Roche and Aznavour

One night, in 1942, Aïda, who used to frequent the Club de la Chanson[1] where young people who wished to pursue an artistic career could get together and try out their material in front of a small audience, returned home in the company of a young man. When I opened the door, she whispered to me: "He's a friend of yours, his name's Jean-Louis Marquet." Unable to make it home before curfew, he stayed the night. It was best to avoid being on the streets after midnight; if there were any attacks made on the occupiers during the night, the Germans would immediately seize fifty or so hostages from police stations and shoot them as an example. Jean-Louis soon became a regular visitor to the apartment. And I, in turn, began spending time at the Club, where Jean-Louis was one of several founding members. It was here that I met Pierre Saka, Lawrence Riesner and Pierre Roche.

The club was starting to become pretty popular with young artists. It moved from the small venue in the 9th arrondissement to a location near the Champs-Élysées, an enormous apartment on the top floor of a smart building on the Rue Ponthieu. We set about

[1] *The Song Club.*

converting the place, building a stage, a kitchen, and offices, so that Zappy Max would be able to teach classes in tap dancing, Jane Pierly in singing, and A.M. Julien in stage deportment.

On the opening night of the Club, in 1943, the directors – Pierre Saka, Jean-Louis Marquet, Pierre Roche and Lawrence Riesner – organised a big cocktail party which was attended by Édith Piaf, Léo Marjane, and André Claveau, as well as everyone who was anyone in *chanson*, not to mention the press. Roche and I used to spend our days at the Club to earn a small regular income. We set up song sessions for young artists and, while Roche accompanied them on piano, I coached them, correcting mistakes they were making, and helped them with their live performance. Every night, the Club was transformed into a cabaret where you could catch performances by some of the Club's pupils or other young artists who had come along to try out their new routines in front of the small audience. Regulars in the audience included Daniel Gélin and Francis Blanche, whose mother, Madame Montana, used to treat us to babas that she baked in the Club's kitchen.

In the meantime, Aïda had passed an audition and was hired as the new revue captain at the Concert Mayol, though management made a slight change to her name: Aznavour became Aznamour. A deeply modest person, she insisted that her outfits cover her from head to toe – a first for the Concert Mayol! Aïda was replacing a comic variety artist by the name of Jean Dréjac, who would later have France humming away to delightful songs of his, such as *Ah, Le Petit Vin Blanc*[2]! I had auditioned there, too, but they passed me over in favour of a pleasing young person who was suitably qualified to thrill the audience by removing her clothes. In an age where images of scantily clad men and women are served up daily on television and in the press, it's hard to imagine the kind of fantasies that were unleashed by the mere glimpse of a breast in those days. Lucien Rimels, who wrote and directed the shows at the Concert Mayol, would sometimes write sketches in verse that tickled me pink. Like this one, for example: four young women would come on stage in long dresses of midnight blue while a narrator began to recite:

[2] *Ah, White Wine*

In the dark, all cats are grey
But beauty's still brunette or blond
The moon lights up the deep night sky
And night lights up the moons anon

As the final line was delivered, the young women would slowly, very slowly, turn their backs to the audience to reveal the heart-shaped cut-outs in their dresses and an exquisite array of four beautifully framed moons.

A Duo Is Born

In the course of 1943, Pierre Roche, whose parents lived in Presles and who was well known in the region, organised a gala in Beaumont-sur-Oise with the help of the Club regulars. We were all on the bill and Pierre, the local star, was scheduled to headline. Line Jack, a dancer at the Concert Mayol, had agreed on this particular occasion, as a favour to Aïda, to come down and introduce the acts. She was a regular visitor to the Club and had heard Pierre and I performing the songs that we were writing for other people. Line, whose speciality was stripping for an audience, not hosting shows, became confused and, instead of introducing "Pierre Roche", announced: "Pierre Roche and Charles Aznavour". We found the mistake amusing, and after sharing a conspirational glance we came on stage together to perform three or four of the songs that we had finished writing... for other people.   The response was such that we were forced to sing the same songs a second time. After the show, all our friends from the Club urged us to carry on as a duo. Jean-Louis promised to set some dates up for us, and Pierre Ani, a cousin of Roche's who was a press agent, offered to take care of our publicity. Our first show was in a nightclub in Lille where I flew into a rage when I noticed that the manager had put up posters announcing "The Rhythm Duo" instead of "Roche and Aznavour", the official name of our act. Before promoters finally learned to spell our names correctly, we would encounter "Roche and Aznabour", "Riche and Aznavour" and even "Roger Aznavour". We lasted for eight years as a duo and made our Parisian debut just around the corner from the Club de la Chanson, in a nightclub on the Rue de Berri where variety stars Andrex and Nila Cara were headlining at the time. One evening, Andrex discovered that he had lost his voice – one man's loss is another man's gain. Jean-Louis rushed over to find us, shouting: "Get your act together! You're on tonight, you're standing in. If you pull it off, you're on for the whole week!" And we did, we sang there until the star had recovered, after which the bookings came rolling in.

We were booked for a fortnight at the Heure Bleue, a club in the Pigalle district, where hoods and heavies would come swaggering in every night. Having stashed the tools of their trade, revolvers, machine guns and whatnot behind the bar, the patrons used to take their seats in gloomy silence, as if they were duty bound, as members of the mafia, to look mean at all times! They would listen distractedly to our set without so much as batting an eyelid. We sang some Charles Trénet songs, including *'Heritage Infernal*[3], which saw me jumping onto the piano to slide across the top on my knees and end up nose to nose with Pierre for effect – we both had rather prolific noses. Our repertoire also included one of Pierre's songs, as well as a song by Johnny Hess, Charles Trénet's former songwriting partner, *Coco le Corsaire*[4], during which – inspired by the film *Treasure Island* – I used to limp as if I had a wooden leg and sported a black eyepatch. As the gents in black never wasted any energy on applause, we assumed that they were totally unaffected by the show. When the fortnight was up, it was good night and thank you, it's been a real pleasure, folks.

We had already started playing another series of gigs, to a more responsive audience, when we had a lovely surprise, in a manner of speaking. An employee from the Heure Bleue arrived in our dressing room and asked, in a rather authoritarian tone, that we resume our show. That audience who had never so much as blinked in approval or disapproval, had had the replacement act fired and expressly requested our return! They made us an offer we couldn't refuse on two counts; we would be getting a raise and were allowed to fulfil our current engagement. The road to success is a mysterious one ...

Next to the Concert Mayol was the The Pont-Aven, a restaurant that served dinner with a show hosted by Jean Rena and Jean-Louis

---

[3] *The Infernal Inheritance*
[4] *Coco The Corsaire.*

Marquet, who was now our impresario. Pierre came from a provincial family of the upper bourgeoisie; he had been interested in music from an early age and his parents, who were very liberal, showed no objections to his entering a profession that, at the time, was inappropriate for what you might call a young man of means. He was into jazz, rhythmic pieces, and had no interest in other popular forms of music. He had done extremely well in his studies and received a good education. I had been born into a bohemian family; I knew next to nothing about jazz – waltz, paso doble, and tango rhythms were my forte. Like Pierre I had had a decent education, but my studies had been as basic as they come. What we had in common was our passion for music and our enthusiasm for meeting pretty, young women, whenever the opportunity presented itself. We hit it off right from the word go and, unusually for a duo, we never really fell out; we were always on the same wave-length.

Jean-Louis Marquet, Pierre Roche and I used to go and pick Aïda up after the performance each night and stop to watch the show. Artists were paid one hundred francs a night and given a sandwich. The Pont-Aven had a well-heeled clientele who came for a "black market" dinner at what was still quite a reasonable price. We used to sit near the restaurant entrance, next to the piano – some people like to sit near radiators in winter for warmth; pianos always seemed to warm the cockles of our hearts. One evening, by some miraculous turn of events, a client who had heard us sing in a club somewhere got Jean to ask us if we would take the stage. We needed coaxing. So, to butter us up, Jean had us served a meal, the likes of which we hadn't seen since before the war. He then went over to the stage and announced: "Ladies and Gentlemen, Jacqueline François!" Jacqueline François was a debutant actress blessed with a beautiful voice; she would go on to enjoy a successful international career. While she sang, she only had eyes for Jean-Louis whom she cornered as soon as she finished her set. They spent several years together, and remained friends until Jean-Louis' death. Marquet would be her first and only true love, something which is rare in our profession. When we had finished our meal, we sang two or three songs. The same scenario was repeated several times a week after that. Jean Rena would trade supper for a show. It was an exchange of friendly services: he held on to his wallet and we filled our bellies.

Micheline Rugel Fromentin

We were often drawn to the Pont–Aven in search of a decent meal, even if it meant singing for our supper. Our stomachs full and our set over, we would peruse the young women who were by themselves, while we waited for Aïda to return from the Concert Mayol. One evening, there was a young brunette there whom I shyly attempted to woo. She made it quite quite clear that, in view of our age difference, insistence was futile. After dinner Jean Rena asked us to sing again, which we did with some success.

A few days later, the young woman, Jeannette, returned to the Pont–Aven with her seventeen year-old, blond, perfectly delightful daughter. She was there to audition. She had a lyric voice which was better suited to opera than cabaret, but popular music was what she wanted to do. Her first song was called *J'ai Deux Mots Dans Mon Cœur*[5], two words in my heart, three little words which we would soon make our own. I asked her to come with me to the funfair at the Place de la Bastille the following day. In a bumper car, when she was aching all over from the collisions I had inflicted on her, I declared my love.

This was how Micheline Rugel Fromentin came into my life. Youth is impetuous and impatient, and I decided to marry her. Our parents found my request premature, citing our youth – I was only twenty one, and my situation was, to say the least, precarious. But faced with our insistence, a decision was reached which was agreeable to all parties: Micheline would come and live with my parents until we reached the proper age for marriage. This kind of arrangement was common practise in the East, so we were following tradition really. It also allowed our parents to make sure that there was no prenuptial consummation! Our traditional–style engagement lasted for almost two years. During this time, I was often away touring; as for Micheline, she applied herself to learning operetta songs in Armenian – although she didn't speak the language. She had a charming accent and would sometimes sing duets with my father.

---

[5] *J'ai Deux Mots Dans Mon Cœur* literally translates to *Two Words In My Heart*, in French *"je t'aime"*, *I love you, counts as only two words.*

CHAPTER 14

Surprise Surprise, I'm a Songwriter!

At Pierre Roche's place, overlooking Montholon Square, where I lived for the most part during the period that Micheline was living with my parents – a two-year engagement is a long wait – we were living it up every night. It was here, after Lawrence Riesner and Francis Blanche had turned down our request for songs, that I set about writing lyrics, I, who until then had only written a few short poems and refrains for Roche to set to music. We now had a set that we could really call our own. Up until that point, we had been singing songs by Johnny Hess, Charles Trénet, George Ulmer, as well as a few songs from Edith Piaf's repertoire, and various hits of the time, but we yearned for more jazzy numbers, songs with more swing. Here's what I came up with on my first attempt:

Been Drinking (J'Ai Bu)[1]

I drank
I gambled on the table

[1] From *J'ai Bu / I've Had A Drink* by Charles Aznavour.

At the wheel, the roulette of life
You won everything
While I lost it all
And so I drank

Roche lost no time in writing the music. There was a general feeling of surprise among our friends, and no one was more astounded than I was; I had the ability, in spite of my lack of culture, to instinctively write verse that obeyed the rules of meter and caesura. More songs followed and we graduated from being duettists to singer-songwriters; we were moving up in the world! I was on cloud nine. Roche, with his two university degrees, felt incapable of stringing two lines together, whereas I, with my humble pass grade school certificate, felt like I had a ticket to highbrow heaven. News travels fast in this profession. The orders rolled in, and I went from being an insouciant singer to a sort of sedulous scribe.

I spent most of my time at Pierre's where there was a constant stream of young writers, composers, and performers of the new generation; and, for the pleasures of the eye, the heart, and the flesh, lovely young girls. In the evenings, we sang in nightclubs; there were a large number of clubs in those days that put on variety shows featuring young singers, entertainers, and impressionists who were just starting out, with or without a headline act on the programme. We returned home at night, often in good company. But Pierre's parents, who had taken up residence in Presles, still owned the apartment and could turn up at any moment to spend a couple of days in the capital. Fortunately, Pierre's sister Anne-Marie, who lived with the parents, would sound the alarm the minute they set off for the station. Suddenly, it was all hands on deck! We'd leap out of bed in a mad rush and queue up for the one bathroom, while our lovely young companions would make the beds and tidy up a little, then, fresh as daisies, we'd wait for the parents to arrive. Thank heavens it never occurred to them to wonder what so many people were doing in their son's apartment at such an early hour! The parents occasionally missed their train and would decide to stay in Presles. There would be another call from Anne-Marie: "False alarm." And we'd all dive straight back into bed with our respective partners for a blissful lie-in.

So we had *J'ai Bu* in the bag, our first composition, and since our inner circle had given it the thumbs up, all we had to now was decide which artist to approach. We were unanimous in our choice of Yves Montand, whose performance at the Étoile had established him as a star in his own right. We all admired him, and, having managed to set up a meeting to present our masterpiece, Pierre and I went to see him in his dressing room. He listened attentively before making a proposition that I categorically rejected: still under Piaf's influence, he agreed to perform the song as long as it ended with the suicide of the drunken protagonist. To Pierre's horrified consternation – as far as he was concerned, no concession was too great if it meant having such a big star perform one of our songs – I replied that if every man who got drunk were to commit suicide then the population of France would be decimated by a good third, and with that, *au revoir*! He turned down another song of mine, some years later, for similar reasons; when I presented *Je M'Voyais Déjà*[2] to him, in the presence of Simone Signoret, he alleged that songs about our profession had never managed to capture the public's imagination.

Years later, Simone admitted to me that this had been a real mistake on their part. Georges Ulmer, a regular visitor at the Roche residence, who generally wrote all his own music, to accompany Géo Koger's lyrics, nonetheless added *J'ai Bu* to his repertoire; he recorded the song and was awarded Single Of The Year for his performance. Heartened by this promising start, Pierre and I got back down to work, and, unconditional fans of Cab Calloway that we were, ventured into more up tempo, jazzy territory. Roche injected his music with swing while I sought words that would echo the *scat*[3] style of singing. If the elders raised their eyebrows in horror when they heard our songs, the rhythms hit a nerve with young people who would sing along with the beat.

Oublie oublie Loulou
Mais oublie oublie Loulou
Oublie-la donc[4]

---

[2] *It Will Be My Day*
[3] *Onomatopoeia sung in a jazzy fashion.*
[4] From *Oublie Loulou* by Charles Aznavour. "*Forget, forget Loulou, Come on, forget forget Loulou, Just forget her*".

Then, one day when we were out window shopping – my favourite sport – we each bought a fine looking taupe fedora. These words had sparked my imagination and the following day I wrote:

The Taupe Fedora (Le Feutre Taupé)[5]

He was wearing a taupé fedora
He was speaking in onomatopoeia
He was drinking iced coffee
Through straws
He had a gangling silhouette
He was smoking perfumed cigarettes
He was walking with dance steps
On Boulevard Raspail

Pierre immediately wrote the accompanying music based on a catchy rhythm; it went down well with the younger generation, who had a thirst for American swing, which they had discovered some years earlier, before our German occupiers had banned all that was related to anglo-culture.

We continued writing jazzy songs, as well as more romantic ones.

All we had to do now was find somewhere to play. During the Occupation, there were few means of transportation, but nothing was impossible for a couple of rogues like us. The Germans had banned all travel to certain seaside resorts, including Saint-Nazaire and Le Havre. However, there were cabarets and cinemas in these very towns that were crying out for artists. Since we knew that trains used to take the precaution of slowing before crossing bridges – which might have been mined by the Partisans – we signed up to play in places where no other artist dared to tread the boards. For example, when the train reached the last bridge before Le Havre, we were able to jump off as it slowed down, find some other means of transport – a tram, a cart, a gas-generator car[6] – and make it to the venue from there.

---

[5] From *Le Feutre Taupé / The Taupe Fedora* by Charles Aznavour.
[6] *Voiture gazogène* – since petrol was scarce during the Occupation, some vehicules were fitted with a generator which turned wood or coal into gas, also known as *charcoal car.*

Since the artists who were booked to play after us occasionally failed to make it across the demarcation line, we sometimes performed at the same establishment for two weeks instead of one. We even spent three weeks in Saumur. Then we were off again – by bicycle, of course, a single bicycle, and *not* made for two – on our way to Angers, where we had been asked to stand in for Damia, one of the great French realist[7] singers, who was unable to make her engagement. It was quite a hike from Saumur; but there's nothing like the prospect of earning the same fee as a big star to motivate you! You needed a permit to travel from one region to another; but while most artists were terrified of being arrested, Roche and I were afraid of one thing only: being out of work. It has to be said: discretion was not the better part of our valour.

---

[7] A genre of French chanson exemplified by artists such as Mistinguett, Édith Piaf, Josephine Baker . . .

CHAPTER 15

Manouchian

Before he was a Resistance hero, Missac Manouchian was primarily known for his poetry in the Armenian community. He often came to our home with his wife Méliné to discuss theatre, poetry and, sometimes, specific actions that had been taken against overzealous collaborators, or high-ranking officials of the occupying army and the Kommandatur, with my parents. They would talk in hushed voices, as if the walls could understand Armenian. Missac loved to play chess, too: he was the one who taught me the rudiments of the game.

In 1944, Manouchian and his group were arrested by the Gestapo. Thousands of posters were printed and plastered on walls across the capital and all over France; circular insets showed the sinister faces of those they referred to as the "foreigners". It was obvious that they had been beaten and tortured. Indeed, we learned that Missac had fourteen facial fractures. Méliné took refuge with us; she was in a state of panic. We waited anxiously for news: it was all bad. The Resistance fighters to whom the Germans referred as "terrorists" were shot by firing squad.

This is the final struggle
Let's regroup and tomorrow
International
Will be the human kind[1]

Nothing But Disillusion

The Germano-Soviet pact had destroyed some of our greatest hopes and brightest illusions. We were fighting for a better future, but the days ahead would bring only disappointment. The Soviets were supposed to open the gates of paradise for us; instead they did an admirable job of creating hell on earth. There were more and more rumours circulating about the role of the Party, particularly in the case of the FTP-MOI[2] Resistance fighters rounded up by the Germans; and there are still unanswered questions. Today, now that the French Communist Party is striving to redefine itself and is no longer a puppet of the Soviet Union, why not resolve the profoundly nebulous, ambiguous Red Poster[3] question once and for all, that is alleged to be such a black mark against the party?

After the execution of Missac Manouchian's group, we were worried sick because when Missac needed someone from outside the group who had not yet been identified, he would call on the Armenian women, including my mother. One of their missions was to transport weapons using a pram, before and after attacks were made, so that there would be no trace of anything if one of the Resistance fighters were to be arrested by the Nazis.

It was a long time after the 1940 Appeal of June 18th, broadcast via the BBC on the programme that would come to be known as "The

[1] From *The Internationale* by Eugène Pottier.
[2] Francs-Tireurs et Partisans de la Main D'Oeuvre Immigrée – Franc Tireurs and Partisans and Immigrant Workers – Resistance group made up of mainly foreign workers and Jews.
[3] L'Affiche Rouge: Plastered on walls across Paris in 1944, the Red Poster showed ten of the twenty four members of the FTP-MOI arrested by the Nazis. They were all executed after a sham military trial. This poster served as a propaganda tool for the Germans and Vichy, portraying the Resistance fighters as foreign terrorists. Louis Arragon wrote a very beautiful poem which he simply titled The Red Poster.

French Speak To The French", and which I had not been lucky enough to pick up on my own radio, that the younger generation, to which we belonged, could be seen walking down the street banging two pieces of bamboo together, chanting: Deux Gaulle, deux Gaulle! Some of our friends ran into trouble with devotees of the new regime; for my part, I got a good kick in the pants from a German soldier on the metro because I was vehemently explaining to Jean-Louis Marquet that it was high time he managed to get us booked at a music hall as the "*vedette Américaine*". There was much talk of Allied landings at that time and the field grey uniformed soldier could not have known that the French expression *vedette Américaine* simply meant "special guest star", the main support act in the programme. I survived the beating and was not shipped off for Arbeit in Germany.

CHAPTER 16

Freedom

Radio London, The French speak to the French[1], De Gaulle, Liberation ... People are draping flags across windows, they're coming, here they come ... Wait! That's not them ... Yes, yes it is! There they are! And up they go again, the French Tricolour and the Allied flag. August 1944, Paris, the entire city is on the streets: there is a mixture of joy and fear; Allied uniforms line the pavements of the capital, tanks roll by; collaborators and militia men are hunted down, rounded up, punished, and sentenced, often summarily. Standing at the kerb on the Rue La Fayette, Aïda, Micheline and I let the Allies know how happy we were; they threw us handfuls of chocolate and chewing gum – at least, when I say "us", I mean Micheline and Aïda – which I stashed away in my haversack. I swapped them for other things that I craved after so many years of going without.

People sought revenge for the miseries of the war: women's heads were shaved; collaborators were hung from lampposts; militia men were hunted down; tradesmen who had grown rich on the black market were disposed of; and Sacha Guitry was thrown in jail simply because he was famous. Personal scores were settled, neighbours

---

[1] *Les Français Parlent Aux Français.*

denounced, people took the law into their own hands, sometimes misguidedly and without restraint, but, more than anything, they purged the sullied towns and countryside of every last trace of field green.

We were free. We could get on with the brighter, simpler things in life. We turned our backs on the horror and faced the delirium and the joy, the waiting and the hoping for prisoners to return. Allied soldiers were discovering the legendary City of Light and needed entertaining – oh la la, pretty mam'zelles, Pigalle, cabarets, the Moulin-Rouge, the cancan – all the folklore of Paris that fascinates and fires the imagination of men the world over The nightclubs reopened – there was a demand for extra attractions, for scantily clad girls, and rhythm, rhythm, rhythm . . .

The occupation years had left a bad taste in my mouth; the post-Liberation period didn't strike me as being particularly glorious either. Since Pierre and I had no scores to settle in all of this, we were out enjoying ourselves with people like Georges Ulmer, Francis Blanche and our Club de la Chanson friends; and more importantly, as concert halls began to open up for business, we concentrated on plying our trade and earning a living. Dates had to be found. We kept our ears to the ground for auditions in the Pigalle district, which boasted the largest concentration of Allied soldiers – carousing, trading, and drinking to their heart's content. We successfully auditioned for a Monsieur Bardy, who became one of Pigalle's biggest club owners. Bardy asked us what our fee was for a three day booking. Three thousand, I told him. "A day?" he asked. Without turning a hair, I said: "Of course!" "Each?" I was on a roll: "Yes, that's right." And just like that, we went from being paid three thousand francs to eighteen thousand, a veritable fortune!

We were free! We could dream of the brighter, simpler things in life. So we posted the bans and the date for our wedding was set at last. I went to the Armenian church at 15 Rue Jean-Goujon, in the 8th arrondissement, to make the arrangements. The Aznavourian family were already well known in the community; I confessed to the bishop that my means would not allow me to ask for more than a simple blessing. He came up with a brilliant idea: if I postponed the date of the ceremony by a week, I would be able to take advantage of the sumptuous floral decorations that had been ordered by young Monsieur Beck, heir to the famous philatelists on the Place de la Madeleine, who was to be married the day before and had spared no expense in planning a lavish ceremony. Micheline and I were married like millionaires. When we left the church, I only had fifty francs in my pocket, just enough to pay for a taxi. After a small reception at my parents' home, we moved in, at 8 Rue Louvois, where we had been given a room by the Parseghian family, cousins of my mother with whom we were very close: Simon, Robert, Armand, Nelly, the Papzian family and the children, Catherine, Shaké, and Minas. The room, which had no running water or toilet, was on the top floor and looked out onto a corridor. We had to wash in the toilets on the landing, although we did have a fireplace. The few pieces of furniture that we owned rattled and shook with every passing aeroplane. But we were young and in love, this was the bohemian life, and bohemian as you know, meant happy.

That I Loved You Was Enough (Il Te Suffisait Que Je T'Aime)[2]

We were twenty, you and I
When under the same roof
We fought misery together
We were still almost children
And looking at us one would say
How very much alike we were

We were hand in hand
Facing destiny's trouble
We resolved our many problems
Empty stomachs and starvation
You satisfied your hunger with illusions
It was sufficient that I loved you

---

[2] From *Il Te Suffisait Que Je T'Aime / Loving You Was Enough* by Charles Aznavour.

CHAPTER 17

The Double Bass

Roche and Aznavour. What were we, if not two young men with a passion for music and the stage? Roche was hooked on swing, and I was smitten, as you know, with the waltz, the tango and the paso doble, which I danced like a dervish. I knew all the words to the songs, even in Spanish, though I could not speak the language! When we started out, small concert halls did exist in Paris and the surrounding suburbs, like the Excelsior at the Porte D'Italie, the Pont de Charenton Casino, or the Saint Martin Casino, as well as in some of the provincial cities; but we mostly sang in cabarets. We earned enough to live on, but we couldn't afford to be out of work for long. Unlike cicadas, it was during the summer season that our pickings were most likely to be slim.

In the summer after the war, seaside casinos were tentatively reopening for business; Pierre and I were concerned that we might not find any bookings. Then a friend, Tony Andal, who was desperately trying to find a pianist to complete his quintet, came to see Roche and begged him to stand in. Without a pianist he could not honour the booking he had for a small ensemble at the Saint-Raphaël Casino, which was reopening for business even though damage sustained during the Normandy Landings had not yet been

83

completely repaired. They had been booked for the whole summer season. The proposition was a tempting one for Roche, but he was confronted with a dilemma: what was to be done with me? Tony's budget for the band was too tight to stretch to a singer.

"If only you knew how to play the double bass!" he said to me, "I haven't hired anyone yet."

Without missing a beat, I replied: "No problem, I just need to practice a bit. I used to play the violin when I was a kid, shouldn't be a problem, plus I have an excellent ear for music."

Tony was less than convinced. Roche reassured him: "You'll see, it'll work out just fine. We've still got three weeks to get him up to scratch."

The contract was signed; now all I had to do was learn to play the bass on the double! Yours truly hadn't touched a violin in six years – Isaac Stern could sleep easy – and now a double bass of all things! Pierre said: "I'll give you the bass parts for a few American songs; you'll see, it's a piece of cake."

Being a musician is a profession; it's not an amateur pursuit, and the day I held a double bass in my arms, the full weight of this realisation hit me. But, post-war, you had to make the most of things and just get on with it! And I got on with it, consoling myself in this way: in view of my height and weight – I weighed about eight stone – compared to the size of the instrument that I intended to use as a shield, I promised myself that no one would even notice me.

So we hired the largest double bass that we could get our hands on, and I threw myself into learning to play it as if possessed; I was not much better than a beginner. I taught myself five tunes: *I Can't Give You Anything But Love, Long Ago And Far Away, Bye Bye Blackbird, Oh Lady, Be Good,* and *Star Dust.* Armed with this slimmest of repertoires, we settled into a charming family boarding house in the proximity of the casino – Roche was joined by his latest conquest, Lydia, who was of Ukrainian origin, while I had Aida and Micheline with me. And let the music play!

On the first night, I played the bass with great gusto, I replaced Pierre on piano for the tangos, and gingerly sang a few refrains, for this was not part of my contract. Things were shaping up well. Whenever the director happened to be in the auditorium, we played

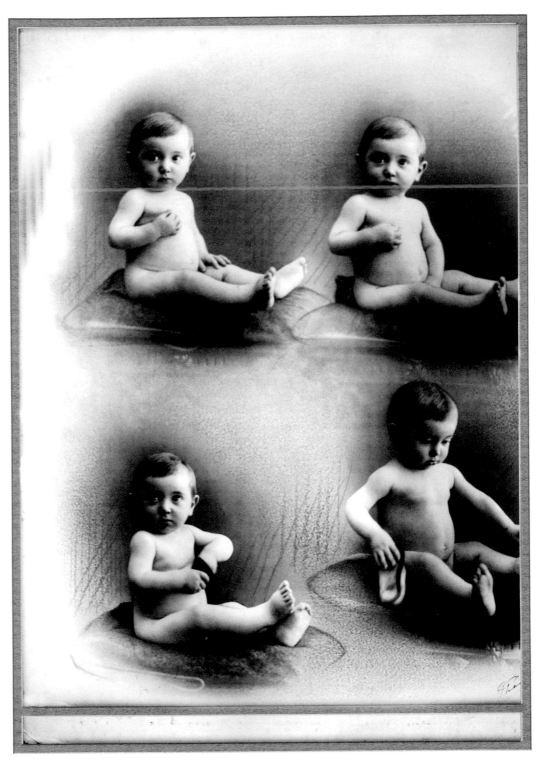

The only existing photo of me naked.

My mother before she married.

My mother as a young girl in Istanbul.

My mother's grandmother, my father, and my mother. Shortly after escaping the horrors of the genocide.

My father Mischa and his father Missak Aznavourian; in Georgia, I assume.

Aïda and myself.

My father holding Aïda, in Salonica.

Berck beach. My mother, me, my father, Aïda standing.

Now you know how I got my husky voice.

Mademoiselle Jeanne's class. I am in the first row, third from the right.

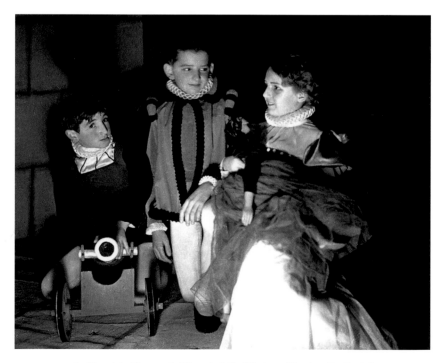

As Henri de Navarre in Margot at the Marigny Theatre. On the left.

1er enfant de chœur

Ch. Aznavour
2. Impasse Béarn (IV)

Date	Répétition	Somme	Signature
15 Février	1	Dix frs	aznavour
6 Mars	8	Quatrevingt frs	aznavour
Date	Représentation	Somme payée	
15 Mars	9 soirés 2 matinés	Cent cinquante frs	75 fr aznavour 79 fr aznavour
22 mars	7 soirés 1 matinée	112. 50	37.50 aznavour 37.50 aznavour 37.50 aznavour
29 mars	7 soirés 1 matinée	112. 50	100 aznavour
5 Avril	7 soirés 1 matinée	112. 50	150 aznavour
13 Avril	6 soirés 2 matinées	105. =	97.50 aznavour

A statement of my earnings from the Madeleine Theatre in Paris.

The Cigalounettes and "Prior"

A spot of camping, but not too much.

My dog. The first in a very long line of friends

My father and a few motivated friends in 1937. The Popular Front. Paid holiday

Our grandfather and his conquest.

My father holding his tar; on his left Missac Manouchian, in front of Missac, Méliné Manouchian; on her left and in front of her the Aslanian couple that were shot by the Germans; then at the bottom, my mother and Badjoui, a governess in Galluis.

It was War, but there would still be music. My father as a voluntary conscript.

Missac Manouchian

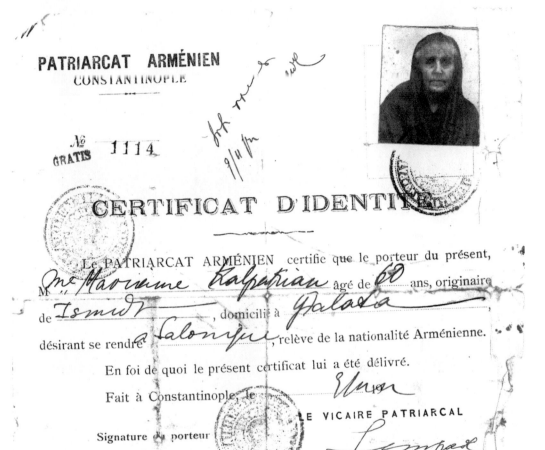

PATRIARCAT ARMÉNIEN
CONSTANTINOPLE

№ 1114
GRATIS

CERTIFICAT D'IDENTITÉ

Le PATRIARCAT ARMÉNIEN certifie que le porteur du présent,
Mme *Marianne Kalpakian* âgé de *60* ans, originaire
de *Ismidt*, domicilié à *Galata*,
désirant se rendre *à Salonique*, relève de la nationalité Arménienne.

En foi de quoi le présent certificat lui a été délivré.

Fait à Constantinople, le

LE VICAIRE PATRIARCAL

Signature du porteur

French influence. The Armenian Patriarchate issued identity papers in French.

Aïda and I performing our
Russian dance number.

Aïda

A.M. Julien directing Aida during acting class.

RESTAURANT Gérard

POUR UNE DEUXIEME SEMAINE "CHEZ GÉRARD"

ROCHE ET AZNAVOUR, fameux duettistes français qui restent à l'affiche du restaurant Chez Gérard pour une deuxième semaine, commen-
çant ce soir.

TOUT QUÉBEC
APPLAUDIT!
ROCHE et
AZNAVOUR
fameux duettistes français
qui font sensation
Chez GÉRARD
Vis-à-vis la Gare Union
L'endroit choisi pour bien
manger et se divertir
ST-GEORGES COTE
maître de cérémonie
Pour réservation, appeler:
4-0549

Ils sont uniques !
Ils sont épatants !
ROCHE et
AZNAVOUR
fameux duettistes français
dans leur
**2e SEMAINE DE
SUCCES**
Chez GÉRARD
Vis-à-vis la Gare Union
L'endroit choisi pour bien
manger et se divertir
ST-GEORGES COTE
maître de cérémonie
Pour réservation, appeler:
4-0549

Devant l'avalanche
de demandes
pour les billets
du récital de
CHARLES
AZNAVOUR
AU THEATRE CAPITOL
les productions
Jacques-Gérard
ont réussi à obtenir de
la grande vedette française
CHARLES
AZNAVOUR
de donner un deuxième
récital jeudi le 23 nov.
au théâtre Capitol
Billets en vente dès aujourd'hui
au théâtre Capitol
Orchestre : $4.50 — $4.00 — $3.50
Balcon : $4.00 — $3.00 — $2.50

SENSATION !
Chez GÉRARD   L'endroit où l'on
mange bien
vis-à-vis la Gare Union
vous présente :
ROCHE et **AZNAVOUR**
LES FAMEUX DUETTISTES FRANÇAIS
Votre maître de   prince des
cérémonie   **ST-GEORGES CÔTÉ**   annonceurs
Faites vos réservations en appelant : 4-0549

With Eddy Constantine, Édith Piaf, Loulou Barrier

Micheline, my first wife, holding our daughter Seda

Édith

Dany Brunet flanked by Victor and François Rabbath.

With Charles Trénet and Jean Cocteau.

the American numbers; until the day he noticed that we were always playing the same songs. We needed to come up with a solution after that. One night – there is a guardian angel for bad musicians, after all – a rather well-oiled punter lost his balance and made a desperate grab for the double bass, which was standing on the small rostrum. Locked in an embrace, they both toppled onto the dance floor to the amusement of the dancing couples; he was unharmed, the sides of the double bass were smashed. It was a gift from the gods. The nearest stringed instrument maker was thirty miles away . . . We made the trip and the good man promised to repair it as fast as he could. This was more than we were asking for, and I had a dickens of a time making him understand that we weren't, no, we really weren't in any great hurry . . .

A month later, I was rushed to the hospital with advanced appendicitis peritonitis for an emergency operation. There was only a duty surgeon there who, for some reason, was not authorised to operate. In light of the urgency of the situation, I signed a discharge form that allowed him to open me up; he made such a fine job of it that the scar is barely perceptible. While I was convalescing, the double bass, which had returned to the fold, was relegated to one of the back rooms where it continued to collect dust until the end of our contract. And quite legitimately – I was too weak to hold an instrument – I finished our three-week engagement as the casino band's official front man.

CHAPTER 18

One and One Make You

In 1947, we were playing the Palladium, an establishment located near the Place de la Bastille. We had written all the songs in the set; Pierre the music, and I the lyrics. *Le Feutre Taupé, Départ Express*[1], and *J'ai Bu* were our most popular live songs. On May 21st of that year, I received the news between two songs: "It's a girl." The moment the show was over, I rushed along to the hospital where I was introduced to the darling little bundle of pink flesh, whom we named Patricia, and later gave a second, Armenian name, Seda.

To My Daughter (A Ma Fille)[2]

I know a day will come
For life is like that
A day I'm dreading
That day you'll go away
I know a day will come
When, sad and lonely
While supporting your mother

[1] *Quick Getaway*
[2] From *A Ma Fille / To My Daughter* by Charles Aznavour.

Dragging my steps
I will return home
To our deserted home
Where you will not be

Is there anything more stupid than a young father at his young wife's bedside where close by a small being lies that has just awakened into life? The idiot feels strange, clumsy, he doesn't know what to say, nor what to do, he almost forgets about his wife, he only has eyes for his first child ... And when the nurse suddenly gives him the child to hold, the new dad becomes even more bewildered; blushing, stammering, he tries to change the baby's position while the little bundle wriggles like a worm; he's not really sure what he should be doing or how to handle this fragile creature. Well, that fine May day, I was that stupid young father; and some years later I experienced the same joy on three more occasions, albeit with a little more confidence.

CHAPTER 19

The Édith Complex

I am not one of those people who keep everything, I have only kept letters sent by friends and those I have admired. That said, a million useless things have accumulated in my cupboards and drawers; the telegrams I received for my Parisian opening nights, for example – this was before the advent of the fax, which, for me, just doesn't have the same emotional impact.

Lately, having decided to have another clear-out, I came across an impressive number of those telegrams. I began putting them through the shredder, when I happened upon the one that Édith Piaf had sent me from the States, where she was performing at the Versailles, a club on New York's East 50th Street. She had sent it to me on my first opening night of importance, at the Alhambra, the night that would either make a *bona fide* star of me, or prove that I was foolish to keep trying and that the media who had been dragging my name through the mud had been right all along.

Printed in black on three white ribbons glued to a piece of blue paper, the colour of a Gauloise cigarette packet, these few words jumped out at me: "Know you will be great success. Regret being far away. Much Love, signed Édith." I hesitated for a long time before consigning that telegram to the shredder of memories. In the end, I told myself that I did not need a piece of paper to bring my memories back to life. Édith has always been close to me, in my heart.

Unique. She was unique. She a heart as big as the Rock of Gibraltar, but she was like the little girl who had the little curl, the embodiment of contradiction. Once you had entered her circle there was no way out, she would cast a spell on you; she would appropriate what you had said the previous evening, adamant that it had been her own idea, and, fixing you with her beautiful clear gaze, she would have died rather than back down an inch. Believing what she chose to believe, she would stick to her guns with every fibre of her small being, this whirlwind of charm, genius and duplicity, with all her strengths and weakness.

We shared a kind of amorous friendship, a close kinship until the day she died, but I never shared her bed. I was drawn into her strange world one night in 1946, and the course of my life changed. Small streams plunge into rivers; and I, for my part, plunged unreservedly into those wild, witching waters, that could not fail to overwhelm a young man who, until that day, had never before encountered a person of such stature.

The Fateful Encounter

That day, Roche and I had been booked to sing two songs on a radio show with a live audience that was hosted by Pierre Cour and Francis Blanche. It would go out from the Salle Washington, on Rue Washington. This venue had no stage entrance, so all the performers were obliged to take a seat behind the stage, before the audience filed in, and await their turn.

We were the opening act of the evening, but, curiously, Pierre's piano had been set up right at the back of the stage as there was an orchestra in the foreground. As for me, I was to sing out front, from the apron[1]. This was the very antithesis of what is required for a duo performance, not to mention an opening act! No sooner had I set foot on stage after the announcement, than I got the surprise of my life: I saw Édith Piaf and Charles Trénet, two legends, together with

[1] The front of the stage.

the prince of publishers, Raoul Breton, all sitting in the front row – Charles had just returned from the States and was going to give Édith a few pointers as she would be making her first trip there in a few weeks time.

We kicked off with *Départ Express*, followed by *Le Feutre Taupé*. My eyes were glued to the front row. Facing any audience used to give me the shakes and my right leg was shaking now as if it had Parkinson's. After a few bars, Édith smiled at me and made a beckoning gesture with her finger like the one she always made at the end of *La Vie En Rose* and which meant: "Come and see me after the show." Try stopping me. Charles Trénet congratulated us warmly; he knew a thing or two about duos, having started out with Johnny Hess under the moniker "Charles and Johnny". Raoul Breton asked me to drop by and see him at 3 Rue Rossini, in the 9th arrondissement, to talk about publishing possibilities; Piaf invited me back to her place, just around the corner on the Rue La Boétie, after the end of the programme. When I asked: "Can I bring my partner along?" her answer was: "What partner?" She hadn't even noticed Roche, a victim of the constraints of live radio. "Very well," she said, "Bring him along too, then."

When Roche and I showed up, we found ourselves in a vast court-yard apartment that looked as if it was expecting some phantom removal man to arrive. The place was sparsely furnished with a few easy chairs, including one black leather armchair from which, once deeply ensconced, the star had trouble extricating herself – a helping hand was needed to rescue her each time – a couple of miserable chairs of no particular style, a large, black grand piano, assorted objects, some records and books lying on the floor, a gramophone player, lyrics and sheet music on the piano, and, I almost forgot, a vast red carpet covering the floor of this large, empty room.

Roche was quite at ease as he walked in, unlike me. I could sense that they had been talking about us before we had arrived. The mocking glances penetrated my chronic shyness. Édith's songwriters and composers, Henri Conté, Michel Emer and Marguerite Monnot, were all present, together with her secretary Faou, her pianist, André Chauvigny, Juliette and Marcel Achard, and her current lover, Jean-Louis Jaubert, a member of the Compagnons de la Chanson, who slipped away early, with Édith's consent. And, of course, Édith herself, mistress of the house, the focus of all attention, whose fragile sparrowlike frame concealed a voracious predatory appetite for love and friendship, enough to root you to the spot forever. It was intense, too intense, all the more so as they were looking at me, judging me, sizing me up and down; is he going to be the next one? Does he have what it takes? How long will he last, poor chap? They whispered, they plotted, they laughed among themselves, then the conversation ebbed and flowed into other realms, there was talk of everything and nothing, of love, of chanson, with a little bitching thrown in for good measure. The conversation turned briefly to Jacqueline François whose career had just taken a remarkable turn. Édith was boasting that she had given Jacqueline a key piece of advice: drop the realist genre and concentrate on singing ballads, which was true. I shyly took advantage of the opportunity and mentioned that she was a close friend. This caused quite a stir. Was I sleeping with her? I swallowed and chose my words carefully: "No, she's in love, she has transports with Jean-Louis Marquet, the very man who takes care of our business."

"Transports?" Everyone burst out laughing, "Did he say transports?!"

I felt as if I were at the court of Louis XIV, a sitting duck for the courtesans. Then Édith said to me: "You mean relations?"

"Yes, it's the same thing!"

She turned to the others and announced: "He's right, it's just a more poetic way of expressing it."

My face must have been the colour of an overripe tomato. Painfully ill at ease, I stammered: "I dropped one of my songs off for you, yesterday."

"Ah, yes," she said; and someone sarcastically added: "And he writes too, does he, music, naturally?" No, lyrics. Lyrics? They were ready to bait me again when Édith stood up for me: "Yes, he does, and rather well at that, let's just say he has an interesting style of writing, it's different."

There was a sudden change of atmosphere; I wrote, so maybe I was one of them. I was assailed with questions: where did I come from? why chanson, why lyrics, how did I go about it? I spoke, I answered their questions, I felt a little more at ease, then came the magic moment when I explained that I had sung and busked in the streets of Enghien; that I used my first earnings from this to buy a second-hand bicycle, and had then begun to frequent the Parisian dance halls[3]. Whereupon, the queen bee shushed them all; as far as she was concerned, I had just uttered words of paramount importance. "You know the *Bal à Jo*, the *Petit Balcon*?" She reeled off the names of all the places she had known before her career had propelled her into a different world. She was wistfully nostalgic about her past on the streets and had long regretted not frequenting the popular bistros and dance halls any more. Suddenly she lapsed back into her native vernacular – that of the street:

"So, can you cut a three step?"

I replied likewise: "You askin'?"

"Standing up? On your head?"

"And sitting down"

"Ok, you devil, let's do it."

She asked Michel Emer and Henri Conté to roll up the carpet, Margeurite Monnot sat down at the piano and the musette waltzes flowed forth; then came the paso dobles, and still more waltzes. The lady had stamina, she was indefatigable, and stubborn with it! She wanted to prove to me that she was in charge, that things didn't stop until the boss lady said so. Suddenly there was something of a boy versus girl thing in the air; neither of us wanted to surrender, we'd die first! She hung on in there, I stepped up the pace, I was almost carrying her but she refused to admit defeat, then finally, she announced, perfectly naturally, in a decisive tone of voice although she was out of breath: "He's the real McCoy all right."

I felt as if I had just been adopted. Juliette Achard, who loved tango, asked me if I danced the tango, too. I nodded that I did. Édith interrupted: "Not tonight, Juliette, another time." Milady didn't give up her new toys quite so easily!

Like Jaubert, Roche had slipped away very early on in the evening. I would soon have to walk home myself to Place Pigalle, but this night I had a spring in my step, especially since Édith had said I was to call her by her first name and had dubbed me with an affectionate

[3] *Bals musettes.*

nickname in her own style: "You will be my little dumb genius." We were to meet the following afternoon to discuss songs. Roche had been invited too, so she meant business. There was only one fly in the ointment, I was married and a father. Édith liked only single men and women. She wanted them all to herself. The man-eater may have believed in God and been religious, but she didn't like sharing, especially when it came to love and friendship.

The following day, I was on time for the meeting, and alone; Roche, who used to stay up all night, was still asleep. Édith was a nightbird and I had to wait for her to get up. Since she only fell asleep in the early morning hours, she needed to sleep late to recuperate. She finally emerged, in slippers and a nightshirt, hair dishevelled and nose shiny from applying *vaseloche*[6] – as she called it – to her nostrils, which were always too dry.

"Ah, you're here."

"Yes, Madame."

"Call me Édith, I told you that."

"Right, Madame ... I mean, Édith."

"Well, I've decided to give you a chance, we are leaving on tour with the Compagnons de la Chanson, my support act; you two will open, and then you'll introduce me after interval."

"What shall I say?"

"It's quite simple:

One name
And in that name
All that is "la chanson"
Édith Piaf!!

"You won't forget that?"

"No danger of that, I'd die first." And thereupon, I made a foolish mistake, the one mistake that I should have avoided at all cost as far as she was concerned, a mistake I never repeated. I asked: "And how much will we be paid?"

---

[6] Vaseline.

The lioness shot me a glare that could have turned me to stone, then furiously exploded: "You ungrateful little wretch! You get the chance to go on tour with Édith Piaf, and the only thing you can say is 'how much'?!"

I had been ready for anything, but not this tempestuous outburst; I stammered: "I have a family to support and ..."

"At your age, in this business, people stay single. Am I married, am I? Anyway, as far as the bread's concerned, you'll just have to wait and see."

"Thank you."

"Yes thank you, or no thank you?"

"Yes, thank you, as far as I'm concerned, but I need to speak to my partner."

"Ahh, the backstage Don Juan!" Milady had sharp eyes and she had immediately noticed that both of Pierre's were riveted on her secretary. "Where is he anyway?"

"He's sleeping."

"If he wants to work with me, he's going to have to learn to get up early. Right, the Rouen train leaves the day after tomorrow at twenty past eight. Be there. I can't stand people who run for trains."

Of Drink and Song On the Road

The night before we left, I decided to sleep over at Pierre's place in Montholon Square, to be nearer to the station, which was ten minutes walk away. That evening, Micheline was singing in a cabaret and we accompanied her there. After her set, we went to a charming place for supper and we didn't roll in at Pierre's until three in the morning.

"Pierre, wake up! We're going to miss the train! Pierre, wake up! We're going to blow it!"

And we blew it: by the time we arrived at the station, the train had left, we were in one holy mess! The SNCF[6] had been on time for once, our luck had disappeared down the track to leave us standing sheepishly on the platform. But I wasn't about to let it slip between our fingers. In 1946, the SNCF had not completed repairs on all the

---

[6] National French Railways.

railways lines and bridges that had been blown up by the Resistance during the war. Trains were sometimes delayed here and there. We managed to hop a goods trains bound for Lille, which, happily, arrived on time at its destination. From there, we boarded a tram which took as to Roubaix and we made our way to the station. As for the train which Édith and the Compagnons were on, it was running late. Making ourselves at home on the brasserie terrace opposite the station, we sat and waited for the group to arrive.

Édith, we found out later, had been furious during the whole journey, swearing that she never wanted to hear a word about "those two losers" again, when suddenly, at the sight of us sitting there at the table with our beers, she let out one of her extraordinary laughs and joined us for a drink. She went through the order of the show again with us: we were to go on stage and perform our short set of songs, then Édith herself would come on to introduce the Compagnons – I don't think that any other star of her calibre, before or since, has ever done such a thing. Appearing on stage prematurely to introduce another group could serve only to diminish the impact of her own entrance during the second half of the show. But Édith didn't give a fig about that, and it certainly didn't diminish her success. After the interval, it would be my turn to introduce Piaf. She used stay in the wings and look after the Compagnons' lighting, and she taught me how to do the lighting for her own set.

This was the programme that we stuck to for the two-week tour that took us from the North of France to Switzerland. Our first show in Zurich was sold out. However, in Geneva, as in all the other French-speaking cities in Switzerland, takings were poor, and we found ourselves short of cash. Édith said to me: "You're like me, we know how to get by; we come from the street, but we're going to have to sort the others out." Édith collapsed with laughter at the mere thought of the Compagnons, those well-bred young men, busking to avoid certain starvation.

Right from the word go, the Compagnons tended to keep their distance from Pierre and I. Our penchant for skirt-chasing offended their "boy scout" sensibilities. As for us, we were convinced that they were all virgins, with the exception of Jean-Louis, naturally, who shared the star's bed. It is true that they had no free time to devote to girls. As soon as they had arrived in a town and dropped off their bags at the hotel, they would hurry to the theatre to rehearse new sketches and songs.

Money problems meant that we were two, three or four to a room. From day one, I found myself sharing with Fred Mella, and a friendship was sparked. We have since remained the very best of friends. Girls liked Fred, but he was extremely shy; so, one night, Pierre and I decided to further his education by inviting round a charming creature who found him most attractive. Then we went off to paint the town red, so that he could be alone with her. When we returned, there was a sparkle in Fred's eye, he had the swagger of a young man who had just passed the test of manhood, with flying colours. Hey, so we used to shock the Compagnons, but we kept Édith highly amused. You could always count on us to have a laugh, drink like fish, and find ourselves some attractive company.

Our next booking was in Belgium, Brussels followed by Liege, where Édith and her nine boys were taking the train to Stockholm to perform at the Berns. Understandably, Jean-Louis did not trust us one bit: he was keen for Édith to remain sober, a difficult task in itself even when we weren't around, and an impossible one if we were. She was happy to indulge in alcoholic excess of any kind: beer, wine, port; we anointed her high priestess and worshipped her by emptying our glasses. Jean Louis was constantly on the lookout for trouble, and we'd make the most of any opportunity we got to throw him off the scent.

The night they were set to leave, Édith, Pierre and I were, alcoholically speaking, done to a turn: our lips were heavy, our pronunciation slow, and we'd burst into laughter at the drop of a hat. When we arrived at the station, Édith leant over to whisper in my ear and ask me if I had made the necessary arrangements. You bet I had, everything was arranged: Pierre and I had gone into her sleeper compartment and discreetly hidden bottles of beer under the pillow, in the pockets of her fur coat, up in the luggage rack and under the mattress. As the train started to pull out, I suddenly realised that Édith had come to mean a great deal to me. I wasn't in love with her, it was worse, I felt dependent. A few days went by and I learned that she felt the same way. She expressed it with a simple telegram: "I never thought I'd miss you so much" followed by "Your little sister from the streets, Édith."

Pierre and I remained in Liege for a few more days. Luckily, the feeling we had of being orphaned was somewhat alleviated when we hit it off with a family of circus artists, the Valentes: Maria, who had a highly original musical act, her husband, her son, and her daughter whose name was Catherine. Catherine must have been about fifteen years old, if that, she liked to dance, so that's what we did. I think I even taught her to dance the *jitter bug,* of which I was a fervent enthusiast at the time.

La Miss

At the end of each contract, we would return to Paris. My little half-breed, Seda Patricia, was starting to chatter away in Armenian and French simultaneously. Micheline was not really the mothering type, she was fond of her daughter but was more than happy to let her sister-in-law or her in-laws look after the child. She and I spent a lot of time at Pierre Roche's; the apartment was always full of people and the telephone rang with increasing regularity, with requests for songs. We used to get an advance of three thousand francs for each song we presented to Raoul Breton. We were writing two or three songs a week, which he would offer to bands like Jacques Helian's, or artists who had record company deals. One day, I wrote a song which was titled: *Three Girls To Marry.* Financially, we were in dire straits. Raoul thought the song was too short: I hurried over to Pierre's and the song became: *Four Girls To Marry.* Still too short! Faster than a shotgun wedding, we came up with: *Five Girls To Marry*[7]. Phew! We almost finished the week without a penny to our names.

Just One Cent (Je N'Ai Qu'Un Sou)[8]

I have just one cent
Only one little cent
One little round cent

[7] *Cinq Filles A Marier.*
[8] From *Je N'ai Qu'un Sou / Just One Penny* by Charles Aznavour.

All round
Pierced by a hole
A fine affair
What can be done
With one cent

One day, what day was it? It was a day like any other, the telephone rang. I heard a slightly husky woman's voice with a drawling, Parisian working class accent: "Mistinguett here, I'd like you to come by and see me about some songs." Our impressionist friends used to think it great fun to play tricks on us by passing themselves off as famous people on the phone. I spoke into the receiver: "Stop playing the fool!" She would not be put off and Pierre asked: "Who is it?" I replied without covering the mouthpiece with my hand: "Some idiot trying to kid us." Pierre took the phone: it was indeed La Miss!

We met her the following day at her home, on the Boulevard des Capucines, a large apartment above the Olympia. After she had explained what she expected of us, she opened up a massive Normandy wardrobe that was crammed full of vinyl: "Here we go, have a dig around in that lot and write me a song in the same style." That wasn't our way or doing things. So Pierre sat down at the piano and I began to sing one of our songs for her, *Bal Du Faubourg*[9], the chorus of which was in a minor key and the verses in a major. When she had finished listening, she said: "That's jolly good, but the whole song must be in major, because," and here she used her hands to emphasize the point she wished to make, "Minor chords get people down in the mouth, majors perk them up."

She was quite a character, La Miss, a really colourful character. She was one of the big stars, the popular artists, who were adulated by the public, her shortcomings were as monumental as her strengths. They don't make women like her anymore in our profession; she had a leviathan capacity for work, a talent to match and colossal charisma ... One evening, she invited us to dinner at her place together with a few of her friends. Everyone was supposed to bring something. We splashed out on a leg of lamb, an expensive contribution given our

[9] *At The Local Dance.*

means, other people had brought wine and cheese, that kind of thing. When it came to the main course, she plainly announced: "I didn't have the meat cooked, it's too heavy to eat in the evening before bed-time." The others, no strangers to the star's sense of extreme thrift, not to say, miserliness, cast knowing glances in our direction.

Similarly, from time to time, you had to go up to the loft where she would parade all the show costumes she had ever worn and collected since the start of her career. After the first couple of times you left it to the others to go and sit around up there for hours in the dust. It was also her wont to pretend to be unable to recall the names of other stars, she would say for example: "What's her name? That young singer with the beautiful strong voice, but who isn't at all beautiful . . . Pi.. pi.. pi..." Someone would say: "Piaf." "Oh, yes, that's it, Piaf," she would echo. Or, "Don't come by tomorrow. I'm going to the ABC to see junior's new show." Junior, was quite simply Maurice Chevalier. She never missed a single of Piaf's or Maurice's opening nights, but it would have killed her to utter their names.

Nightclubbing

There were lean times and times of plenty, and tough times in between. We found ourselves playing in clubs where the show wouldn't start until the often drunk and disorderly patrons turned up at some point between midnight and five in the morning. Slumped in the empty, soft seats, yawning and dozing, we'd wait for a punter, or rather the next mug, to step up to the door. At this point the doorman would push a hidden button which rang a bell inside the club, and Sleeping Beauty would awaken: the band launched into a catchy tune, the staff looked lively, the performers pasted on inane smiles, and the hostesses made themselves more enticing and sympathetic than ever, devilishly artful teases who would make the client feel at home, and consequently, deep in his pockets! The club would be awash with an artificial wanton gaiety. To keep the cove and his party happy and captive, they'd send on the floor show who would often have to prostitute themselves on the dance floor for half a dozen punters or less, more interested in thighs and buttocks than verse and music. It created an edgy, ambivalent atmosphere, part cheap dance hall, part funeral parlour, crazy nights indeed.

We came across quite a few clubs like this in our time! Why did we agree to perform in dives like this? Only because the agent who had booked the dates had assured us, and banked his commission, that we would be working in a top class establishment – top class, my foot! And to top it all, we'd discover once we arrived on the premises that we were going to have to camp out in the joint from 10 p.m. to 5 a.m. without permission to address so much as word to the hostesses. It got better; there were no drinks on the house and we had corkage to pay as a bonus! The worst club we encountered was in Antwerp, the Casbah or the Algiers, the name escapes me now, but it was the pits. We continued working in nightclubs after this, but we checked our contracts and made sure that we only had to be there to play our set, unlike the hostesses who were obliged to work from 10 p.m. until closing time. Finally, after this experience, it was back to Paris briefly before I played Marseilles for the first time.

For our one and only booking in Marseilles, our set at the Variétés Theatre was incorporated into a Ded Rysel revue that had enjoyed a successful run of five hundred nights in Paris without our help. On the first night, a member of the audience, who had not detested the show, came backstage to congratulate us, adding sadly in the local accent: "Oh, it's subtle stuff, really very subtle!" Which we translated to mean: "Oh this will never work." As it turned out, we didn't last a week; the takings were indeed subtle, really very subtle.

Yoohoo! Here we are!

With Édith in the States, Pierre and I wanted to surprise her by turning up in New York unannounced, and sitting in the front row of the Versailles just to see the look on her face when she spotted us. But things didn't go quite as planned.

On this second trip, Édith was to perform again at the Versailles. This was the big year when Cerdan was set to fight Tony Zale, the titleholder in his weight class. Naturally, we had a few drinks to celebrate before she left, when, between rounds, she said to me: "Shame you're not coming with us." Quick as a flash I replied:

"No such word as can't in Armenian, and definitely not in Franco-Armenian."

"You're on!" she said.

The day after she left, I took two songs that Pierre and I had just written round to Raoul Breton's office, including *C'est Un Gar*[10], which Édith was due to record when she returned to Paris. "How much?" he asked. I had done the sums carefully: two single tickets for New York, a few dollars to tide us over until we found work – we just didn't have a clue: one hundred and eighty thousand francs – old francs[11], of course. Raoul started coughing – he always coughed when you asked him for an advance:

"One hundred and eighty thousand francs is a huge advance! I never pay out more than two or three thousand per song, and that's for hit songwriters."

"Yes, but this is so we can join Édith, whatever, if you can't manage it, we can always go and see Beuscher!" There was no way that Raoul would lose any of *his* songwriters to the competition. Reluctantly, then, he handed over the advance. Once our bags were packed, I went to Temple market to buy a pair of python skin shoes and changed our francs into dollars at the bank: I was raring to take on America.

[10] He's The Man
[11] In 1958, General de Gaulle deflated the "old" franc by two zeros. On January 1st, 1959, the "new" franc, was officially introduced, at a value of 100 old francs.

CHAPTER 20

My Father's Barrow

So we were all set for the Americas – has a nice ring to it. Broadway, jazz, musicals, places we knew from films, and maybe even Hollywood, it was all going to be ours from now on – dream on, Charlie boy! We had some nerve. It's true that we were young and impetuous, not to say oblivious. I did the sums in my head: my parents had arrived in France, in 1923, to wait for a passage to America, it was now September 1948; almost twenty five years to the day, I was bound for that promised land. Not as an emigrant, but a tourist, not down in the hold of some shabby, broken down old tub, but on an aeroplane – if you please! – and not entirely without design as Edith was supposed to meet us when we arrived. There was a problem however: how would my family survive in the meantime, until I found work and was able to send money home? My father was considering taking on a small stall at the Saint-Ouen flea market. He was convinced that everything would work out just fine, especially as Micheline's father, who had a shop in the Rue des Rosiers, would be able to give him some good advice.

And so it came to pass ... We decided upon the Malik market. From that day on, my father began attending sales in the Rue Drouot auction rooms in order to pick up all manner of sundry objects that

were sold by the basket at a good price. It was all there, crockery and
cutlery, sheets, lamps, and heaven knows what else, everything including the kitchen sink! Once he had stocked up, he would hire a
coster's barrow and, harnessed like a mule, make his way from the
Rue Drouot back to the flea market, huffing and puffing, sweating,
struggling, but unflagging in his determination. Pulling that bloody
barrow when it was loaded up was no simple task, not to mention
pushing it uphill, to the top of Montmartre, and then wheeling it
back down again while braking like crazy. I used to help him as much
as I could by pushing from the rear, but I felt guilty knowing that he'd
have to pull it along by himself when I was gone. But you do whatever it takes to support your family's needs and bring up your children. Setting pride aside, you swap the stage for the street, the glory
for the daily grind, burying the hopes and dreams of your youth,
which were born in the lands whose language you spoke, where you
had neighbours, cousins and friends, lost now or scattered across the
globe, deep in your heart together with your memories, good and
bad alike. That image of my father with the barrow is etched in my
memory; it hurts me even now to picture it. But my father, he pulled
that barrow of his as if it were the most natural thing in the world,
and he did it with a cheerful heart; he knew we would make it, and
we did.

So off I went to buy the tickets for our trip, but it turned out that
all the direct flights were full. We were offered two tickets to
Amsterdam where they said we could find seats on KLM to take us
the rest of the way. So off we went to Amsterdam thinking that we
would get a connecting flight for New York straightaway. Alas, we
arrived just as Queen Juliana's coronation was in full swing; there
would be no seats available for some time. The company booked us
into a hotel in the city; a day passed, then another, our dollars began
to dwindle. Every day we'd pack our bags and make for Schipol airport in the hope of finally catching a flight. In the meantime, I suggested to Roche that we go and visit his family at the palace; he'd told
me that, through his mother – she was a Châtillon de Coligny – he
was a distant, very distant, cousin of the Royal Family of Orange.
Without skipping a beat, he retorted:"You've got to be kidding, on a
day like this!"The city was in the throes of jubilation, it felt as if all of

the Netherlands had come to the party. In the midst of all this bound-less joy, I must have been the only one sulking. They finally found us two seats for America, and, after more than fifteen hours in the air plus a stop in Gander, I caught sight of the statue of Liberty through the porthole. Like Rastignac, I could not help but say triumphantly: "America, we're ready for you now"[1]

They eyed us suspiciously at immigration. Crazy French! The hippy era was yet to come and young people did not travel then as they would in later years. Who were these two hare-brained nut cases trying to enter the States with no money, and, more importantly, no visa nor return ticket. We had quite simply forgotten that you had to have a visa or a work contract to get into the country, and we had neither. There we were before the airport authorities, incapable of understanding a single word of what we were being asked. I said to Pierre: "You studied English at college, can't you tell me what they are on about?" Cool as cucumber, Pierre retorted: "They are not speaking English, but American, which we were not taught." As for me, I wasn't aware that there was a difference. Finally, they found an interpreter for us.

"Did you not know that a visa is required for entry into the United States?"

"If we'd known, we would have made the necessary arrange-ments."

"Do you have a return ticket?"

"No."

"What did you come here for?"

"We came to join Édith Piaf."

She didn't seem to know who Édith was; Édith hadn't been in the States for long. "Where is she?"

"In New York."

"New York is a big city, I suppose she has an address?"

---

[1] At the end of Balzac's short story "Old Goriot" (*Le Père Goriot)*, an adaptation of Shakespeare's *King Lear*, Rastignac looks down upon the city and says «Paris, I'm ready for you now." *(Et maintenant, Paris, à nous deux !)*. Charles Aznavour played Old Goriot in French film made for television in 2004.

"We're not sure, but we do know the name of her impresario, Mr Fisher."

There were dozens of Fishers in the telephone book. Our translator, who worked for the customs authorities, did everything in her power to treat us kindly. She finally located the right Fisher, who informed her that Madame Piaf was currently appearing in Canada and would not be able to do anything to help us until she returned. We remained in the customs offices for several hours; no one was paying us any attention anymore, when suddenly a tall black colossus motioned for us to follow him before asking us to climb into a long, dark limousine which looked like a hearse. For a split second, we thought they were going to give us the VIP treatment. And some day pigs might fly! I noticed, once inside the car, that there were no handles on the inside. It was like being in one of those gangster movies, we were locked in, trapped, prisoners. After a good half an hour's drive – we sadly contemplated the receding city lights in the distance – the car boarded a ferry. The statue of Liberty stood before us, we passed her on our way to Ellis Island – used to pen up illegal immigrants from all over the world. We were taken to a long dormitory where some forty people were sleeping and were shown to two iron beds. We fell asleep in spite of the chorus of resonant snores emanating from our fellow detainees. When I awoke, I discovered that it was a veritable Tower of Babel: besides English, I could hear all kinds of languages: Yiddish, Polish, Italian, Greek, some of them had been living there for months and were making the best of their situation, happy to wait as long as it took to be granted admission into the States rather than be sent back home to their country of origin, to poverty and hardship. There were no cells here, the beds were all right, there were showers, healthy and plentiful meals which we lined up for in single file with a tray, the guards were indifferent, there was no brutality. We'd hit the jackpot!

We'd spent the day twiddling our thumbs, when Pierre noticed an old, locked piano in a corner. We asked if we might use it. No problem, no problem at all. As soon as we lifted the lid cockroaches came pouring out in serried droves. Pierre played, we both sang. A small audience gradually formed, and some, who had come from Europe, spoke in French with us. On the third day we were summoned and driven in the same kind of limousine to New York where we would be heard by a judge, with the help of an interpreter. Round two:

"Why are you here? Do you intend to make an attempt on the President's life?" – as if I would be daft enough to reveal such an idea if I did – "Are you a member of any political party? What is your profession?"

"We're songwriters."

At the time, Pierre and I, together with a young, unknown comic who answered to the name of Bourvil, had been hired by Pierre Grimblat, to sing on the radio programmes he produced. Purely for our own pleasure, Grimblat and I had translated the songs of an American musical that was making a big splash on Broadway, *Finian's Rainbow*. The judge asked me to sing a few lines for him, and I was happy to oblige. Smiling, he granted us a three-month residence visa that would have to be renewed on a regular basis until we found work. And so it was proven that music not only has a soothing effect on behaviour, but on judges, too. We returned to Ellis Island to pick up our suitcases, leaving the island to shouts of warm encouragement and applause from the other "prisoners". A taxi, whose shock-absorbers had given up the ghost, dropped us off in Times Square with our bags. Wow! The real thing was better than the movies; it was lit up like a Christmas tree, and there was a smell of sugar in the air like at Luna Park. An immense billboard, four stories high, showed the gigantic head of a man smoking, exhaling. The square was teeming with street vendors selling hot dogs, cowboy hats and army kepis from the Civil War; our attention was drawn to a large Coca Cola vending machine: for five *cents* it automatically dispensed a cold drink – the kind of machine that hadn't been introduced in Europe yet. Theatres and cinemas flanked the square, posters announced Nat "King" Cole over here, Artie Shaw & His Band over there, and films, films, films with five showings a day ... We feasted our eyes on it, our ears, too, as the loudspeakers in front of the shops were pumping out an endless stream of the latest hits.

We walked into a small hotel on 44th Street, the Langwell, where we rented a room for the modest sum of seven dollars a week, which was about all we had between us. We were approached by a Frenchman: his name was Lucien Jarraud, he was an acrobat and had an act with his partner called "Crick and Croc". He came to our aid as the hotel manager did not speak our language. Lucien managed to convince him to extend a line of credit to us until we found work.

The majority of the hotel guests were Europeans, they were all in show business and they were all late in paying their bills to some degree, but pay them they did, without exception; the manager agreed to trust us. This was no luxury hotel: it was noisy, the walls were a faded pink, multiple layers of paint had formed blisters on the walls and were peeling off as one, the sink was more grey than white, the bedsprings were shot, but what did it matter, we were in New York, we'd dreamt of this all through the Occupation years. This was the country where entertainment was king, the home of all the artists we admired and still admire to this day. We had high hopes of carving out a niche for ourselves; this was the start of a new life, and it was looking rosy, fate was smiling upon us, we were young and full of hope, we'd be sleeping in five star hotels in no time! There was no doubt in our minds, and that was all we needed. We only had a few dollars left, but we had faith. That same night, we spent some of those dollars on tickets for a Broadway cinema where Artie Shaw's band was playing before the film. Then we gorged ourselves on hot dogs on Times Square and promptly collapsed from exhaustion.

The following day, we dashed over to Carnegie Hall to see a brilliant jazz concert by Stan Kenton & His band, featuring vocalist June Christie and the incredible trumpet player, Maynard Ferguson, with arrangements by Pete Rugulo. On another evening, when we had gone to see The Rockettes at Radio City Music Hall, a young woman in a nurse's uniform came up to me in the cinema foyer, while Pierre was buying the tickets. Magnanimously, I took a dollar from my pocket, thinking that she was collecting for a charity. She spoke to me – naturally, I didn't understand a word – refused my dollar and led me towards some other people dressed in white, before rolling up my sleeve and tapping a good pint of blood faster than I could say ouch! It seemed that I had just agreed to donate my blood – to goodness knows what cause! Though still a little dazed, I thoroughly enjoyed the show.

As we left, a man came up to me and pointing to my python-skin shoes, asked: "How much?" He wanted to buy them. They were brand spanking new and looked a million dollars. After haggling for quite some time, I got fifty for them. We dropped by the hotel, which was close by, and I changed shoes. He walked out of there pleased as Punch, while I was fifty greenbacks better off. The money made Pierre and I feel like millionaires for three or four days until our pockets were empty again. Fortunately, our French friends at the hotel used to invite us along to receptions with generous buffets and where there was no shortage of drinks; Lucien rarely failed to make the most of this.

During the course of one of these evenings, Roche disappeared; we looked for him in vain, the first day, then the next … It wasn't so much that we were worried about him, but he was our treasurer and had the last of our funds in his pocket. We were concerned, but we had a pretty good idea of what might have befallen our aristocrat. Once we had exhausted our meagre resources, which we had replenished by collecting the deposit on empty Coca-Cola bottles so that we could go and drink a ten cent beer at Martin's and help ourselves to the small hors-d'oeuvres they served on the side, little cubes of cheese and pretzels – there was nothing left to do but sit back and listen to our stomachs rumbling. The telephone rang at last: "What are you playing at? Where are you? What are you doing?"

"You'll see, come on over!" He gave us an address near 70th Street. Not bad! It was quite a hike on foot, but, if hunger can move mountains, it can certainly get two starving wretches moving. We found ourselves in a sumptuous apartment where our Pierre received us in a silk dressing gown, and introduced us to his beautiful, rich companion before opening the door of a well-stocked refrigerator. With a trencherman's appetite and without waiting to be asked we pounced on the food, before sprawling out on the deep, soft sofas, and dozing off like a couple of yobs.

Édith returned from Canada at last. We went straight to see her. You could have knocked her down with a feather: "What the hell are you doing here?"

"We came to see you. We kept our bet!" Which made her laugh a little, but not that much. She finally softened and said to us: "Well, we'll try to find some work for you."

In the meantime, Berlitz in hand, I prepared the conversation I imagined us having with the important publisher that Raoul had told us about. This was how we met Lou Levi. A charming secretary opened the door and showed us into Lou's office. The exchange got off to a chaotic start, I had been answering his questions blindly until he suddenly asked: "And how about the Marquise?" I had no idea then that Raoul's nickname for his wife was the Marquise and assumed that he was referring to the song, *Tout Va Très Bien, Madame La Marquise*[2]; so I replied:

"She is dead."

He studied me, dumbfounded. "Dead?"

"Yes, dead."

Whereupon, I became completely confused and incapable of uttering an intelligent word. Lou sent for his right-hand man, Sal Chiantia, who, thank heavens, spoke French and was able to clear up the misunderstanding. Lou took a liking to us straightaway and, after listening to our songs, bought two of them for a handsome advance in beautiful dream-green notes.

Suzanne's Umbrella

It's Raining (Il Pleut)[3]

It rains
Umbrellas are sad compagnons
Like enormous mushrooms
Come out one by one from the houses
It rains
And the whole city is wet
The houses catch a cold
The drainpipes have a runny nose
It rains

Pierre and I wrote this song that was performed by The Compagnons de la Chansons, and coincidentally, I got to know Suzanne Avon, who

---

[2] *Everything Is Fine, Madame!*
[3] From *Il Pleut /It's Raining* by Charles Aznavour.

would become Fred Mella's wife – though we didn't know it then – because of an umbrella. They have been my dearest friends now for over fifty years.

I knocked on Fred's door. He opened up: a furtive shape darted into the bathroom to hide. But since I had caught sight of her, she came back into the room, a little embarrassed; neither her family, nor anyone else knew that she had travelled down from her native Montreal to join Fred in New York. As we were coming to Montreal, Suzanne was afraid that I might reveal their secret. Are you kidding? I'm as silent as the grave, especially where love is concerned. For example, I never ask questions like: "How is your wife," or "How is your husband?" So much happens so fast in this business. Although I did once ask a triumphant seventy-something with a pretty nymphet on his arm: "Is this your daughter?" I had put my foot in it, she was his new fiancée! After Suzanne had left for Montreal, Fred realised that she had left her umbrella behind and asked me to return it to her; I willingly obliged. Fortunately, when I returned her umbrella on the night we opened night in Montreal, it was pouring with rain. It simply looked as if I were lending her my own umbrella, and appearances were safe.

CHAPTER 21

The Snows of Yore

Returning (Retour)[1]

Lakes and plains
Mountains and forest
My memories are leading me
Under the skies of my home

Roche and I arrived in Montreal with a recommendation from Édith Piaf, partly because she thought we had talent, partly because she knew that our act would go down well there, and partly to get rid of us so that she would be free to devote herself to Marcel Cerdan, her great love of the moment.

Marcel

Édith tended to live a reclusive life. Not because she didn't like being around people, but because she didn't care much for going out. She would hole up in her usual capernaum, or the one that she created for

---

[1] From *Retour / The Return* by Charles Aznavour.

herself on tour. She had no interest in sports; walking, swimming, and skiing were not part of her world. Marcel Cerdan was the exact opposite. He enjoyed going for a run, being in the open air, and preferred the company and conversation of men. He would quietly agree to read the books that Édith foisted upon him in her role as his Pygmalion and listened to the records that she recommended, but it wasn't his cup of tea. When he needed a breath of fresh air, to escape from backstage at a theatre or the star's subdued rooms, where the only real subject of conversation was music, he would sometimes come over and hang out with us, "Roche and Aznavour" and Fred Mella. One day, at the Langwell Hotel on 44th Street, in New York, for some strange reason, Fred and I had put on boxing gloves to try our luck against the great Marcel. The sight of us putting up such a Lilliputian fight made him laugh; he only had to raise his fist to keep us at arm's length. Having failed to beat, or rather, lay a single finger on the world champion, we set up a Fred Mella vs Charles Aznavour match in the hotel bedroom that we were using as a boxing ring. It was a short affair: I inadvertently caught Fred on the side of the head with a blow that damaged his eardrum, rendering him temporarily deaf. He regained his hearing a few days later, thank heavens. I would have hated to have deprived the Compagnons de la Chanson and the public of my friend's talent. We came to a mutual decision that, thereafter, we would stick to doing what we did best: singing.

We touched down in Dorval; the airport was brand spanking new. It was 1948. We were so stricken by the cold, to which we were unaccustomed – the kind of icy cold that chills you to the bone and makes you want to get right back on the plane and head for warmer climes, anywhere on the planet – that I would have been happy to see an open fire in the arrivals hall. But we were already beginning to warm up by the time we reached immigration. One, Canadians know a thing or two about heating their buildings; two, a warm welcome awaited us: "You're French, from Paris"? Yes, we were indeed – this being important as anyone who was French, even if they came from the depths of the countryside and had never set foot in the capital, used to pretend that they came from Paris, for the sale of appearances.

We were met by Roy Cooper, our Canadian impresario and Monsieur and Madame Longtin, the owners of Quartier Latin, who,

I was told, had been opera singers before they opened their club in West Montreal, in the heart of the English quarter. The car was heated – it was heaven! To think that heating in cars was still considered a luxury in France! We were shown to our lodgings in a "tourist room" on the corner of Sherbrooke and Mountain Street, a stone's throw from the place where we would be performing twice an evening for a fortnight. As it happened, the two weeks were extended to four on the night of our first show as the venue was sold out: anyone who was anyone in Montreal had come to check out Piaf's protegés. The Piaf stamp of approval was a guarantee of artistry.

The audience was made up of French-language singers, composers, poets, radio people, the press, of course – and to our great delight – a pool of pretty girls, each lovelier than the next. Our set was a mix of romantic and up-tempo songs, which was novel in France but par for the course in "Canada". The French had not yet begun to differentiate between Canada and the province of Quebec; de Gaulle's cry of: "Long live free Quebec!" was still to come. After we had played our fifty-five minute set, the audience was even more enthusiastic; the atmosphere was charged. It was the first time that French artists had performed something other than the traditional style of song that had been imported by André Dassari and Georges Guétary; whereas we had more in common with Charles Trénet and certain American singers. The applause was so overwhelming that it was hard to leave the stage. I was dripping with sweat, my shirt clung to me like a soggy rag. After the first show, everyone wanted us to come and sit at their tables: in one evening, we met the cream of the region's French-speaking artistic community.

The following day, towards noon, a small press conference had been arranged. I say small, but the whole of the French-speaking press was there. This had never happened to us before; there was no time to look intimidated, we had dozens of questions to answer, questions about us, France, Piaf ... The one which most surprised us was: "What do you think of Canada?" Hey, fellas, slow down, we haven't been here five minutes, give us a little more time to make up our minds. To begin with, we often had to ask them to repeat their questions, the unfamiliar accent threw us. But we soon became used to it and found it absolutely charming after a while.

115

The day after that, the Deyglun family took care of us. The father, originally from France, was a known and respected author; the mother, Janine Sutto, a famous actress; and the children, charming young people. Friendships were forged, and, little by little, the Deygluns introduced us to the Montreal establishment. We met many beautiful young women which only served to reinforce our attachment to the region. We soon made quite a reputation for ourselves in Montreal as a couple of rollicking Casanovas, to the extent that Suzanne Avon, still somewhat prudish at that time, would refuse to admit that she knew us, when people asked about us, for fear of tarnishing her reputation.

News of our show had reached club owners in the East of the city – the French-speaking districts – some of whom were persona non grata in France and enjoying a second wind in the club business here, with a slew of less recommendable activities on the side. The nostalgic ones among them had opened musette dance halls. They would bring over famous accordionists like Fredo Gardoni and Émile Prud'homme.

The Martin brothers were two such owners: Marius, who owned the Ceinture Flechée on the Rue Saint-Catherine, and Edmond, who co-owned the Faisan Doré on the Rue Saint-Laurent with his brother and Vic Cotroni. They may have been Catholics, but these actually rather likeable characters were certainly no choir boys, far from it. One night, Edmond, the most artistic member of the "gang" turned up at the Quartier Latin to see what he could get out of these two tearaways. He came straight out with an offer of a long-term engagement at his club, where he wanted us to start in three and a half weeks time. We wanted to check the place out first and arranged to meet up the following day. After a copious meal at Edmonds we embarked on our reconnaissance mission at the club. It was a kind of first-floor warehouse dance hall, a room devoid of charm, tastelessly decorated; the walls were hung with immense, unbelievably hideous portraits of sinister-looking felons, Cheri-bibis[2] by the dozen; and

---

[2] Chéri–Bibi, a character created by Gaston Leroux who appeared in a series of books including: *Cheri-Bibi, Cheri-Bibi: Mystery Man , Missing Men: The Return of Cheri-Bibi*, and *The Dark Road; Further Adventures of Cheri-Bibi*.

there was a vast dance floor in the centre, surrounded by velvet ropes like an elongated boxing ring. It looked more like a dive than a cabaret.

When I told Edmond that it would be impossible for us to perform on the stage, if you could call it a stage, his eyebrows shot up like two circumflex accents, all the more so since he had doubled the fee that we were getting at the Quartier Latin. "Think about it," he advised us, "You'll have seven hundred people out there at every show, where you're playing right now, there's got to be two hundred and fifty all in."

It wasn't exactly a persuasive argument as we always put artistic concerns ahead of financial ones; but considering the fee he was offering ... "What is it you need, then?" I explained – as Roche was already on the other side of the room chatting up a charming crea-ture who worked behind the bar – that the dance floor would have to be divided into two parts, a circular curtain would have to be installed in order to mask the cavernous depth of the unusable space and create a feeling of intimacy. He would also need to add a curtain at the front of the stage, two spotlights with coloured filters – essen-tial for creating ambiance during the songs – and two follow spot-lights to ensure that the performers were properly lit.

We were not the only ones who would benefit from all this para-phernalia, as some of Quebec's most popular artists were going to be performing there including Jacques Normand, Lise Roy, Gilles Pellerin; and later Monique Leyrac, Jean Rafa, an entertainer from Paris; and later still, Fernand Gignac, who must have been all of fif-teen years old. The refurbishment would mean that we would not be able to start on the set date, moreover, we had a subsequent booking at the Café Society Down Town, in New York. Edmond Martin would have to be a man of action to accept our conditions in the cir-cumstances. It turned out that he was; he shook on it and postponed the opening night.

CHAPTER 22

Somewhere a Village

The few weeks we spent in New York gave us the opportunity to meet all the French artists who were working there. We struck a chord with Florence and Frédéric, a couple who were both dancers. Of Armenian origin, Frédéric Apkar was well-versed in the ins-and-outs of show business – he later became a highly successful producer in Las Vegas. Knowing that we wanted to play a gig in town, he had secured an audition for us at the Café Society Down Town, and we bagged a three-week contract over the Christmas and New Year holiday period. So, once our residency at the Quartier Latin in Montreal ended, we caught the train for New York, that "palace of our illusions[1]", to fulfil our engagement. We were getting ready to settle down in our couchette berths, which were hidden from view by a curtain, when the train started slowing. Customs officials were boarding the train to check passengers' passports. You needed a visa to enter the States, naturally, and ours had expired. There was no discussion, we were kicked off the train with our luggage in the open country-side, miles from the nearest inhabitants. So there we were, standing

---

[1] Reference to *Le Palais de nos Chimères / The Palace Of Our Illusions* by Charles Aznavour

there in the snow like a couple of twits, frozen to the marrow, and wondering just what we were going to do.

Is there a guardian angel for heedless young lunatics? Probably. In fact, one just happened to be passing in his car and gave us a lift to a kind of corner store in the middle of nowhere, where we were able to drink something hot, eat a hotdog, warm our bones a little and, more importantly, make a panicked call to Edmond Martin, who came and picked us up himself. The following morning, it was all hands on deck. We needed visas and we needed them fast. Once again, Edmond called in a few favours to save time, and, two days later, we made our debut at the Café Society Down Town in the legendary Greenwich Village, the artist's district. It was the only club where black and white artists performed on the same bill – the headline acts were a young singer who had sold a stack of records, Patty Page, and a humorist whom we later saw in a number of musicals and comedies, Jack Guilford. It was the Christmas and New Year holiday season, and even more than usual, people were looking to have a good time. We were billed as major French artists. At that time, French acts were enjoying a lot of success in the United States: Jean Sablon, Charles Trénet, Édith Piaf, Les Compagnons de la Chanson – whose name Ed Sullivan, the host of most popular variety show on television, could never pronounce and who would say "And now, ladies and gentlemen, Les Champignons de la Chanson[2]."

CKVL[3] radio even had a new segment – for once, English songs had to take a backseat! Jack Tietolman had a nose for these things and realised that the tide was about to turn; he gave French songs their rightful place on the airwaves. It was called the "The French Quarter Hour"; all day long, you could listen to songs that were being played on radio then in France: Édith Piaf, Lina Margy, Lucienne Delyle, Charles Trénet, Maurice Chevalier, Luis Mariano, Georges Ulmer, Yves Montand, Tohama – a highly popular Belgian songstress and a champion record seller in France, Belgium and Canada – and dozens of others, including Line Renaud with her *Cabane Au Canada*[4], a song

[2] Translates to *The Mushrooms of Song* instead of *The Companions of Song*
[3] In North America, radio stations are identified by a series of letters.
[4] *My Canadian Cabin*

which offended the Canadians a little as they were proud of their modern cities. Their reaction was: "She sure ain't never been here shovelling winter snow!" A new French revolution was brewing, this time on the other side of the Atlantic, a sweet revolution borne on an army of verse and melody.

French acts were headlining all over the city, top of the bill, but five songs was our sorry lot, not one more: the show was timed down to the last minute as the place had to be emptied and the audience ushered out before those who had come to see the second show could take their seats. On Christmas Night, a pretty young woman came running up to me and kissed me full on the mouth, a kiss which took my breath away, and without so much as a by-your-leave; then with a big sigh, she uttered a languorous, "Oh, French Kiss!", and disappeared forever.

We were singing all our own songs and we had added *Pigalle,* a hit by George Ulmer. We didn't bring the roof down, but they liked us enough to extend our contract from three to five weeks. During the final two weeks, we were lucky enough to perform alongside the wonderful Sarah Vaughan who was headlining, and whom we listened to religiously every night. Emboldened by the positive feedback we were getting we turned down any small bookings we were offered. This proved to be a mistake as we didn't receive any further offers. It was high time to return to Montreal which waited for us with open arms.

CHAPTER 23

Back To Our New Cradle

Talk about a building site: it was crawling with workmen! Martin had wagered that everything would be ready by opening night and had no intention of losing his bet! Nail this, break that up, bring that here, hang this up there ... the old dance hall was being transformed into a local variety theatre, but American-size. Hale, hearty fellows built like hundred-year-old maples were working relentlessly to give the Faisan a fighting chance of being up and running on time. The final curtain was hung, and the Faisan Doré, located on the first floor of a building on the corner of Saint-Laurent and Sainte-Catherine Street, was ready for our opening night. For Roche and I, our real career began in Quebec. "There's a certain type of client in every city," Edmond used to say, "who never sets foot in nightclubs. They are the ones that I want to bring in."

He really had some front; the club was situated in a very working-class area, and I was convinced that the only punters he'd ever see in his establishment were the usual good fellas. I have since learned not to draw hasty conclusions. As it turned out, right from the first show all the tables were taken, champagne had replaced the beer, the place was littered with luxurious furs and evening finery; arms and necks dripped with expensive jewelry. Edmond had positioned his own boys all around the room. No other shady characters were allowed in to rub shoulders with the "swells" – intellectuals, students, future lawyers, doctors, people who would go on to become ministers and officials in the province, like René Lévesque, for example. The evening was a triumph. Edmond was like the cat that got the cream, and he was lapping it up.

The second show was just as successful, this time the audience were more working class. Things were looking good. Together with Jacques Normand, we wanted to come up with something else besides music hall numbers; we decided to do a finale with the whole troupe. And so it was that, every week, we'd get together with the Canadian artists, change the show finale and perform a marathon medley of all the French hits of the time, to the great delight of the audience who would join in and sing along on the choruses. Between sets, we'd be invited to have drinks with clients who, in time, became friends; some of them would even have drinks sent over that we'd knock back on stage during the medley sequence. We were easily downing between twenty-five and thirty whiskies a night. Roche and I could hold our drink, that was the rub. Whenever I felt my heartbeat quicken, I would put it down to the exertion of the performance. My friends, however, began to worry and urged me to go and see a French doctor, who was now in his seventies and had lived in Montreal for a very long time.

Doctor Dufeutrel asked me a series of questions about my work, my sleeping, eating and drinking habits, without offering any com-ment. After he had given my chest a cursory listen, he opened a mas-sive cupboard to reveal dozens of bottles, liqueurs and alcohol of countless brands and types, and invited me to join him in drinking a toast to friendship between Frenchmen. I tasted banana cream liqueur for the first time, a horrible, cloying drink. When I put down my empty glass, he looked me straight in the eye and said: "If you want to live to a ripe old age and stay healthy, that must be your last drink."

"For how long?"

"It will take at least three years to cleanse your arteries of all the alcohol damage they've sustained." No alcohol passed my lips for three years. I even turned down sweets or chocolates that contained liqueurs. But three years later... Well, that's another story!

A Hymn To Love

That morning, a single, but crushing event made every media head-line: Marcel Cerdan's plane had crashed while Édith was waiting impatiently for him in New York. I was in Montreal when I heard the news and, knowing that she would need the support of all her friends at a time like this, I asked for a few days off and made it to New York as fast as I could. The atmosphere in Édith's suite, where all her friends and colleagues had gathered, was somber; she had been locked in her room in complete darkness for two days and refused to come out, eat or drink. For those two days, The Versailles remained closed; on the third day she finally emerged, like a sleepwalker; she had cut her own hair short, very short – she looked like Joan at the stake. Ashen, but determined, she immediately went over to Robert Chavigny, her bandleader and orchestrator, and asked him to arrange a new song that she intended to sing later that evening.

The Versailles auditorium was packed to the rafters, there was not a single empty seat, they even had to add chairs, and the waiters were having trouble making their way through. The death of Marcel, Piaf's great love, had been front-page news in all the papers. So, in addition to Édith's fans, there was a crowd of the curious, who had never heard of the little sparrow from the streets of Paris who answered to the strange name of Piaf. The atmosphere was strange, it was subdued, people in the audience were practically whispering. The lights dimmed, and a deep dramatic and harrowing silence descended. Édith made her entrance, pale but steady; she started by singing a few songs from her usual set, then the band played a very short introduc-tion, and Édith's powerful, impassioned, moving voice rose up and sang these words:

If the sun should tumble from the sky
If the sea should suddenly run dry
If you love me, really love me
Let it happen, I won't care[1]

---

[1] From *If You Love Me / Hymne A L'Amour* by Édith Piaf, English translation by Geoffrey Parsons.

The Hymn To Love, a hymn to her great love, gone but not forgotten, that she implicitly dedicated to Marcel. She sang from the depths of her heart and soul, everyone there was transfixed; the staff, the audience, even those who could not understand a word of French, they were all deeply moved; women were crying, men were crying, too. When the song was over, a deathly hush descended, and time seemed to stand still, then in a single movement the whole place was on its feet for a standing ovation so deafening and sustained that they must have been able to hear it and feel it as far away as Times Square. An ovation for Piaf and, why deny it, for Cerdan, too, while up on the small theatre balcony behind the projectors where we were sitting, those of us who were close to her, her friends and unconditional admirers, all, without exception, had tears streaming down our cheeks.

Our Quebec Cousins

Roche and I spent two and a half wild and crazy years of our young life in Montreal, where we carried on like a couple of sailors on shore leave. I played the field a bit; it was normal at that age, but I only remember one young woman now, Monique Leyrac. She was, maybe, seventeen years old ... She had dark hair which she wore in plaits and looked like an Indian straight off the reservation. This was not one of those long, harrowing affairs ending in a dramatic break-up. It was something simple, an enjoyable moment of my life. We were working in the same establishment, which brought us together in a casual, but charming way. We had two shows a night, three on Saturdays and Sundays – a matinee and two evening performances – and no day off. We used to finish extremely late, almost daybreak.

It was traditional to go and end the night in a spaghetti house, or at Ruby Foo's, a Chinese restaurant on the outskirts of the city, where Quebec's French-speaking showbiz crowd used to hang out. The English-speaking community, which had monopolised on the Montreal clubs until then, did not associate with this new race that was slowly but surely making off with a sizeable slice of the Anglo-American pie. We began to notice how talented Monique was, and we'd listen to her sing with affectionate interest. Since then, a dazzling career as an actress and singer have made her one of Quebec's leading cultural figures.

We were fully integrated into life in *La Province*[2], working in Quebec in summer, and Montreal in winter, alongside Jacques Normand who became "my Quebec cousin" and remained so until the end of his days. We took part in radio programmes – he and Roger Baulu were undisputed stars of the airwaves – and gala performances deep in the heart of the province. I was still writing lyrics. I had no intention of breaking up "Roche and Aznavour", but I was itching to write. As for my partner, he was flitting from flower to flower, with an average rate of conquest that put mine to shame. As I saw it, there was a time for everything.

I had brought Aïda – who was now working at Marius Martin's club, La Ceinture Fléchée – and Micheline over, and intended for my parents – who were bringing up our daughter, Seda Patricia, in pure Franco-Armenian tradition – to join us. Micheline liked Canada, but she only wanted one thing: to return to France. She missed Paris. I, in turn, was homesick for my city, in spite of the easy life that this country afforded us and our continued success. Roche made fun of me: "We'll go to Paris for a holiday, with our fortunes made, and you'll see, you won't be able to get back to the life we have here fast enough."

For the first time, perhaps, he seemed to be in love, with a young woman who had recently joined the Faisan Doré troupe and promptly captured his heart. It must have been serious as I soon found myself wearing tophat and tails in a church, where a priest blessed the union of Monsieur Pierre Roche, a prime specimen from the Oise region, and Jocelyne Deslongchamps, purebred Quebecois, for better and for . . . the stage?

Jocelyne would go on to perform in France and Canada under the stage name Aglaé. I accompanied them on their honeymoon, to Paris, where, fresh off the boat, and reunited with my country, my parents, my friends, my neighbourhood, the professional milieu I had known, and Édith, I decided not to go back to Canada, leaving Roche and his

---

[2] *La Belle Province* is an affectionate French name for the province of Quebec.

young wife, a little put out by my decision, to return by themselves. But he never reproached me for it. As I have mentioned, Roche had a certain nobility about him.

After eight years as a duo, during which time we never quarrelled or fell out with one another, it was with much sadness that we ended our partnership that had thrived from Paris to New York, and then in Canada, where we quickly made the transition from French unknowns to francophile darlings.

Nous Nous Reverrons Un Jour Ou L'autre

We will meet again one day or another
If you want to as much as me
A rendezvous
One day, anywhere
I promise I will be there
For Christmas or for Pentecost
In Rio de Janeiro or in Moscow
We'll be crazier then
And we'll laugh at everything more
We will meet again one day or another
I'm insisting on it

CHAPTER 24

Back To Square One

Whether you believe it or not, I am a shy soul, a tad self-conscious in any case, so much so that when I returned to France, in the 1950s, I took to hiding behind dark glasses when I played my songs for the artists who came to Raoul Breton's, looking for the next big hit, as I hammered away, execrably, at the piano — my playing has improved since . . . at least I hope it has! I was a chain smoker, too: no sooner had I finished one than I was already lighting up another. I had a voice like a foggy London night, straight out of a Conan Doyle story; like a used 78 that sounds as if it is about to give up the ghost.

Raoul Breton, who would introduce me as the new house genius — the original being Charles Trénet — used to receive artists in the small office with the blue piano that still has pride of place in the house, and on which Charles Trénet, Mireille and Jean Nohain, and Gilbert Bécaud wrote many of the songs that captured the hearts of music lovers and other listeners. These performers were to become the travelling salesmen of my humble creations. I had just returned from Canada; Micheline and I had quickly reached a mutual decision to part ways; Pierre Roche and Aglaé had returned to Montreal; and although I had been adopted by Édith Piaf and accepted as a permanent fixture in her private capernaum, artistically speaking, I felt like an orphan. Life as a duettist was harder to forget than I had imagined.

My First Client

I'm Coming Home (Je Reviens)[1]

I'm coming home
To those I love
Coming home
Unchanged
To the place
Of my tender Bohemia
I'm coming home
Speedily
Coming home
I assure you
From as far away
As the adventure has taken me
I haven't
Found glory
Or gold
But I am
And this I swear
As rich as a lord
I'm coming home
From all my travels
Coming home
A little wiser
Just enough
To never leave again

Leo Fuld, my first client – let's call him that – walked through the door of Raoul Breton's publishing company, still bathed in the glow of his burgeoning Parisian fame and triumphant performance at the

---

[1] From *Je Reviens / I'm Coming Home* by Charles Aznavour.

Alhambra music hall. Unknown to French audiences, and scarcely better known among the Jewish community in France, word of mouth had made him almost famous. His set was mainly composed of songs in Yiddish and Hebrew. Originally from the Netherlands, he was living in the United States. His gift touched the "goyim" too.

In the early 1950s, people were still subdued, they had not yet completely recovered from the war years. But those who had suffered more than the rest, deeply wounded in body and soul, who bore the consequences of the suffering endured in the concentration camps, those who had lost most of their family, and who clung to the shadows as if they were ashamed of what had happened to them, these survivors of the worst of all crimes, rendered fragile, still unable to express themselves entirely freely, fearing to assert their Judaism as if the black uniforms of the Gestapo might rise up again at any moment, they welcomed him as a mouthpiece. They came from Belleville, from République, the Marais, the flea markets of Saint-Ouen, Temple market, the Bastille, from modest suburbs and upmarket districts alike, they flocked to hear the first committed Jewish artist who was singing not for a religious feast, but for an international audience, finally allowing them to rediscover their injured pride. They would have given anything to be there, to celebrate together without being afraid to say: "Leo Fuld is one of us." Tickets were even being sold on the black market.

Hungry for live music hall performances, I had slipped into this crowd, some of whom tapped me on the shoulder, convinced that I was one of them. And I was one of them, not through religion, but through fellowship: had my people not also suffered a tragic fate in another time and place?

So, that day, Leo Fuld had walked into Raoul Breton's legendary publishing house, where I went to work every day, come hell or high water. From behind a pair of dark glasses, the inevitable Gauloises dangling from the corner of my lips, stained yellow with nicotine, Raoul, who had met Leo in the States, welcomed him in and introduced him to the whole team. Leo wanted permission to translate some of Charles Trénet's songs so that he could perform them in Israel, which had recently been recognised as a state. Raoul led him into the small office.

I behaved so shyly back then that people thought I was sulking. Raoul urged me to play some of my compositions for our visitor. I banged away at that poor piano to the best of my ability and sang three or four of my songs, including *Parce Que*[2]. Leo thought them interesting and wanted to hear me play to an audience, so that he could see how they went down. In those less than glorious days, I was performing nightly at a club famed for its attractive and rather scantily clad young ladies, the Crazy Horse. Fernand Raynaud and I used to go on between the striptease numbers. Since we performed several "masses" every night, as we liked to call them, to supplement our income, the last one of us to arrive would always inquire of the other: "What's the audience like tonight?" For strangely enough, if one of us went down well, the other did too. Especially since half the time some loud, vulgar voice, pickled in champagne, would shout "Get your kit off!"

This was the rather special cabaret where Leo Fuld came to see me perform. While things went well that night, he was nevertheless disappointed by my set, which did not include any of the romantic songs that he had heard me play, only the uptempo numbers like *Le Feutre Taupé* and *J'Aime Paris Au Mois de Mai*[3]. In his opinion, I was on the wrong track and this kind of set would never get me anywhere. I was a singer of dramatic songs, a child of Piaf rather than Maurice Chevalier; if I were to perform what he had heard me play a few days earlier, the road would perhaps be hard, but ultimately more rewarding. I didn't need any more convincing, I had felt this for some time, but I was obliged to play uptempo sets to get bookings. I had no option but to be a light-entertainer if I wanted to continue earning a living. But Leo's comments had hit home and I made some changes to my repertoire. Overnight and for several years to come, I was an artist without a future. I left the Crazy Horse and my sole regret was no longer being able to join Sim and Fernand in helping the lovely, very lightly dressed young women with their limbering-up exercises just before they went on stage!

[2] *Because.*
[3] *I Love Paris In The Month Of May*

Many years later, when I made my debut in America, Leo came to see me and gave me some excellent advice on how to introduce the songs I sang in French to an English audience.

Chez Patachou

After Leo Fuld, Raoul had a visit from his former secretary, who, for some years now, had had the Paris smart set, and indeed the world and his wife, lining up to hear her sing and see her cut off the patrons' ties. Henriette had become Patachou and owned her own nightclub up on the Butte Montmartre. She, too, came and sat down beside me at the blue piano. I sang her several of my songs. She chose *Parce Que* and said to me: "You smoke too much, three packets of Gauloises a day, no wonder your voice is so trashy. I've a proposition for you: stop smoking for four weeks and I'll take you on for an indefinite period up at Chez Patachou, deal?" Deal!

Four weeks later, she came back to see me and she wasn't happy: "You're not taking this seriously, I asked you to stop smoking, you obviously haven't done so, your voice is even worse now than it was four weeks ago."

"I honestly did give up, ask Raoul Breton, he'll back me up." Which she did. She hired me after all and lifted her futile ban: "You'll start at my place next week. There's just one condition: I sing *Parce Que.*" I'd have happily given her all the songs in my repertoire, I was so thrilled to be performing in a club every night that was packed to the rafters with an international top-drawer clientele.

Maurice Chevalier was there during the first day's rehearsals. I sang *Jézabel, Sa Jeunesse, Poker*[4] and one or two other songs. It was obvious that I had still not come up with the right song sequence for my set. Maurice, whom Roche and I had met during the war, came to see me towards the end of the rehearsal and helped me arrange my set list so that it would appeal to the audience who were basically there for Patachou. Advice from an artist of his stature was bound to be sound. And the audience's reaction on the first night confirmed it. After the

---

[4] *Jezabel, His Youth, Poker.*

show, Maurice, who knew that I lived at Édith Piaf's place in Boulogne, asked me to drop him off on the way. I was obliged to call a taxi and spend some of my evening's pay. When I told Édith what had happened, she said to me: "It's true that he is a little tight-fisted. Take my car after tomorrow." And so it was, in Édith's car, that professor Chevalier became my mentor, as he revealed to me, more or less intentionally, the secrets to an international career.

CHAPTER 25

Édith, Always Édith

For years after his death, Édith clung to the memory of Marcel. She used to pray for him, she thought and spoke of no one but him. She even sent me to Casablanca one day laden with toys for his children. Those of us who were close to her did not like to see her alone. Édith always needed to have someone to love.

Whenever I returned to Paris, I used to frequent the fashionable clubs of the time, particularly Maurice Carrère's, as I really liked his house band, whose leader, Léo Chauliac, was Charles Trénet's former pianist, and the resident singer, an American girl who went by the charming name of Marilyn. There was also a male vocalist there whom, I reckoned, might just be Édith's type, and, why not, a possible candidate for the new "boss". He had a fine voice, and sang well in French, with a warm American accent . . . I decided to introduce him to her. She was performing nightly at a new club on the Champs-Elysées. But I had to find the right pretext, as Édith still wasn't interested in meeting another man. Luckily, Eddie – for it was indeed Constantine – unwittingly conspired to help me: he had attempted to translate *L'Hymne A L'Amour*. I seized the opportunity and lost no time in outlining the plan of action: "I'm going to tell Édith about you. When I bring you into the dressing room, you go in, you wave hello, and as you say *hi*, flash her one of those devastating smiles of yours." Everything went according to plan. When we saw Édith's conspirational smile and her wink, we all knew that a page had been turned in the family history, that a new chapter was being written, but that Marcel would never be forgotten.

With Édith, you couldn't afford to make mistakes about anything, whether it was a film, a play, a book, or a restaurant; if she didn't like it, you'd get the "Well, I can't say I'm surprised coming from you, with your lack of sensitivity" treatment. One evening I had just returned from the cinema, when she asked me what I had been to see, I braced myself and charily replied: "*The Third Man.*"

"Is it as good as they say it is?"

"Better than that, as far as I'm concerned."

"And as far as I'm concerned?"

"I think you'd enjoy it, though I couldn't swear to it."

"Right, we'll go tomorrow, and heaven help you if it's rubbish!"

The following day, we all made our way to a cinema on the Avenue de L'Opéra where *The Third Man* was showing. Our Édith was captivated by Orson Welles and, having discovered that the original version of the film was being shown alternately with the dubbed version, dragged us all back there again the very next day, and the next, and so on and so forth for almost a fortnight. Well, we had all loved the film, but you can have too much of a good thing, and we had just about had our fill. We thought we were saved when we had to leave for the States again. But we had overlooked Édith's tenacity; when she decided that she liked something or someone, there would be no escaping it or them for days on end. As soon as we arrived in New York, she asked Constantine to buy a paper and check where *The Third Man* was playing. It was still showing at a cinema deep in the heart of Brooklyn. We crammed ourselves into a couple of taxis: "*Orson Welles, Here we come!*" Édith would always sit close to the screen, surrounded by her entourage. On the pretext that my eyes were sore, I went and sat at the back of the small cinema, where by Jove, I gave into jet lag and fell sound asleep. At the end of the film, I was still lying blissfully in the arms of Morpheus when I suddenly felt myself being roughly shaken, and a voice I recognised said: "So, you little bastard, sleeping through a masterpiece are you? That's a punishable offence! From now on, you'll have to go without the film. We'll see it without you!" All our friends eyed me enviously as we made our way back to the hotel.

You'll have noticed by now that Édith could be obsessive about things: we might eat the same thing for a fortnight, drink like fish, go on the wagon, see the same play ten times over, adopt someone and see them constantly, then suddenly drop them like a hot brick. The child of the streets/street urchin had learned to recognise and appreciate many things, she was intuitive and had very discerning taste. When passing judgement on something or appraising it, she always expressed herself incisively in a manner second to none.

Since she was particularly partial to Furtwängler's renditions of Beethoven's symphonies, I gave her one of the recordings that she didn't yet own for her birthday. There was an immediate commotion: "OK, kids, we're going to listen to a masterpiece. Eddie, switch on the record player, Loulou, turn the lights down, and you lot, stop talking. Let's listen." We were all sitting in the half-light, inspired looks on our faces, when the music broke the silence. But the turntable must have been playing at the wrong speed. After a few minutes, our Édith began shifting around in her armchair as if she were trying to get comfortable, before calling out: "Right, get the lights, Loulou." When we could see again, she took the record, told Loulou she could have it, and said to the assembled company "You have to hand it old Beethoven, when he got it wrong, he didn't mess around."

One day in New York, Édith was in a foul mood, we had a difference of opinion about something quite futile – it must have been a play or a film – that quickly escalated into a something serious. I only remember that I stood my ground. Which was, of course, exactly the wrong thing to do with Édith. Vexed, she said to me: "Well, if that's the way it is, you can take the first boat back to France." As it turned out, the Transatlantic Company just happened to have one leaving the following day. After a curt goodbye on both our parts, I left the hotel and the United States. The ship had barely made it out onto the open sea when a telegram arrived for me: "I miss you already." That was Édith all over.

CHAPTER 26

Montreal and Back Again

Quebec was my second home, and so I was off to Montreal again, where I was always sure to find work. I had not long arrived when I received a telegram: "Getting married. Would like you to come home," signed "Édith." I was back in no time, arriving at her place around ten in the morning. "Madame is still sleeping, but please come in, someone else is already waiting for her." He had dark hair, a rather nervous disposition, nails bitten down to the quick; he was sitting at the piano, but he was not playing, he was biting his nails. I introduced myself, he introduced himself:

"Gilbert Bécaud."

"What's your line of work?"

"I accompany Jacques Pills, but I'm really a composer and my dream is to write soundtracks. Jacques and I have written a few songs for Madame Piaf, that she should be including in her set once she's recorded them."

"What are you up to here, today?"

"I'm waiting for Jacques."

Right, I hadn't realised that Jacques was in bed with Édith and that he was the new boss. Since the lovers took their time to emerge, Gilbert and I had plenty of time get to know each other better, hit it off and talk about, guess what? Songs, of course, with the idea of working together, which, I think, proved to be constructive.

Now, I'd cut short my trip to attend Édith's wedding, but I should have known that there would be complications: where she was concerned, nothing was ever simple! And indeed she ended up deciding that she wanted to get married in New York. And off we were again, crossing the Atlantic once more. Marlene Dietrich, who was in New York, was waiting for Édith; she had agreed to be one of the marriage witnesses.

When I returned to Paris several weeks later, I met up with Gilbert and our partnership produced songs like *Viens, Méqué Méqué, Terre Nouvelle, C'est Merveilleux L'Amour, La Ville*[1], and a host of others. He was married to a young actress whom he'd nicknamed Kiki, she had recently fallen pregnant and he never left her side – which naturally irritated Édith. Jacques Pills, Gilbert Bécaud, Édith and myself set off on tour across France in two cars: I was driving the second car, with poor Kiki as my passenger, suffering from frequent bouts of nausea.

Gilbert and Édith were not on the same wavelength. For example, Édith had the curious habit of ordering a set menu for everyone, to save time in restaurants – the menu she wanted. Gilbert, who was still unfamiliar with our mistress' character, would insist on choosing something else in spite of the kicks I gave him under the table. As a result, the atmosphere during dinner was always strained. When Gilbert resigned from being piano accompanist to successfully make a name for himself in his own right, another pianist took his place, and we set off on tour once again. This time, I shared a car with the show's producer, Édith used to call him Papa Lumbroso.

Love Is A Wonderful Thing!

Love Is A Wondrous Thing (C'est Merveilleux L'Amour)[2]

Love – it's marvellous
It's fantastic
It's too complicated

[1] *Come, Méqué Méqué, New Ground, Love is A Wonderful Thing, The City*
[2] From *C'est Merveilleux L'Amour / Love Is A Wonderful Thing* by Charles Aznavour.

To be explained
It comes, it goes, it runs
It's lunatic
Love is marvellous
Happy or unhappy
It's a dilemma
That gives lovers
Many problems
It's a dangerous game
But when you're in love
It's marvellous

For the new show, I had been given a proper slot as the opening act; Jacques Pills followed my set. Édith came on in the second half. That particular night, in Royat, the show was about to begin, but Édith and Jacques still hadn't arrived. We were starting to get pretty worried when our two newlyweds turned up in an extremely advanced state of inebriation. Édith was talking gibberish and Jacques couldn't stop laughing. The audience were tired of waiting. Papa Lumbroso pushed me towards the stage: I was to sing five songs to keep the audience happy when all they wanted was Édith. I sang and from the wings someone signalled to me: no, they're still not fit to come on stage. Someone was whispering the titles of my songs to Papa Lumbroso who stood at the back of the venue and announced them. But the audience could take me or leave me: after another three songs, they were clearly unhappy, four more songs and there would have been a riot. I made my exit praying that Jacques would be ready. He was, more or less, but there was a new dilemma, Édith absolutely wanted to go on stage and introduce him. We had a hard time dissuading her. Jacques managed to appease the audience's impatience a little, which allowed Édith time to pull herself together. A goodly number of coffees and other concoctions were employed to – let's not mince words – sober up Madame, before I announced her after an unusually long interval. Her appearance met with thunderous applause, as always. Her first song began with the words:

Walking way above the storms
Looking out from the foc'sle[3]

But this is what came out of her mouth:

Wacky way brother stumps
Lucky farmer foxhole

or something like that. Since she had just returned from the States, the audience assumed she must be performing a song in a foreign language, and applauded confidently. By the second song there was some discomfort among the crowd. By the third song, which should have been *Je Hais Les Dimanches*[4], she had trouble articulating the first verses, stopped, suddenly, and holding her forehead, managed to blurt out: "My mind's gone blank".

It was a catastrophe. The audience were whistling, shouting and heckling. Édith left the stage to the sound of jeering. So I went on – I was very badly received – to explain that Édith was suffering terribly from jet lag and the fatigue of travelling, but if they were patient, she would come back on with renewed vigour.

The audience's reaction had sobered Édith. She had found her fighting spirit again, the spirit of the small girl on the streets who become successful through sheer determination and hard work. Fifteen minutes later she made the sign of the cross again and like a feisty little cockerel, reappeared on stage, determined to win back her star status. The audience were cruelly cold, and it took her song after song to reverse the hostile current. Her set was usually composed of fourteen songs, but Édith had to sing twenty-five songs to win back their hearts and earn their applause. I was waiting for her in the wings, hoping for some small word of thanks. I should be so lucky! She hurried straight into Jacques arms to tell him: "My darling, you saved the evening."

Years later when I reminded her of this anecdote over dinner, she smiled and admitted: "I know perfectly well what went on that night, but you know what it's like when you're in love ..."

[3] *Le Chant du Pirate*
[4] *Sundays Not My Day*

CHAPTER 27

Patrick

The Piaf tribe was about to up and leave for the United States again when I met Arlette, a pretty, young dancer. We were like ships passing in the night: farewell, we had some good times, I'll be seeing you. When we returned to France, Arlette came to see me a few months later to tell me that she was pregnant and had made up her mind to keep the baby. Why not? I took care of all the birth expenses. When the child was born, he was given the name of Patrick. I was left with a tiny seed of doubt all the same: was this child mine? So we went along to the hospital, and there, according to my mother, there was no doubt about it, this was indeed my son. Nothing can compare with a mother's natural instincts for proof of paternity. I offered to officially recognise the child; sweetly, Arlette laid it on the line: either we got married, or she would marry a man who was in love with her and prepared to give the baby his name. For my part, I hadn't the slightest intention of getting married; what is more, my divorce from Micheline had only just come through. Overnight, Arlette disappeared from my life.

Many times, gripped by a feeling of guilt and wanting to see the child again, I took steps to try and trace Arlette – to no avail. I subsequently learned that they had gone to live in the provinces. The years passed. Nine years later, Arlette wrote to me asking if we could meet up. She confided to me that her husband, a confirmed drinker, was abusive to Patrick, and that, recently, he had even thrown the fact that he was not the boy's father in his face. Arlette was at a loss as to what to do and implored me to help. I discussed it with my family – Aïda, my parents, and especially twelve-year-old Seda, and the decision was unanimous. "He can come and live with us."

Seda, more than anyone, was delighted to find herself unexpectedly blessed with a little brother. Patrick moved into the family home in Mouans-Sartoux, near Cannes; he was a charming child, a little secretive but very loving. Some years later, he started at the Armenian school in Sèvres where he learned to read and write Armenian well. When he came of age, he decided to move out. I bought him a small studio flat. It was here, that he was found dead on the eve of his twenty-fifth birthday.

There was no autopsy. The evidence was strewn around him: diet pills and beer cans. What more is there to say? I treasure the letters he wrote to me from school, always with a few neatly written lines in Armenian at the bottom of the page.

Patrick now lies buried alongside my parents in our family vault in Montfort-l'Amaury.

Putting these few words to paper brings tears to my eyes; I think of him always.

CHAPTER 28

You Need a Good Nose For This Business

In New York, a friend of Édith's, answering to the name of Reine, was the proud owner of both an art gallery and a broad upper Belleville[1] accent. We were having a drink with her, when, suddenly, she looked straight at me and blurted: "You know, you got a nice pair o'peepers, you'd be quite a looker if it weren't for that hooter of yours." Édith looked at me in agreement. But what was the problem with my nose, my hooter, my conk, my proboscis, my ruby rose, my beak? What was so special about it? If it didn't bother me, why should it bother anyone else? It was mine, my nose, and that was the end of it. The bridge was a bit battered, it was a little on the prominent side, obscuring my face somewhat, which prevented people from noticing that I did occasionally smile, it was perhaps a trifle large for my stature, but useful for all kinds of things like breathing, inhaling perfume or scents of cooking, and easy to blow. It was no average nose,

---

[1] Belleville is a multi-cultural, working-class neighbourhood in the north-east of Paris.

you know, and it gave me personality. It wasn't Cyrano's, Pinocchio's or Cleopatra's, it was mine, and it was the nose of my kin, not Jewish nor Bourbon, but an Armenian nose.

Reine resumed: "I know a surgeon that can do wonders. He's a good *yidde* like me, and even though he's right busy, I'm sure he'd do a good price for one of us."

"But I'm not Jewish."

Momentarily taken aback, she added: "Just don't tell 'im, afterall, he ain't operatin' in yer trousers is he?"

"Anyway, I don't have the money."

Édith spoke up then: "It'd be good thing for your career. Go on, I'll pay for your snout."

An appointment was made with Irving Goldman, the miracle worker, who showed me a photograph album of Hollywood stars before and after their operations, then arranged an appointment at the clinic for the following week.

The night before the operation, after the second show at the Versailles, we found ourselves in a French restaurant in front of a bottle of Bollinger, Édith's favourite champagne, and, in the early hours, by which time we were pretty sloshed, Édith suddenly shed a tear and said: "I wonder if we are doing the right thing. It's true your nose never stopped the girls going for you ... When all's said and done, I like you as you are."

This was not the time to start having doubts, I was due in the operating theatre in only a few hours. Rather perturbed, I ended up entrusting my proboscis to the marvellous doctor's hands all the same, and I emerged from the clinic the following day with a bandage across my nose which made me look as if I had been in a fight. As it happened, Famechon, a young French boxer, had won a match the previous night in Madison Square Garden. On the street, passers-by, noticing my black eyes and the plaster across my nose, congratulated me as I walked by.

A few days later, still sporting my bandage, I left for Paris by myself. It was understood that I would go and meet Édith when she returned. Two weeks later at the airport, I found myself in the midst of a throng of friends, admirers, photographers and press. I tried standing right in front of Édith, but she immediately turned her back

146

on me every time. Incensed by my insistence, I overheard her saying to her friends: "Who's the brat that's hanging around?" I replied:

"But it's me!"

She looked at me, let out one of her enormous laughs: "If I hadn't heard your voice, I never would have recognized you."

That simple operation changed my life. I've never been less than delighted with the amputation – my new profile allowed me to believe that I, myself, might finally be able to sing some of the love songs that I wrote for others.

CHAPTER 29

My First Music Hall Appearance

In the 1940s, the Pacra, a small venue on the Boulevard Beaumarchais, a stone's throw from the Place de la Bastille, was not the largest theatre in the world, far from it. It must have had all of two hundred and ninety seats, but it was a well-known, important music hall in those days when no Parisian neighbourhood was complete without one. During the 1952/1953 season, there were three show-days a week; so including the matinees, we had five performances in all. The wages reflected the size of the establishment; the headline act was paid twelve thousand francs for the three days, the main support act, nine thousand. It was barely enough to cover the musicians, the travelling expenses and the agency fees; you could hardly go mad on what was left over.

The two impresarios with exclusive booking rights for local music halls of this kind were Brown, whose wife was a variety singer called Fanny Brun, and Zam. I don't remember who signed my contract, but I was hired as the main support act. Rose Avril was headlining. One day, Rose had arrived at her manager Bizos' place in tears and announced that her father had passed away. When she explained what had happened, everyone present burst out laughing. To be fair, the incident could not fail to provoke hilarity. The good man was in the toilet and had pulled the chain; the shoddily fixed reservoir promptly fell on his head and killed him. In light of this reaction, Rose subsequently, and judiciously, took to saying that her father had died in a hunting accident[1]...

But let's get back to my booking. On the opening night of the show, a Friday, the auditorium was packed to the rafters with regulars. Given the number of seats, anything less would have been a disaster! Naturally, all my friends, brought along by Raoul Breton, were sitting in the front row, and, for the first time, my set was a great success. That same evening, the agent offered me a second date in six months time, again, as the main support act, with Tohama headlining on this occasion. When this performance was also met with enthusiasm, I was asked to come back and headline. But I wasn't interested in taking risks for an extra three thousand francs. I came back and sang for a third time at the Pacra, and decided that from then on, I would have to set my sights on more challenging venues.

---

[1] *Accident de chasse:* chasse is the French word for both toilet chain and hunting.

CHAPTER 30

How To Get On the Radio

Jean-Jacques! I was fond of you, and our stormy relationship never stopped our mutual liking for each other from developing, over the years, into a real friendship. You didn't want to hear about Aznavour, but you had never listened to him. You simply didn't get it, you, the producer whose radio shows introduced the public to so many songstresses and singers before they became famous. You were a professional, and one of the best; I would even go so far as to say that you were one of the people who changed the voice of radio. You sailed from success to success, invulnerable. Those we think are invulnerable are always the least so. It took a great many years for us, your friends, so sure that we knew you, to realise this. It was only when we found you lying there, with a rifle bullet lodged in your mouth, that we understood just how fragile you were.

We got off on the wrong foot, you and I. I was starting to attract my fair share of admirers, my records were doing well, I was selling out theatres and yet, to all intents and purposes, I never got played on the radio. As for you, you never played my records on Radio Luxembourg, and no one had a hope in hell of building a career, even a small one, without getting on the radio. However much Raoul Breton kept trying, it was hopeless, for stubborn was your middle name, and when your mind up was made up there was no changing it.

I took advantage of a professional mistake you made and twisted your arm into playing my records three times a day for a month on the radio. You had produced a film, and, the day before it was released in a handful of Parisian cinemas, including the Normandie on the Champs-Elysées, I discovered that you had used one of my songs, *Parce Que*, without obtaining the rights from Breton Publishing. I immediately entreated Raoul to have the reels put under seal, to force you to come knocking at our door, which proved to be no easy task, as you were most indignant to begin with.

Who was this little worm who dared take on the great Jean-Jacques Vital? I didn't budge a hair – I still had quite a bit back then – I let time do its work, as indifferent to your problems as it was to my little blackmail scheme. The first screenings were set for two o'clock that afternoon. It was only at noon that you resigned yourself to accepting my conditions. You later confessed to me that it was only at that point that you became interested in the small potato that you took me for. I have never been a yes man, and this forged our enduring friendship, until the day when, alas …

We miss you Jean-Jacques, and I perhaps a little more than many of the others, because friends, true friends, can be counted on the fingers of one hand, and to be friends for thirty years, takes exactly that, thirty years, and nothing less.

CHAPTER 31

And What of Love?

I always had a soft spot for very young women, androgynous looking girls, a little naive, a little lost, with nothing to their names,
whom I could easily impress with my generosity and whose
Pygmalion I could become in spite of the little I knew. I had a fantasy
in which a young woman, naked under a borrowed raincoat, would
come to my home, where I would provide an entire wardrobe for
her. Once this was accomplished, I would have her return the raincoat to its owner. Everyone has their fantasies. Fortunately, I soon
grew out of this one. In those days, the age of consent was twenty-
one, and I risked the magistrates court for every one of my love
affairs. The age having been reduced to sixteen since then, old-timers
can sleep easy in their impotence.

I changed enormously when I became a father for the second time,
and then a grandfather. I regard these young girls as children who
have grown up too quickly. I have a sense of the ridiculous. Age, as
well as a marriage that I believe to be exemplary, have taught me the
limits of decency. I am dumbfounded when I read, in a certain kind
of publication, about the passionate love affairs of octogenarians
whose fresh young fiancées claim to be desperately smitten with
these terribly rich gentlemen, who are nonetheless close to cashing in

their final chips, if not about to do so, and potential clients for the nearest funeral parlour.

Do they really believe it or are they just pretending, to impress the world and escape their solitude? You have to admit that it's odd that none of these wonderful creatures seems ever to fall desperately in love with a little old retired post office worker who only has a modest income to live on. Love, for geriatrics, moves in the most mysterious ways.

I have never been a Don Juan, a Casanova, a first-rate seducer, it's true. I have had girlfriends of all creeds and colours. I have been married three times, but, when I really think about it, I don't believe I have truly loved more than four or five women. When I say "loved" I mean the kind of love that you never forget for as long as you live; not a single detail, not the name, not the first time you met, not what it felt like, nor anything along the way from the first feelings of love to the final break-up, the impulsive behaviour, the raised voices, the dirty tricks.

In The Name Of Youth (Au Nom De La Jeunesse)[1]

In the name of youth
Seasons of the good days
My thoughts were running
Towards laying down my weakness
To the sun of love

Évelyne was stunning, she was elegant, confident, and cultivated – less than she would have you believe, but reasonably well, all the same. Roland Avellis, The Singer With No Name[2], introduced us on the terrace of Fouquet's[3]. Swayed by youth and beauty, I went out of my way to see a lot of her, with Roland's help. Little by little, I arranged to meet her on her own. She introduced me to a young designer who was starting to make quite a name for himself, Ted Lapidus, with

---

[1] From *Au Nom De La Jeunesse / In The Name Of Youth* by Charles Aznavour.
[2] *Le Chanteur Sans Nom.*
[3] Famous restaurant on the Champs Élysées in Paris.

whom I forged an unshakeable friendship. And so, as dating evolved into flirting, and flirting evolved into nights, love moved into my life. I introduced her to Édith, but they were not made to get along. Évelyne was not the kind of person who could fathom Édith's way of life, and, more importantly, if they were both in the same room, no prizes for guessing who was in the firing line! I did end up leaving Piaf's place all the same – for the second time and without slamming the door – to move in with Évelyne at the Acropolis hotel on the Boulevard Saint-Germain.

CHAPTER 32

Taking the Helm

When it came to her love life, Piaf was hard work for a man of strong character like André Pousse, who didn't like to be pushed around. I have to admit that of all the tenants of Édith's heart, he was the one that I felt closest to. He wasn't in the business – at least he wasn't at that time, as he would go on to become artistic director at the Moulin Rouge – and worked as a sports manager, before embarking on and carving out a nice little career for himself in cinema. What is more, his way of life was the antithesis of our leading lady's. He and I got on like a house on fire. Édith was in the habit of sleeping late into the morning; André, a sports fanatic, was used to getting up early, and would be driven to distraction waiting for the rest of the household to emerge.

The day he elected to leave the house, where a sporting man like himself was bound to feel stifled, I decided to go with him, acting upon the advice of Raoul Breton, who felt that I would never seriously make a go of it in the business as long as I remained under Piaf's sway. One morning, when the chaotic rhythm of the life we led there had become too much for me, I said to him: "I hear you're leaving."

"Yes, mate, I've had enough, I'm out of here. How did you know?"

"There are rumours in the house. If you leave, I'm leaving too, I don't want to live here with a new boss."

We were very fond of Édith, but her way of life was beginning to paralyse us. Eyeing me sceptically, André packed up his things, and it was only the next day that he learned that I, too, had packed mine. Édith never held it against me; she always knew that, one day, I would decide it was time to set out and follow my own path.

Then my troubles started. People in the business, convinced that Édith had sent me packing and imagining that they were doing her a favour, shut their doors in my face. No Piaf, no dates. As a result, my records were regarded as unprofitable, unsaleable. I had joined the ranks of the so-called marginal artists.

Swings and Roundabouts

In September 1950, while Évelyne was on tour, I decided to move in with Florence Véran, Richard Marsan and Billy Florent who were squatting – before the term was invented – a huge apartment on the Rue Villaret-de-Joyeuse, just around the corner from Porte Maillot. As they were often late in coming up with the rent money, the owner wanted to be rid of his tardy tenants. In an attempt to flush the tenacious occupants out, he simply cut off the hot water supply. But water is never too cold when you are young! We got used to it in no time. We, that is, because I had moved into the last unoccupied room. During the day, I would go off to Raoul Breton's like a state employee goes to the office, then, in the evenings, Richard and I would hang out in nightclubs where, over a glass, or rather a bottle, we'd sit and put the world to rights in the company of a few part-time entertainment workers[1]. We were particularly harsh in our judgment of the people in the business. Richard and I would roll in late at night, rather soused; he'd be in the doghouse with Florence, while I was sometimes in good company.

---

[1] *Intermittents du spectacle*: workers in the entertainment business in France who do not have steady employment and who receive money from the state between contracts.

My contract at Chez Patachou was up; we needed to find work and quickly. I don't know who came up with the idea of putting together a threepenny show, but we were quickly decided and baptised it *The Three Notes*[2]. We fleshed out the formula, touted it round the entertainment agencies, and, since we weren't asking for a great deal money, it wasn't long before we had a string of dates set up in the Maghreb. First stop: Morocco, Casablanca. The show went like this: Richard would come on, tell three jokes, then introduce me, I was accompanied on piano by Florence who would subsequently sing her own set while continuing to accompany herself on piano. Finally, I would introduce Richard and take my place at the piano to accompany his impressionist act.

First night, Le Jardin d'Hiver in Casablanca. I don't know whether it was the sound of my voice with its oriental undertones, my way of singing or the songs themselves, but I was suddenly as if borne aloft by the large audience in this open-air club, who did not want to let me leave the stage. At the end of the night's performance, after a short meeting, we unanimously decided that from then on I would headline the show. The next day, Jean Bauchet, the director of the Moulin Rouge in Paris and the Marrakech Casino, who had attended the show, offered us a contract at the casino. I already had *Poker* in my set. The gamblers, who, it must be said, are more at home with gaming tables than cabaret dancefloors, would actually come and listen to my song before dashing back to take up their positions in front of the green baize. It was, apparently, the first time that anything like this had happened at the casino.

The Marly brothers were the most influential impresarios for thousands of miles around: Maurice in Tunisia, Isidore in Algeria, and Sadi in Morocco. At that time, because my small stature was considered to be a major obstacle to my career, I had had two pairs of *elevator shoes* sent over from the States which gave me an extra three inches. One day, when Richard and I were in Sadi's office, I saw him lean over towards Richard to whisper in a sorry voice in his ear: "He's got a club foot." At these words, I crossed the other leg, which prompted him to say: "Poor chap, he's got two club feet!"

---

[2] *Les Trois Notes.*

From Casablanca, we carried on touring: Marrakech, Fez, Port-Lyautey – Kenitra today – Rabat, Oujda, Algiers, Oran, Constantine, Tunis. I had finally been able to put a little money away, which allowed me to return to France and replace my old banger of a car which had suffered a great deal on the bumpy North African roads. And for the cherry on the cake, Jean Bauchet had concocted a very attractive contract for me to headline at the Moulin Rouge. After years of slim pickings, more prosperous times were on the horizon. I no longer had any regrets about going solo as far as Pierre Roche was concerned, and I continued to spend time with Édith, still with her clown of a boyfriend in tow, The Singer With No Name. As for Éve-lyne, she was on tour in the Middle East: Beirut and Cairo. In Egypt, you couldn't go wrong, at that time, with blond hair and a bodice ... Since telephones were not what they are today, I used to write her passionate letters; I was head over heels in love.

My First Olympia

Back on European soil, I met up with Évelyne and we moved into a place on the Rue Sainte-Rustique, up on the Butte Montmartre. By this time, I could just about afford to pay an accompanist. I found one: Jean Leccia, a Lyonnais of Corsican origin, seventeen years old, looked fifteen, an excellent, stylistically open-minded musician of great sensitivity. With Jean on piano, I started playing gigs at a few left bank cabarets, in the run-up to the Moulin Rouge date booked by Jean Bauchet.

Then the day of the rehearsal with the full orchestra arrived. I introduced my music director, but when they saw Jean, the experienced musicians categorically refused to be conducted by someone who looked like a young child as far as they were concerned. The dormant Lyonnais in him rose up in arms, and the Corsican took to the maquis: he began to scowl and sulk. When they found out that some of my songs had been orchestrated by him, the musicians changed their tune; the atmosphere became more relaxed, but they stuck by their original decision. Things were looking good for the shows. Right from the first night, my new songs were enthusiastically received, and Bruno Coquatrix, who had always refused to book me at the Olympia finally asked me to play there. My glass of champagne ranneth over. The wheel of fortune seemed to be turning in my favour. It was time; my perseverance and determination notwithstanding, I began to worry.

So Évelyne and I were living together. While I worked on ideas for new songs, she made a pretty good job of looking after the flat and was fantastic in the kitchen. But then the inevitable happened. After a few weeks, she started giving me advice about my profession, and I have to admit that I can't stand women who, just because they share a bed with an artist, suddenly believe themselves to be vested with some new wisdom as well as a mission as an *eminence grise*. All that "in my opinion, you ought to do this, sing that, meet so-and-so, stop seeing whatshisname" drives me up the wall. From Paris, to Lyon, from Lyon to Saint-Tropez, we were on the verge of moving in fashionable circles. She would have loved, I'm sure, to be part of the so-called jet set. I really didn't give a damn, I enjoyed it, but I had more important things to do with my life.

In view of the importance of my Olympia appearance – this was going to put me on the map! – I wrote a new song that appealed to Raoul Breton and my entourage. Raoul Breton reminded Jean-Jacques Vital that we had a sort of gentleman's agreement with him. Since the song seemed to be taking off brilliantly, the latter, with Radio Luxembourg on board, even went beyond the bounds of his promise.

On My Life (Sur Ma Vie)[3]

On my life
I swore
To love you 'til
My dying day
The same word
Was soon to unite us
Before God
And all mankind

---

[3] *From Sur Ma Vie / Believe In Me* by Charles Aznavour

I presented the new song to Bruno Coquatrix; he felt it was perfect for my debut at his music hall.

He had an international programme at the Olympia at that time: Brazilian ballets, the American, Sydney Bechet, Marceau, the French mime, while I was the Armenian support act . . . Funny, but then why not? As the gig was a success, he immediately offered me another booking, on the same bill as Roger Pierre and Jean-Marc Thibault. This show went down even better than the previous one, and Bruno Coquatrix asked me to headline at the venue the following season. But our talks were short-lived because Bruno refused to pay me the same as the American artists. I knew what price he was willing to pay for Frankie Laine and since I was selling almost as many tickets, if not more, than the illustrious singer, I insisted on the same contractual terms. He was still getting a good deal as there were no costly travelling expenses or hotel bills to cover. In light of Bruno's flat refusal, I accepted Jeanne Broteaux' offer to play the Alhambra – where my last performance been decisive – twelve months later.

Several months previously, I had written the French version of Frankie Laine's big hit of the moment, *Jézabel*. As it turned out, our first nights coincided on the same evening, Frankie Laine at the Olympia, and I at the Alhambra. Of the two shows, the press dedicated their front-page coverage to Frankie's, and although I played to a packed venue every night, I was continually shot down by the critics. I ventured a phone call and offered to take Frankie out to sample some of the fine restaurants of our capital, if he had a free evening. To my great surprise, he was free every day. Since no one at the Olympia had bothered to check what he wanted to do before the show, I took him and his wife to Parisian restaurants and museums, as well as jazz and South American music clubs. They accepted enthusiastically, much to the delight of the paparazzi photographers and the press who were wondering which one of us would come out on top. I freely admit that the journalistic scales were tipped well in Frankie's favour. But none of this had any importance for us, our daily outings evolved into a friendship. When my run at the Alhambra was over, I decided to set off on tour across France.

As for Bruno Coquatrix, besides being one of the most downright stubborn people I have ever met, or worked with, he was one of the most likeable, but also one of the toughest. He had a reputation, amazing intuition and the Olympia was the perfect platform for launching an artist's career, but in spite of this, our beloved Bruno had decreed that I was not right for his theatre after seeing me perform at Chez Patachou. The years went by, and what he had failed to see in me, had not gone unnoticed by the public. And five years later when the theatre was going through a rough patch, I didn't hold it against him; I had never lost my respect for its owner nor my affection for the Olympia. They were both irresistibly charming.

In the meantime, Évelyne and I had decided to marry, with a civil wedding at Chez Carrère, a fashionable restaurant in Montfort-l'Amaury. Neither of our families were present, just a handful of friends. When she realised that there would be thirteen of us at the table, she absolutely insisted on having a fourteenth person. So I called the Town Hall and the mayor, whom I knew well, agreed to join us. Maybe destiny was trying to tell us something as – we didn't know it then – our marriage would end in divorce. Which number is supposed to be unlucky, is it thirteen or fourteen?

CHAPTER 33

Delusions of Grandeur

As a young man, I wanted a car to match the status of the "star" I believed myself to be. What a fool! Since huge American cars and bright colours were all the rage, I went to see the Buick dealer on rue Guersant. I probably didn't look as if I could afford to buy a car of that calibre, for the salesman – as snobbish as they come – looking me up and down – given my height, easy for him – barely condescended to provide me with any information, he really had to force himself. Inside I was fuming, but I tried to contain myself. Finally, I could bear it no longer, under the weary eye of the salesman, I took my leave with the firm intention of teaching him a lesson. I walked straight into the neighbouring garage which had a splendid south sea blue Ford displayed in the window, and drove away shortly thereafter at the wheel of the wonderful machine, right under the nose of the ill-mannered salesman, stunned and speechless at the sight of the sale that had just slipped through his fingers.

After getting Évelyne settled in Saint-Tropez, I set off on tour at the wheel of my celebrity car, with Claude Figus, who was more or less acting as my secretary, and Jean Leccia, my pianist-arranger and band leader. The further north we travelled, the less successful the show was. It was a disaster in the East. For the last leg, in Périgueux, where we were supposed to arrive by five o'clock in the afternoon to prepare the show, we had to get up very early: there were no motorways then in the South, and we had no option but to take the tightly winding country roads.

Over the course of the tour, I had become quite exhausted. So I didn't hear the lorry approaching in the opposite direction, a twelve tonner loaded up with bauxite that emerged from a bend in the road. We must have both been driving at about forty miles an hour, and we had no time to brake. And so it was that death kissed my beautiful blue bonnet full on the mouth. My two companions, who were dozing in the back, were thrown against the front seat; as for me, I gripped the steering wheel so tightly that my elbow bones broke my skin. The dashboard collapsed onto my knees and — since cars back then were not fitted with safety belts — my head smashed against the windscreen. I felt no pain, I was just dazed. The radio was making a crackling noise like an engine about to explode. During the impact, my wristwatch had become hooked on the steering wheel where it still hung, swinging back and forth.

There was little traffic on this small road, but finally someone stopped and immediately telephoned for help. "Whatever you do, don't move," the driver said when he returned. Are you kidding? I was completely pinned in place! I waited forty minutes like this, worrying like crazy about the show I would not be able to play. At last, an ambulance arrived. Everyone got to work, they cut through the bodywork to get me out, and we set off for the nearest hospital. When we had driven almost thirty miles, the driver realised that he had been going in the wrong direction. We turned around. After another forty-five miles, we finally arrived at Brignoles hospital. As there had been time to announce news of the accident on radio, several photographers were waiting for a shot of the victim. Publicity is bread and butter; I flashed them one of my best smiles which must have looked more like a pained grimace, and, duty done, blacked out.

Évelyne, who was lapping up the sun and high on Saint Tropez nightlife, showed up with a small local following in tow. Naturally, she didn't bother to get in touch with my parents and my sister, who were in Mouans-Sartoux and without transport. Fortunately, Philippe

Clay, who was a close friend, drove across a good part of Provence to fetch my family.

Driving (Rouler)[1]

Driving
Push the pedal to the metal
Burning rubber like the devil
Vainglorious, victorious
Revelling in your skill, you feel
Driving
Like a racing champion at the wheel
On a winding country road
Overtake
A line of cars at breakneck speed
Smash into a wall or tree
Or, better still, a family car
Injuring women and children
The holiday over before it begins
As laughter turns to tar
And weekenders watch as you drop
Like a wretched, mangled dog
At the side of the throroughfare

Some weeks later, I left the hospital imprisoned in a neck-brace and white plaster, with both arms stretched out in front of me as if I wanted to hug somebody. I was encased in this shell from my neck to my waist. I was a heavy smoker in those days; someone gave me a very long cigarette holder, as I couldn't reach my mouth with my hands. I needed someone to help me move around, lift me out of chairs, open doors … Unable to remain inactive, I began hanging off the wardrobe as best as I could, as a means of moving my arms around inside their white shell. I also practised changing gear in the 4CV Renault that I had bought – for the very reason that it was the only car with the gear stick really close to the driver – by whacking it with my plaster cast.

[1] From *Rouler / Driving* by Charles Aznavour

167

It was at that time that Claude Figus introduced me to Dany Brunet, who would later accompany me everywhere for many long, happy years. He was a former long distance lorry driver, solid in every sense of the word, physically and morally, always optimistic and of good humour, especially when there were pretty girls in the vicinity. Dany had the speciality of regularly falling in love, and like all love-struck people, he wanted to know what the future held for him and the girl of his dreams, who at the time was a young Greek woman living in Greece. My mother used to read his coffee grounds for him, and strangely, the accuracy of her predictions would surprise even a sceptic like me.

This accident which nearly killed me brought my existence and my songs that spoke of love, life and simple everyday things, to the attention of a huge audience, who decided that I had something to say. In the space of a few days, I received three postal sacks of letters wishing me good luck and encouraging me to keep my spirits up. All the letters were kind, except one, anonymous, that stood out from the rest: "Your voice was already broken, now you've broken your arms, when are you going to break your neck?" When I think that there are people who actually take the time to write, to buy a stamp, so that they can express their rancour and nastiness, I am stunned.

As soon as I was able, flanked by Dany and my plaster casts, I set off back to Raoul Breton's publishing house and took my place, uncomfortably, at the famous blue piano. Twisting myself so that I could lay my hands flat across the keys, I started writing songs again in anticipation of my new season. I was feeling optimistic and threw myself into a song with a jazzy beat.

Jamming (Pour Faire Une Jam)[2]

Some nights when I feel downcast
There is a little place I know
Where I meet friends
To have a jam

---

[2] From *Pour Faire Un Jam / Swing* by Charles Aznavour.

I came up against a lot of reticence on the part of the Parisian music hall and cabaret directors. This didn't stop me playing three or four clubs or cabarets on the left bank, in addition to playing a cinema – between the newsreels and the film – in one evening. By the final sets, the sixth or seventh of the evening, I had no voice left to speak of, but I kept on singing and the spectators often assumed that what they were hearing at the end of the night was my normal voice. Not that I had a crystal clear voice, no, it was husky, I had a voice like broken glass. I had consulted two or three throat specialists about it, the verdict was always the same: "Don't kid yourself, you'll never be able to sing, one of your vocal chords doesn't vibrate." It's their imagination which isn't vibrating I thought.

The Ham (Le Cabotin)[3]

A ham I am, behold me in all my splendour
I was born to perform
Give a me bare, cold stage to play upon
I will bring the rafters down
A ham I am, behold me in all my splendour
The gift is in my blood
Give me four bare boards, the smallest crowd
And my talent will shine
My talent will shine

I spent the weekends at the Breton's house in Méré, in Les Yvelines. My domestic life with Évelyne was in bad shape, and I realised just how different her world was from mine. She couldn't bear her new name, Aznavourian – Aznavour was bad enough ... She often criticized my family, whom she really didn't know, and completely ignored my daughter. Monsieur and Madame Breton were just about acceptable in her eyes. She set about changing my behaviour, my way of living, the people I saw, who, according to her, were beneath us, she wanted to mould me – she would have her work cut out! We didn't argue. Worse, we just drifted slowly further and further apart. Raoul

---

[3] From *Le Cabotin / The Ham* by Charles Aznavour.

Breton took me out for drives in the surrounding countryside and I set my heart on a small house, the old blacksmith's forge of the Chateau de Galluis, also in les Yvelines. She was up for sale for three and a half million old francs. Raoul advanced me the money to buy it, and I lost no time in starting extensive renovation work on it in spite of the fact that I was broke and still in plaster. Strangely, the longer the renovation work went on, the less I was able to picture Évelyne living in that house. I was right. I later bought the land opposite so that I could build a house for my parents. Aïda had just become engaged to a young composer of Armenian origin, Georges Gavarentz, who also owned a lovely little cottage in our village. We were over the moon to be reunited.

All things, even the good ones, must come to an end. I could see, even with my head stuck in the sand like an ostrich, that we were not really made for one another. The problem with Éyelyne was that she came from a different world, that she was already the wife of the star that I had not yet become. She wanted to give me advice, and I loathe it when someone else tries to do my job for me. As far as she was concerned, after all, I was an unrefined individual, not untalented but in dire need of guidance. Évelyne made a show of her education, she felt superior, terribly proud of her two A-levels with which she admonished me at every opportunity – had she really passed them? One day, after she had seen me in *La Tête Contre Les Murs*[4] she decreed that I would never be a decent actor and that I ought to stick to songwriting if I knew what was good for me. She weighed things up, drew her own conclusions, and tried to impress them on me. I made it a point of honour to maintain my peace of mind in order to pursue my profession as best I could and in my own way.

The day before I left to play a date in Lisbon, without a word – men are often cowards when it comes to big decisions – I packed my things and left the Montmartre apartment that I shared with Évelyne. I met a charming actress on the plane on my way back who had just come from a festival in Rio de Janeiro, Estella Blain. We chatted during the flight and flirted a little. When we left the plane, the film press

---

[4] *The Keepers*, directed by Georges Franju.

were there to welcome the actors and actresses who had attended the festival. Photos were taken, and Évelyne saw them. Feeling slighted, she lost no time in filing for divorce; she wanted to get in first. Nothing had happened at that point between Estella and I, but the photograph, oh, the photograph! I have always wondered if she would have accepted a divorce so readily, even at my cost, if it had not been for this tabloid revelation.

CHAPTER 34

Up and Running

When you come from nowhere and success suddenly grabs you by the shirt-tails, two serious afflictions are waiting in the wings to catch you out: big headedness, the symptoms of which are pronounced swelling of the head, the britches and the boots, and which to my mind is incurable; and delusions of grandeur, which life itself can treat, and even cure with a drop in the popularity ratings and a series of unexpected setbacks. I was not spared from the epidemic, but the lessons learned from our family history meant that I was only infected by delusions of grandeur. I was not trying to impress my neighbour, but myself. First there was the acquisition of the old forge and the furniture sold to me as antiques; then there was the Rolls-Royce, not just any old Rolls, but the beautiful, big, actually, huge model, the one which would have had trouble getting through the rue de la Huchette, the same as the Queen of England's. Hey, fellas, you're either a star or you're not, you must be equal to the task, or you'll look like a third-rate act from the Pacra.

Things got more and more out of control as time went on. In addition to Dany, my eternally staunch and devoted stage manager, I hired William, a professional Rolls chauffeur with the requisite Welsh accent, Berdjoui, the governess, Eddy Kazo, my secretary, and Annette and Louis, housekeeper and cook respectively. On another occasion, in the grip of a sudden bout of Caucasian fever – my people did come from the Caucasus, after all – I was consumed with the burning desire to own some horses. So off I went, with Dany by my side as ever, to pick out some fine animals. He soon developed a passion for horse-riding, and, quickly proved to be an excellent horseman. He lived the same life as I did, his readiness and efficiency were unfailing, on horseback, on tour, as part of the family. My relationship with him was not one of employer to employee but that of a close friend, a brother almost. For the upkeep of the animals, the cleaning and feeding, I also hired Pierre, from the village, as groom.

It was open house and open homestead, I lived like a nabob; no sooner had money come in than it was gone, disappearing into the pockets of suppliers. I was working like a Trojan and spending like a madman. When the Rabbath brothers came on board as my accompanists, I was paying a total of ten monthly salaries in addition to my ex-wife's alimony. At that point, I had two options: end up crushed by debt, or could get a grip. I chose the second option.

I couldn't really afford to employ a trio, on top of all the other expenses I was incurring. I generally used to hire a pianist and then use the venue's house musicians to create a fuller backing sound. I had auditioned several pianists; the last one was called Pierre Rabbath, and he had exactly what I was looking for in an accompanist. I was about to offer him a contract when he announced that he could not abandon two of his brothers, who, unable to find work in France, had decided to return to Lebanon. "Unless," he added, "you would be willing to employ all three of us." François was a bass player, one of the best, Victor was a drummer. Even at preferential rates, the monthly salaries put a real strain on my budget. But to hell with the figures!

We hit the road, the five of us plus Dany, for an extensive tour. Tunisia, Morocco, Algeria, Greece, Belgium, Switzerland, Spain, Portugal, Egypt, Lebanon, we could get by anywhere, we spoke seven or eight languages between us, except for Dany who, besides French "jus' didn't geddit". The only problem was in the Maghreb: a Rabbath had a hard time making himself understood here! Although they were able to understand the locals, the latter had difficulties with the literary Arabic that my Lebanese trio spoke. We were a very tight-knit group, we were in each others pockets, so to speak, twenty four hours a day; we played epic games of chess which would start before curtain up, spill over into the interval, and which continued on occasions after the show was over. I certainly had my fill of Tartakover[1] and so-and-so's move and whatshisname's move! When we returned to Paris, we couldn't wait to get back on the road again; we were always ready to jump at the chance to travel the globe.

---

[1] Saveilly Tarakover (1887–1956) was a great chess player and an incomparable tactician.

CHAPTER 35

The Ancienne Belgiques

I was starting to make a decent living. I wasn't up there with the emirs of the Persian Gulf, but it was enough to be able to travel in comfort, dress in style, and eat at the best tables listed in the little red book[1] – the French one, of course, not the Chinese. Georges Mathonet and his brother Arthur presided over the fates of the Ancienne Belgique theatres, Arthur in Antwerp and Georges in Brussels. They had seen me play at their venues when I was starting out, and had always refused to book me as a headline act since. But, season after season, my name sold a few more tickets each time. Any venue that was putting on a top headline act every week really ought to have me on the bill at least once a year. And yet, dear old Georges Mathonet turned a deaf ear to the sound of my name.

His audience began to wonder why I was the only artist who never played in Brussels, at the Ancienne Belgique. And they overcame George's obstinacy for he finally sent a booking offer to Jean-Louis Marquet. The latter proudly announced the news to me as if we had just won the war. The sum that he was offering met my usual asking

[1] *The Michelin Red Guide.*

price, which was four thousand Belgian francs per day. As I had a score to settle with our friend Mathonet, I asked for eight thousand. Mathonet's refusal was immediate, case closed. By the following year I was making the eight thousand I had asked for. Mathonet confidently sent a contract offering such a fee to Jean-Louis. But I had not finished my fun; I sent back the reply that I would not budge an inch for less than sixteen thousand. Again, the response was negative. When my fee finally reached thirty thousand – which is what Édith was paid when she played the Ancienne Belgique – I responded to the new offer from Belgium by sending word to Malthonet that I wanted more than Piaf. Tired of fighting and left with no choice, even if it meant losing money, he said to Jean-Louis: "Alright, fill in the figure you want." Imagine his immense relief when he discovered my asking price: one franc more than Édith Piaf. One small symbolic franc for me, a nice little lesson for him.

In the course of our lunch with the Brussels press at Chez Son Père, he said to me over coffee: "You really put me through the wringer." I then related the whole anecdote, which the press had the good grace not to publish and, from that day on, to the end of Georges' days, we remained firm friends. And I still look back on the Ancienne Belgique years with fond remembrance.

CHAPTER 36

Tonight or Never

Luck, like misfortune, never comes singly. I was due to return to the stage for the first time as the headline act at the Alhambra. "A tall order[1]" as de Gaulle would have said. I was feverishly preparing myself while Aïda and Georges Garvarentz provided moral support. I was not exactly scared, but I had suffered so many setbacks that I sometimes had my doubts: what if they were right after all? In my dressing room, I was pacing back and forth, then I went to see what was happening on stage; nothing seemed to calm my nerves. Finally, I went out for a cup of tea at the bistro on the corner. I walked round to the front of the theatre where my name was spelled out in blazing lights; that snapped me out of it. This was no time for weakness, this would be the deciding night of my career.

I took my car and drove over to embrace my daughter and my parents. When I got back to the theatre, I opened the telegrams that I had received, as is customary in our profession. The brief messages from the Compagnons de la Chanson, from Montand and Signoret, Jean Cocteau,

---

[1] Refers to de Gaulle's answer of "Vaste programme!" in response to the cry of "Death to the idiots!"

Jacqueline François, Juliette and Marcel Achard, Charles Trénet, some PTT[2] telephone operator girls and groups of women factory workers were a comfort to me. Then little by little my friends and colleagues began to arrive: Jacques Vernon, Androuchka, Jean-Louis Marquet, La Marquise and Raoul Breton. I felt encouraged by their support.

While the band accompanied the opening act, I started getting ready: I applied a light coat of make-up to hide my pallor and dressed in the blue suit that Ted Lapidus had specially designed for the song upon which I had staked all my hopes – the one Montand had turned down, on the pretext that songs dealing with our profession had no earthly chance of being hits.

By the interval, I was already in the wings; then came the crucial moment as the band launched into my introduction. I walked on stage. The applause was sparse, very sparse. I could only count on my unconditional fans and my friends. More than anything, a first night draws everyone who is remotely connected to the business. One song, two songs, six songs, nothing, this audience was as cold as ice, it was enough to make you want to turn and run without looking back. I was sweating blood, I was shaking from head to toe, but I put every-thing I had into it. We planned to introduce a false curtain at the end of the seventh song, this was supposed to be my smash number. Particularly, since I had come up with a rather revolutionary setting for the song, for that era, as people were not yet experimenting with lighting effects. I launched into the song:

It Will Be My Day (Je Me Voyais Déjà)[3]

At eighteen I left my home town
Ready to fight the struggle of life
Light of heart, with little baggage
And so certain to take Paris by storm

During the previous songs, I had gradually removed my tie and my jacket, unbuttoning my cuffs so that I could slowly dress again:

---

[2] *PTT* - The French Post Office and Telecommunications Service
[3] From *Je Me Voyais Déjà / It Will Be My Day* by Charles Aznavour.

I could see myself on bills and posters
Ten times bigger than anyone else
My name printed there
I could see myself applauded and rich
Signing autographs for crowds of fans.

At the end of the song, when I was fully dressed once more, the spot-light facing me would shut off just as a whole row of spotlights hidden down at the front of the stage switched on to dazzle the audience in the stalls, I would then dance off stage silhouetted against this screen of light. As if the audience were sitting on the other side of the stalls, and the curtain was at the front of the stage. Yet, where I expected applause, I heard nothing but deathly silence. I reached the stage right upright support where Jean-Louis Marquet was standing: "We'll try a different line of work after this," I quipped, to which he replied: "Go out and take a bow anyway and finish your show."

As I made my way to the front of the stage, head hung low, and the curtain was being raised again, I heard the sound of chairs snapping shut. Was the audience leaving? Drenched in sweat, I stood at the front of the proscenium; staring into blackness. Gradually I was able to make out the front rows. Then I suddenly realised that the whole place was on its feet, they were bringing the house down. The tout-Paris, as tough as it gets, were giving me one of the happiest moments of my life. We were face to face, this first night audience, who had come here to witness my downfall, and I; there was no fight left in me now, I was ready to burst into tears.

The end of the show was a dream. The curtain calls were relentless; I could have easily sung another ten songs, but it would have been a mistake to overdo it. I left the stage to endure the hypocritical cries of "I always said you'd make it" and "You're the greatest", and the whole spectrum of falsehoods that you hear on a night like that. I had been through the mill too many times to be taken in by it, but I still enjoyed it immensely. The humiliation is over, no more nights lost in self doubt, a star is born, I thought. But don't kid yourself, son, the hardest is yet to come. Success is one thing, staying successful is quite another. I was only thirty three years old and, as you would a in fifteen-round boxing match, I wondered: my God, how long will I be able to keep this up?

PART 2

CHAPTER 37

Camera! Action!

I inaugurated my acting career with two films that failed to capture the public's imagination. After the second one had been released, I told my agent: "Don't bother coming back with any projects where I have to sing; I want to be an actor in my own right."

Then, one night, in 1957, at François Patrice's club in the Rue Ponthieu, a strange individual came up to me at the bar: "How would you like to be in a film where you don't have to sing?" I instantly took a liking to the man that I had assumed to be a pest. His name was Jean-Pierre Mocky and he had the following proposition: he had adapted Hervé Bazin's novel, *La Tête Contre Les Murs;* the director – Georges Franju – had hitherto only made short films; it was a small role. "But," he said, "it'll get you an Oscar." Well blow me down!

After I had read the script, I agreed to accept a hypothetical share of the profits in lieu of a salary. We didn't make any money with this film, and I didn't get my Oscar, but my brief appearance did earn me a Crystal Star[1] for Best Actor.

[1] The Brussels Film Awards.

Mocky's big dream was to direct and he offered me another role in the first film he was to make himself, *Les Dragueurs*[2], in 1958. The film was a success and the offers came flooding in. First up was no less than François Truffaut. He had come to see my show at the Alhambra, where the programme featured a madman of sorts, Serge Davri. With infinite modesty, he intimated that he would like to offer me a leading role in one of his films. I was still shy at the time, and our conversation was punctuated with silences. A few weeks later, he came back to see me and explained that he had found a book by David Goodis whose protagonist corresponded perfectly with what he had in mind for me. He was also considering roles for Serge Davri and Bobby Lapointe. And so it was that I made my appearance in *Tirez Sur Le Pianiste*[3], in 1961. Then came André Cayatte's *Le Passage du Rhin*,[4] Denys de La Patellière's *Un Taxi Pour Tobrouk*[5], the same year, followed by Jean-Gabriel Albicocco's *Le Rat D'Amérique*[6], opposite Marie Laforêt, in 1962.

I made one film after another, with a host of different directors including Julien Duvivier and René Clair. I have to admit that, in this respect, I was very lucky. To top it all, unlike the music press, it was not the wont of the film press to tear me apart. I felt more at home in the world of cinema. The stress of the singer's lot turns you into a kind of tightrope walker who, come hell or high water, dare not lose his balance; you are dependent on trends and radio programmers' tastes, on the sales performance of your latest record, the number of tickets you sold when you last played in Paris or the provinces; but, most of all, you run, you keep chasing *the* song that will make it possible for you to hold out for another season or two. No singer has the right to grow old, unless he writes his own songs and his songs achieve posterity. For him, every new artist who takes the stage is a threat.

Cinema is different, theatre even more so; actors perform together, singers sing alone. In cinema, once the film has been shown to the

---

[2] *The Flirts.*
[3] *Shoot The Piano Player.*
[4] *The Crossing Of The Rhine*
[5] *Taxi For Tobruk*
[6] *The Rat Trap* aka *The American Rat.*

critics, the actors have finished their work; you make a film, it is released, and you are already busy making another one. In music, you go out on stage alone and solitude awaits you when you come off; it's a wonderful profession but it's a tough one. In cinema, you spend your days filming in the company of your fellow actors, and more often than not, people stay in touch once the film is finished. In any case, such was my trade in the days when I was just a young star.

CHAPTER 38

Random Memories

I wanted to see something of the world, rub shoulders with other cultures. I would often accept overseas contracts for less than my usual fee out of pure curiosity, to make the most of every opportunity I had to see and learn. Not only was I a *saltimbanque*[1], but I was turning into a vagabond because of it. With one eye glued to the viewfinder of a camera or a cine-camera, I travelled, eyes and ears primed; going from one style of music to another, from one language to another, from one place to the next.

I learned effortlessly, everything flowed into me. Without actually seeking to retain anything, I absorbed the most important things nevertheless, everything, at least, that could be of some future use to me. I never made a conscious effort to learn a foreign language; each new land and each new culture gave me something I could use: English, Italian, Spanish, a smattering of Russian, a dash of German. I learned to say "Hello," "Goodbye," "Thank you," and "How much is that?" in ten or so languages; I learned how to sing in five of them. I made a mental note of what different audiences wanted from me. I used to sing more or less the same songs everywhere, but the set

[1] An itinerant acrobat/circus performer

varied from country to country: in one place I'd sing entirely in French, in another I'd sing a few songs in the local language; elsewhere, the audience would follow short translations. There were many times that my artistic and business entourage reproached me for not staying in France to bolster sales of a recently released record that was starting to take off. But I preferred to let the records do the work for me, and get back out on the road as if the devil himself were hot on my tail. I wanted to combine the pleasure I derived from singing with that of travelling; I was, in my own sweet way, an explorer of nothing and everything, the Stanley and Livingstone of not much at all, but it filled my head and my heart, the black boxes of my existence. The films of my vagabond wanderings will never be shown in public, but I often close my eyes and watch them, and there in the dark room of my memory I rediscover perfumes, sensations, and images that have enriched me beyond measure.

Greetings, Maurice Dekobra!

Back in the days when the journey from Paris to Menton train took a whole night to complete, as a young star, I had treated myself to my first ever first-class ticket, in a couchette compartment on the night train, to make a date at the Monte Carlo Casino. I had seen prestigious international artists met with half-hearted applause at this venue in the past, and I was worried about what fate had in store for me. Before I left, Jean-Louis Marquet had spoken to Raoul Breton and broached the question that was bothering him: how much should he ask for my fee.

"How much do you usually ask?"

"Three thousand francs."

"Well, ask for thirty then," replied Raoul. "After all, you have to open your mouth the same way to say one or a thousand"

But let's get back to my trip. I had read some Maurice Dekobra, and I had a fantasy about meeting the "Madonna of the Sleeping Cars[2]". I had boarded the train well ahead of departure time and I was

---

[2] *La Madone Des Sleepings*, by French novelist Maurice Dekobra.

watching the passengers from the corridor opposite my compartment
– well, the female passengers anyway – when, miracle of miracles, I
saw the Madonna appear in the neighbouring compartment. She was
young, gorgeous, perfect from the tips of her toes to the crown of
blond Venetian hair that tumbled freely about her shoulders. She was
meticulously dressed, Italian-style. When the train pulled out, she
came and stood at the window to watch the landscape rolling by, like
many travellers do. I could not help but look at her, but my lack of
confidence at that time prevented me from approaching her. It was
she who initiated the conversation, in a delicious Italian accent:

"Are you who I think you are?" she asked, gracing me with a smile
that could have stopped a train in its tracks. We conversed for about
half an hour; I was like a strutting peacock inside, I was beginning to
think that I might be related to Maurice Dekobra. But when I finally
resolved to ask her:

"And where are you off to then?" I was alarmed to hear her reply:

"I'm going to *sheeet*."

Caught off-guard, not knowing what to say, I added: "And where-
abouts?"

Then with the broad, sweeping gesture of a tragedienne she confessed: "In high places, I'm going to *sheeet* in very high places."
Nonplussed and thinking that I must be dealing with a high class
hooker, travelling first class for a better choice of mug, I cut our conversation short and, to her look of surprise, locked myself away in my
compartment. A dozen or so years later, when I started to pick up
some Italian, I learned that *sciare*[3] means to ski and realised that I may
have let a fleeting but delicious affair slip through my fingers; that
delightful girl had simply Gallicised the word, as people often do
when speaking a foreign language abroad, she had been on her way
to go skiing up in the mountains. I have often taken the same train
since, but never again have I seen the "Madonna of the Sleeping
Cars."

---

[3] The Italian *sciare*, to ski, is pronounced with a soft shh sound, like chier in French
which means to shit.

There Are Trains (Il Y A Des Trains)[4]

There are trains
That fill you with sudden desire to leave it all behind
To break free and leave without looking back
Without a word, without a thought, erase the past
From your mind

There are trains
Sleeper trains, overnight trains where the mood is right
For love unencumbered with hollow words
A chance encounter with a passing stranger, whose name
You'll never know

The Alhambra: Tales Of Love and Glory

In 1962, when I returned once again to play the Alhambra, success and love were waiting in the wings. Androuchka was a familiar face around the place who, like many homosexuals, was always surrounded by pretty girls. It was always a pleasure to run into this charming entourage, but up until then his protégés had not stirred any special feelings in me. That evening, he arrived backstage at the Alhambra with a young girl of around sixteen or seventeen on his arm; her name was Claude. I was due onstage a few minutes later and in the midst of a game of chess with Dany. This was my way of forgetting that I was about to perform in front of three thousand people, of defusing the stage fright that used to plague me.

As soon as she appeared in my dressing room, all blushes and shyness, I lost all interest in the game. I wasn't sure how to react as there was so little time left before curtain up, so I placed a thick towel in her hands and said: "Here, take this, you can stand by the side of the stage and pass it to me when I come off between songs and need to dry my face." Stage fright made me sweat profusely. She conscientiously tended to this responsibility every time I came off. After the

---

[4] From *Il Y A Des Train / There Are Trains* by Charles Aznavour.

final curtain, once I was backstage and dried my face properly, I gave her a brief, chaste kiss as a token of my appreciation.

And so Claude came into my life, and I, of course, became part of hers. Cheerful and carefree, she had everything I needed to be able to relax. She was slightly myopic and had to wear glasses, which makes a woman look very sexy. It tickled me pink to see her doubled up like a hairpin, leaning over a table to try and find what she was looking for.

After the Alhambra we went off on a romantic holiday to New York and Miami before joining the set of *The Rat Trap*, the film based on Jacques Lanzmann's book *The American Rat*[5] and directed by Jean-Gabriel Albicocco, in which I held the beautiful Marie Laforêt in my arms. We made a wonderful trip at this time – Paraguay, Chilli, Bolivia. And then – hell, that's life! – one day, Claude and I went our separate ways, there was no argument, no resentment, and we both cherished tender memories of the salad days spent in each others company.

From One Claude To The Next

I said goodbye to Claude but I was not alone for long. If my memory serves me correctly, at the time of *Que C'est Triste Venise*[6], I had put Françoise Dorin's lyrics to music, and the song began a rather enviable run of success as *Com'è Triste Venezia* on the other side of the Alps. I was spending my days then – or at least my nights – with a beautiful blonde of barely twenty who looked about sixteen, a romantic, mischievous ingénue who was still in the habit of sucking her thumb. Once a month, for a week at most, she'd take leave of my Galluis haven to go and pose for a photographer in Rome.

As success would have it, I found myself in a RAI studio for the promotion of my song in Italy. Since my charming companion had had the good sense to rent a *pied-a-terre* for herself in the Italian capital, she naturally invited me to share her Roman lodgings. She was out that particular day, and I had stayed in by myself, immersed in

[5] *Le Rat D'Amérique* also know as *The Rat Trap*
[6] *How Sad Venice Can Be.*

reading, when the telephone rang. The ringing persisted, so I picked up. A young, male voice with a charming local lilt asked me if Claude were home – yes, I had forgotten, of course, to mention that her name was Claude: I had changed lovers, but love had not changed its name … We all have that office telephone reflex, and mine kicked in: "Who shall I say is calling, please?"

"Gian Franco."

"I'm afraid she isn't back yet, but I'll be sure to tell her that you called when she returns." He was about to hang up, when, I ventured, pointblank: "May I ask you an indiscreet question?"

"Yes, of course," he said, delighted to be able to prolong the conversation.

Without hesitating, I said: "Are you her lover?" A short silence ensued. There was no drama, but a great deal of humour in his reply which, when it came, was frank, amused, full of curiosity and preceded by a small laugh:

"Yes, and you?"

It was my turn to laugh, then we both laughed. It was then that I realised that I was more flattered to have a beautiful girl on my arm than I was in love. And I said: "So she has a lover on both sides of the border."

"I trust," he said, "that it ends there."

I replied that I as far as knew she only travelled back and forth between Rome and Paris, and suggested that we meet up for a drink. We arranged to meet on the terrace of the Via Veneto. We hit it off straight away. We never mentioned anything to Claude; since she was happy this way, why upset her time in Rome and Paris, or spoil her secretive love life for her. It's only by reading these lines, if she reads them, that she will learn that Gian Franco and I were neither fooled nor jealous, and we didn't mind playing at *Jules and Jim,* François Truffaut's film, in our way. My romantic ingénue turned out to be an ingenious libertine.

A Foreign Affair

I wanted to tour overseas. I sat down with my record company, Barclay, and we decided how to go about it and where to start. I decided to visit Spain and South America first. So I had a number of my songs translated, and Eddy Barclay managed to find a label to represent us, initially in Argentina, then, gradually, for all the other Spanish-speaking territories. It wasn't long before my songs were making their way up the charts of several countries, *Venecia Sin Ti, Con, Isabel, Quando No Pueda Mas*[7].

In the meantime, I was appearing on Italian and German television, as well as on Guy Lux' and Maritie and Gilbert Carpentier's shows in France.

It was in Brazil, where I had been asked to attend a charity gala for a humanitarian cause presided over by President Kubitschek's wife, that the idea of giving a recital first came to me. I had Jacques Loussier on piano, François Rabbath on bass, and Victor Rabbath on drums. Jacques, who had been looking for a new angle with a view to pursuing a solo career, suggested that we try his *Play Bach* concept – jazz interpretations of Bach – to open the show. The evening was a success for all concerned. I decided from then on to continue doing recitals; Jacques Loussier went on to make a name for himself worldwide with *Play Bach*.

In the Brazilian club, Machado, I noticed a voluptuous young woman in the ballet; I arranged to be introduced to her. She joined us at our table after the show, but my attempts at communication were fruitless: she spoke neither French, nor English, nor indeed any Spanish, and I, besides a *un cafezinio, muite obrigado*, could not speak a word of Brazilian. But love has its own secret language that has no need for words. We had a beautiful love affair, Marlène – for that was her name – and I in the space of those few weeks that I spent in Rio. Every evening, after my show at the Cocacabana Palace, I would go and sit in the club where she worked. Many years later when I returned to Brazil, I learned that she had been the companion of a highly placed government official for a while and that, one day, God alone knows why, she killed herself.

---

[7] *Que C'est Triste Venise, Avec, Isabelle, Quand J'en Aurai Assez.*

Good Times (Les Bons Moments)[8]

We shared some good times
We shared some great times
Crazy joy, some strange pains
Living together
Amalia

I have always enjoyed working in Belgium, whether it's in Wallonia, Brussels or Antwerp. I love the Belgian audience who embrace you with unaffected enthusiasm. I have a passion for *anguille au vert*[9], the beer there is excellent, the country is cheerful, and I am happy to spend time there. It was in Knokke-Le-Zoute that I had one of the most passionately artistic encounters of my life, a feeling that was fortunately instantly mutual.

One evening, arriving in the main room of the casino a little early for my set, I had the chance to watch the act that preceded mine, that of a unique Fado singer, who was blessed with an extraordinary personality, so very different from Edith and yet so like her in the way she surprised and caressed an audience. Although she sang in a foreign language which we could not understand, we were all completely captivated. At the end of the show, Monsieur Nellens, the casino owner, invited us to supper, she and I, and once again, there was magic in the air. The following day, it was she who came to see my show, then we went and dined in a bistro that had a piano; we sang long into the night. The following day, she left for a gala in Monte-Carlo. The separation was painful, but so that we might keep in touch, I asked her to agree to be the support act for my show at the Palais D'Hiver, in Lyon.

She asked me to write a song for her, which I did, a song of passion and drama.

---

[8] From *Les Bons Moments / Times We've Known* by Charles Aznavour.
[9] Eel poached in green herb sauce.

I8 Mai ,jour anniversaire de ma naissance.

Mon cher Gérard,patron ,ami et camarade non syndiqué,

Merci de votre charmante lettre. Je pense que
votre "Break-down " sera une petite concession
que vous aurez faite a la mode. Ici, la depression
nerveuse est tres bien portée et on serait mal
considéré si l'on n'avait pas chacun son petit
" Break-down" .

Bonne idée de vous reposer un peu tout de même....

Moi pour tout repos je vais passer apres demain deux
jours d'enfer dans ce New-York que je deteste. Mais
il faut,avant mon départ pour le Mexique que je paye
mes impots . Aie,Aie,Aie.......
Je viens de terminer une série d'émissions
radiophoniques avec la Charmante et trépidante Carmen
Miranda. Elle viendra peut-etre cet étéau Canada....
On me propose à Mexico $2000 par semaine
pour aller au Chili en Juillet. J'irai en Septembre
car je me fais une grande joie de montrer le beau
pays de Québec a ma mére qui arrive demain a New-York.
Tachez de me trouver au lac Beauport un chalet
avec trois chambres dans le plus joli coin.
Je viens de faire une chanson nouvelle que je
créérai chez vous. Titre :Mon vieux Cinéma muet.
Je vous engage...a engager les duettistes Roche
et Asznavour. ILS SONT EXCELLENTS,pleins de talent
et font leurs jolies chanons eux memes. Vous verrez
le succés qu'ils auront. Si on pouvait les avoir tout
l'été ce serait charmant.

Ecrivez moi de vos bonnes nouvelles directement a
Mexico City Cabaret El Patio. Adresse sufisante.

Avec mes bonnes et chaleureuses amitiés

Quelle chaleur aujourd'hui !   FOREST 3300   Charles Trénet

A letter from Trénet to Gérard.

With Madame and Monsieur Raoul Breton, "the prince of publishers, and publisher of princes" according to Charles Trénet.

With François Truffaut on the set of "Shoot The Pianist".

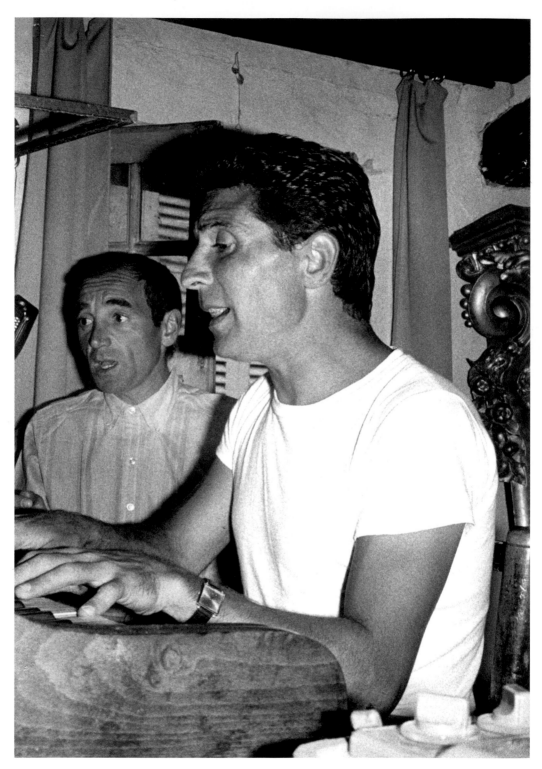

Writing songs with Gilbert Bécaud.

At the window with Fred Mella, Jean Berthola and Georges Brassens.

With Liza Minelli during rehearsals.

Ulla Thorssell, before she became
Madame Aznavour.

Sammy Davis, Petula Clark and Aïda. Witnesses at our wedding in Las Vegas.

Patrick.

My father, my mother, a cousin, Patrick, me, Seda, Fred and Suzanne Mella, Michel Mella and ?

A royal performance.

Summit meeting with Bill Clinton. With Hillary and Liza in the background.

First Legion of Honour. Awarded by President Mitterand.

Second Legion of Honour. Awarded by President Jacques Chirac.

The Lebanese President presenting me with his country's highest honour.

Four Armenian speakers. Rosy Varte, me, Aïda, Lévon Sayan. Legion of Honour award ceremony.

With Levon Ter Petrossian, first President of the young Republic of Armenia.

With Robert Kotcharian, current President of the Republic of Armenia.

In Georgia with the Archimandrite and the new Armenian Catholicos.

Le Catholicos, Jean Paul II and myself, in Armenia.

To Die Of Love (Ay Mourir Pour Toi)[10]

I can die of love
When your hand is touching me
Leaving my head on your shoulder
To sleep with all my joy
I can die of love
Offering you my very last moment
And leave this world without regret

It had a slight fado mood to it, and was rich in the drama and pathos that suited her so well.

Singing these words was her greatest gift to me. Amalia Rodrigues – for it was she – remained a close friend until the day she left us. A few weeks before she died, I was fortunate to be able to dine with her once again; we talked of everything and nothing, of fados, the past, and the romantic friendship that we had shared for a while.

Liza

It must have been a Wednesday or a Saturday afternoon, the usual days for matinee performances at the Broadway theatres. Aïda, Georges Gavarentz, and I were set to go and watch our third performance of one of my favourite American musicals, *Fiddler On The Roof*, with the wonderful Zero Mostel leading the cast, whose talents had been much vaunted to me by Maurice Chevalier, usually rather chary with his compliments.

I was getting ready while vaguely watching a television talk show – the best way to understand the tastes and expectations of a foreign audience is, first of all, get out on the street and walk around the city, then switch on the radio and the television. When the next guest came on, however, I was transfixed – a young woman of highly promising talent, seventeen years old at most, no Hollywood beauty, but a woman of strong personality and boundless charm, the daughter

---

[10] From *Ay Mourir Pour Toi / I Could Die For Love* Lost by Charles Aznavour.

of two show business giants, Judy Garland, a legend, and Vincente Minnelli, one of Hollywood's greatest film directors. Her name: Liza Minnelli, easy to remember. She sang accompanied by two partners; one slim, elegant and romantic-looking, the other, rather plump, short and comical. The talent and youthfulness of the trio was dazzling, but she was the one whose screen presence really hit you. In the space of the first bars, Aïda, who was also watching the show, called me on the phone in a state of excitement, to tell me that a future star was on television. I stayed glued to the television set until the end of the number, without ever imagining for an instant that I was destined to meet her.

I was doing the rounds of the talk shows, there were invitations and cocktails; a party had been organised in my honour, by whom, I no longer recall. In any case they were well-connected in the business whoever they were. I arrived sufficiently early to be able to stand at my host's side and greet the guests as they arrived. I shook hands with the celebrities, then, since these people all knew each other, they gradually banded together in small groups, glasses in hand as they munched away on the petits-fours brought round by the waiters.

I remained alone in a corner of the room – I didn't know any-one – wondering what on earth I was doing in this excruciating situation and planning to make a discreet getaway. Besides, discreet or indiscreet, who would have noticed my absence? Certainly not the host of the evening! The introductions had been made, pho-tographs had been taken for the people pages of the magazines, everyone had done their job; the rest could be filed under futility! Suddenly, two immense black eyes boldly underlined in kohl of the same colour were staring right at me, and a pair of voluptuous lips declared:

"I saw you the other day, I couldn't understand a word, but I think you were great, and so different to anything I've seen before."

I repaid the compliment: "And likewise, I saw you on television the other day and *I* thought *you* were great." All in English, if you please.

She held out her hand and said, simply: "I'm Liza."

Suddenly I was no longer alone and friendless, I had a companion who was talking, laughing, listening to what I had to say, who wanted to know how I went about songwriting, and who found my style "fantaaaaastic", especially *Les Comédiens*[11], "very original". She would have liked to have continued our conversation, but was leaving the next day for Los Angeles where she was booked to play the Coconut Grove. After chatting for a good hour, we each went our separate ways.

At the end of my New York engagement, I was asked to appear on a Hollywood television show. Would I accept? You bet I would! It was a godsend, with Californian sunshine, a bungalow and the Beverly Hills Hotel swimming pool thrown in for good measure. As soon as I was settled in my suite, I consulted *Where* magazine and read: "Liza Minnelli at the Coconut Grove." I reserved a table for three, had a spray of roses delivered to the star, and that evening, Happy Goday, Jacques Vernon and I watched the show. It goes without saying that all three of us were extremely impressed by this young woman's theatrical talent and intelligence. When the show was over, we made our way to her dressing room and, naturally, we talked of our mutual passion for the stage and song, of our respective sets, of what we liked and what we loathed about the business. We were on the same wavelength. Since we are both loquacious, she and I, we talked long into the night. She is a nightbird, I am just the opposite, all the more so on this occasion since I had to be on good vocal form for the following day's show.

"I'll come with you, as long as it doesn't bother you," Liza suggested. Good lord! The diva, a bother? You'd have to be mad!

The following day, at rehearsal, she was there. I was to sing three songs *You've Got To Learn* and *Happy Anniversary,*[12] in English, and *Les Comédiens,* in French. I found the backdrop for my performance most curious indeed: a bistro terrace, a few tables, a few extras wearing berets, one of whom was carrying a bread baguette under his arm, a bicycle in one corner ... In short, everything I hated: a caricature of France created by over-imaginative foreign designers who have patently never seen a Vincente Minnelli film set!

I called the studio director and made it clear that I had absolutely

[11] *Les Comédiens.*
[12] *Il Faut Savoir* and *Bon Anniversaire.*

no intention of performing in this ridiculous stage setting designed for Americans who had never been further than their own backyards. Nick Vannof, who happened to be a charming man, attempted to calmly convince me that the designer had come up with this wonderful backdrop specifically with me in mind. So I asked him a very simple question: had the artist in question ever seen one of my shows? The answer was no, but he was a highly creative man ... There were only a few minutes left before the final rehearsal, I stuck to my guns: I would have left the set rather than flirt with ridicule. Finally, unable to replace me at such late notice, they agreed to stand me in front of a neutral background, no extras and no bistros – out with the bread baguette and the 1870s Austrian moustaches!

"You've got some nerve!" Liza said to me.

You bet I had! I refused to play the typical French singer for an ignorant audience just to get on one more television show, however prestigious that show might be. Then Liza added: "It's funny, when you get mad, your English improves!"

After the recording, which went ahead after all, we went for a bite to eat in a French restaurant. Liza enquired what my plans were for the following day; I replied that I was leaving for Canada where I had a series of shows at the Place des Arts lined up before embarking on a tour across country. That evening, we parted company a little more tenderly than usual.

Montréal, it always feels like coming home; I have friends there, a faithful audience and a whole host of memories. Memories of my days as a duo with Pierre Roche, of the drinking sessions, and getting away from it all in this country that will surprise you in any season, especially in the spring when the sun, like a celestial Prince Charming, awakens nature after many long months of sleep. He melts away the seemingly eternal snows to reveal the earth, as if by magic, and when autumn comes, he drenches the land and the forests in swathes of crimson and gold. I have always had a special place in my heart for this Quebec, where Roche and I had our first real taste of success.

At the Place Des Arts, a handsome venue seating three thousand people, Jacques Vernon, who was acting as my agent and secretary, but was, first and foremost, a friend, announced as I came off stage after the final curtain call: "I've got a surprise for you. When you've changed, you'll find out what it is."

The surprise was Liza, in flesh and blood. I think she set this up back in Los Angeles with Jacques who had kept it secret. She came along for the whole tour; she was a fountain of joie de vivre, tap-dancing during rehearsals with Jacques Vernon, a dancing teacher by profession. After Canada, I followed her to Las Vegas where she had some dates booked. And then, by Jove, our nomadic life brought this sweet affair to an end, an affair that with the passing of the years has evolved into true, lasting friendship.

The Hollywood Of My Dreams

Beverly Hills. On my first visit, I stayed at the Beverly Hills Hotel, the legendary establishment frequented by the biggest names in literature, politics and cinema. In spite of my modest means, I had rented a large bungalow, one of those that had caught our imagination as kids when we discovered the stars who lived in them in the Gaumont and Pathé newsreels.

Beverly Hills in the rain is more like Cambrai[13] than a Californian town. To prove that a French star had no reason to envy the local celebrities, I had hired a driver who drove me around in a limousine. Truth be told, I hate those long, lugubrious limousines, with their smoked glass windows, that look like hearses. It's strange, stars will do anything to get themselves noticed and then hide away behind smoked glass and dark glasses. Anyway, I overcame my reticence and bowed to tradition.

What tradition, you may well ask? The one that states that appearances are everything. The *in* place for lunch was the Brown Derby. My American agent had arranged to meet me there. It was pouring with rain, and, as you well know, if it's American, it has to be larger, bigger, more plentiful, and more generous that anything European – it was a veritable deluge. I stepped out of the limousine, the porter came out to meet me, protecting me with his umbrella, he too was a giant. As I walked with my head bowed to protect my face against the

---

[13] Cambrai – dull town in Normandy.

rain, I saw the glint of a star encrusted in the pavement with a celebrity's name engraved in the centre. Strange folk these American artists, I thought to myself. They buy a business and then emblazon their names outside the entrance so that everyone knows who owns it. It was only later that I learned that the whole city was paved with such stars, in honour of those who bring fame and fortune to the Mecca of cinema.

CHAPTER 39

Back to my Roots

A t the end of our tour of the Soviet Union, we had planned to go to Armenia. It had taken some insistence on my part when we were signing the contract to visit the country of my origin. I wonder what the authorities were afraid of. Admittedly, I had refused to submit my lyrics to the board of censors. But what could they have censored anyway? *Après L'Amour*[1] perhaps. That's exactly what I wanted to avoid. So, I neglected to submit the lyrics of the songs I intended to sing until the very last minute.

We landed at Yerevan airport. As the cabin door opened I was quite unprepared for the blast of bitter cold that engulfed me. What a fool I was! What an ignoramus! There I was thinking that Armenia was a hot country. It was snowing cats and dogs! Well, I had wanted to come, and here I was. As I came down the steps someone thrust a large bouquet of flowers into my arms. It had been hard enough to make much out through the blizzard, now I couldn't see a blind thing. I handed the bouquet to the nearest reception committee secretary and, having kissed him on both cheeks with frozen lips, I made

---

[1] *Don't Say A Word*

sure to retrieve my cumbersome gift before turning towards the officials who had come to greet me, as they uttered words of welcome, in Armenian, of course, and followed by: "Welcome home, we are happy that you have returned."

Returned? I had never set foot in Armenia, no more than my parents had; they, like me, had both been born on foreign soil. I had barely managed to make it past the officials than I ran into a crowd of some two hundred people, members of my family, they said. I had not imagined there could be so many of them in this country that even my grandparents had never seen. There were endless cries of "*Charles djan, sirheli Charles arhperh djan*", and let me shake your hand, let me hug you tight, let me pat your cheek! They all had something to say, they all wanted to arrange for me to come by to meet the other family members, the children, the old folk, and heaven knows who else ... I was buffeted back and forth, it was worse than the stage door at the Olympia ... Someone managed to get me into a large, black limousine, of the kind used by eminent Party members.

Aïda, her hat and coat askew, after the same cries of "*Aïda djan, sirheli Aïda*", barely made it to the limousine. And we were off to the hotel where, at last, we figured, we would get some peace. Think again! The lobby was bursting at the seams with people, every one of them a close relation of a distant relative. We had never imagined that after the genocide, which had eliminated a million and a half of our people, after all – half the population of the country – they had been quite so successful in renewing the race. Talk about a "revenge of the cradle!²"

We had a great deal of trouble in reaching our room. I had barely sighed an "ooph" of relief than the telephone began to ring, and ring, and ring. We disconnected all the plugs. I intended to have a quiet bite to eat in the company of my sister and the musicians, once I had taken a bath. Little did I know! We were official guests. I no longer remember what we ate, but, when it came to the drinking, I was dealing with professionals. They were world champions! Every time a

---

² *Reference to the women of Quebec who it was alleged felt a collective desire to take revenge on the Conquest of 1760, and the anglophone population, by having as many children as possible.*

glass was raised it had to be accompanied by a small speech; and I was expected to play my part in this.

But we were no strangers to this kind of dinner-table sport. To help me get through this almost impossible situation, I looked to my father for inspiration. He made, I think, one of his most memorable toasts on the occasion of my daughter Seda's baptism – we still called her Patricia at that time. She was nine years old, in 1956, when a date was finally set for her to be baptised.

After the requisite visit to the Armenian Apostolic church, it was on to Le Lilas, the famous Armenian restaurant on the rue Lamartine, with family and friends, around forty of us in all. We had my father's sense of organisation to thank for the gargantuan meal and an endless supply of bottles – vodka, raki, red wine. He officiated at the head of the table, the perfect *tamada*, that indispensable master of ceremonies for all Georgians and Armenians; no glass may be raised without the tamada's say-so, and a speech by him is the *sine qua non* for enjoying any drink, and even then, you must wait until he has finished his monologue before raising the glass to your lips! A *tamada* has to be a poet, an orator, even something of a braggadocio, and any talents he may have as a rhapsodist or singer are more than welcome. My father was a master in the art, he had the ability, glass in hand, to keep an audience spellbound for hours on end. For Patricia's baptism, he gave us his greatest performance.

There were people of all creeds and races among the guests. Between the mezes, the national dishes, the cheeses, the deserts, the coffees and the after-dinner drinks, we spent nine hours at the table without a single thought of complaint. Papa poured all of his lore and talent into moving, amusing and captivating his audience, all the while building to a crescendo. First, toasts were raised to those around the table, honouring their strengths and making fun of their foibles. Then we drank to the restful peace of the souls who perished in the genocide, and each of us then dipped a crustless piece of bread into our wine glass before placing it on the edge of our plate. We drank to all those who deserved to be Armenian and whom my father had naturalised, just as he himself hoped to be naturalised as a French citizen.

After each speech, the glasses were filled; homage and praise flowed forth. We drank to our local neighbourhood, to the stone bridge that my parents had had to cross, to the boat that had set them down in Marseilles, to the railway that had brought them to Paris, to France, of course, to the Parisian suburbs that had welcomed them, Alfortville, Issy-Les-Moulineaux, and so on and so forth. I wondered just where my father's imagination would lead us. Between speeches, guests contributed poems and songs. Nine hours. Nine hours of sitting, nine hours of drinking, yet neither the speeches nor the drink proved to be too much for anyone. Glancing at the bottles that the waiters had lined up behind me, I was curious to discover how my father was going to end his performance. And he did it with panache, bringing this day to a close, after we had made three final toasts to water, gas and electricity. The *tamadas* from France could hold their own against their peers abroad, and I am sure that this first and brilliant performance has never been equalled.

My father was in the habit of giving nicknames to his friends and acquaintances; there was "Bedros the Bear", for example, and "Écheque Simon" which translated to "Simon the Ass", and many others besides. Simon was far from being a stupid man, it was simply the luck of the draw, and while he lived in France all his friends called him "Écheque Simon." He had arrived in Armenia around 1947 and he was head waiter at the hotel restaurant. He came up to me: "I am Écheque Simon." As soon as Aïda and I recognised him, we were delighted to see him. He then quietly said to me, "Your grandmother is in the hotel lobby, and the officials are refusing to allow the members of your family to come through."

Aïda and I got up from the table to go and meet my father's mother. She was a tiny, sturdily built woman with a very loud voice, ninety-six years old; I could have lifted her up with one hand. After an affectionate exchange, she explained that all the seats for my show at the opera had been allocated to Party members and that there wasn't so much as a folding aisle seat left for the family.

Party or no party, the next day, I delivered an ultimatum – or rather two ultimatums. There was a common or garden piano and a Steinway on stage at the opera; since I wasn't a classical musician, the former had been designated for my use. They soon realised that my Armenian blood would not prevent me from vehemently exercising that most Parisian of arts, complaining and shouting. In Armenia, like the USSR, people were terrified of anyone who threw their weight around verbally. The piano was duly changed. As for my family, I obtained seven seats in the centre of the front row, and a few Party bigwigs had to be relegated to more modest seating. My tiny grandmother, accompanied by six family members, sat in the front row every night that I sang. So I had my grandmother opposite me in the venue the whole time that I was there. In Yerevan, students had tagged the opera walls with the words: "The Party get the tickets, but Aznavour belongs to us."

I didn't get to see anything of Yerevan during my short stay. The thick snow buried everything. To console me, someone quoted a Russian Tzar who had experienced something similar when travelling in Armenia: "Well, I was deprived of the sight of Mount Ararat, but Mount Ararat was also deprived of the sight of the Tzar." You don't have to be a Tzar to utter such silliness, I say "The snow hid Mount Ararat from me, but I've made up for it since." It certainly isn't Proust, it won't make history, but it's the truth.

CHAPTER 40

Solo in the USA

It was a crazy idea that I just got into my head. I set off for New York, where I wanted to present a couple of my songs in English and take in a few shows. Howard Richmond, a publisher whom I'd known for some time, and who had already had a few songs of mine on his books, had been briefed: I didn't need much, just a recording studio. I brought two backing tapes with me, nothing else. Howard arranged for one of the best music men in the business to look after things for me, Happy Goday; and there we were, all set to lay down some tracks in the studio, and me with my execrable accent – I still hadn't mastered the tonic accent, which you need to do if you want to be understood.

Art Luboff, the proprietor of the Village Gate, a famous Greenwich Village jazz club, had very much enjoyed François Truffaut's film *Shoot The Pianist*. Always keen to discover new musicians and came along to one of my recording sessions. *Tu T'Laisse Aller*[1] made a big impression on him, he enquired whether I was the one playing on the backing track and was most surprised to learn that my voice was my instrument, not the piano. He invited us over to his jazz club that

[1] *You've Let Yourself Go*

same evening. We went along to hear a singer whose name was unknown to me at the time: Nina Simone. She was quite something, the lady played piano like few others. He introduced us, explaining to Nina that I was a French singer-songwriter whose writing style was quite unlike hers. She and I arranged to meet up a few days later in Richmond's office, where she chose two of my songs to record the next time she went into the studio, *Íl Faut Savoir*[2] and *L'Amour C'est Comme Un Jour*.[3] On the same evening, Art Luboff asked me if I liked his venue, and when I replied that it was perfect for vocalists, he said that this was why he had invited me and that if I agreed, he would like to book me for a week for two thousand five hundred dollars. He was very surprised when I told him that I had stopped playing clubs some time ago and only performed concerts in theatres. He explained that in the States, even the biggest stars were happy to play occasional club dates. "Anyway," he concluded, "if you change your mind and you want to play here one day, the stage is yours."

It was after this trip that I decided I wanted to tour in the land of show business. "Hang on," countered Jean-Louis Marquet, "they've asked for Jacqueline François, but never for you. She's sold a lot of records, so the interest is there. But Barclay has never tried to release your records anywhere outside of Europe and the Middle East."

I had some money put aside. I suggested to Jean-Louis that we put together a world tour, and specifically, a tour of the States. We could invest the income from the countries where I was well-known into America, where I was going to have to put up the money myself. "Madness!" he retorted. "Sheer madness" cried my friends and those close to me. Madness, yes, but in this business, can you do without it? In the meantime, Jean-Louis had met the man who was representing Ray Charles in Europe. Of Polish origin, he was ready to give it his best shot, and did not feel that I was throwing money down the drain with my investment. The tour was shaping up well, with dates in Spain, Belgium, the Netherlands, a few concerts in the USSR, and from there, destination New York where I had hired Carnegie Hall,

[2] *You Got To Learn*
[3] *Love Is New Everyday*

followed by Washington, Boston, Philadalphia, Chicago, San Francisco, and Los Angeles.

We encountered our first obstacle as soon as we arrived in the States: my Soviet visa did not make a good impression. They wanted to know what I had been doing with the Communists, if I was a Party member. I denied this quite honestly: my left-wing leanings of the time did not make me a member of any party. My rule of thumb is to listen to men and women of all political affiliations, but to stay well away from power. The audience is my party: white, black or yellow, right-wing, left-wing, rich or poor, heterosexual or gay. We finally arrived in town, where Herb Rosen would be taking care of the record company side of things since Barclay had managed to get me signed to the Mercury label, thanks to our friend Quincy Jones. As far as radio promotion was concerned, I was in the devoted and capable hands of that extraordinary music man, Happy Goday, who became a close friend.

Our second hurdle was no minor one; the press had been on strike for several weeks, and it did not seem likely that they would be going back to work anytime soon. Which left television. The most important and influential talk show was hosted by Jack Parr. He had heard about me from Geneviève, who for a long time had owned a club up on the Butte Montmartre where a number of us used to go for a drink after our respective shows, including Jacques Brel, Raymond Devos, Pierre Roche and a host of others. Geneviève had subsequently moved to New York to make a name for herself. Thanks to her, Jack Parr knew all about my Carnegie Hall date and every night, for over a week, announced on television that a certain Charles Aznavour would be playing a show which was an absolute must, he said. He did such a good job that Sybil Goday, Happy's wife, who never missed a new act, unable to get tickets for herself and her daughter Mace on the day before the show, called up the person in charge of the box office whom she knew well. The conversation went as follows:

"I want two tickets for Charles Aznavour."

"Charles who?"

"Charles Aznavour."

"Hang on a second, I'll check for you."

211

Returning to the phone, the man said: "It's sold out."

"Get away, nobody's heard of him."

"I know, but it's still sold out."

"Come on, stop kidding me, find me a couple of tickets."

"Sybil, I swear it's totally sold out. There isn't even any room in the aisles! But I might be able to fit you in on stage, behind the artist."

She ended up with two chairs where she had a back view of me. And so it was that I first trod the boards at Carnegie Hall in New York, in 1963, with three hundred people, most of whom were American, sitting around me on stage. There were many people who had enjoyed *Shoot The Pianist,* and many musicians in the audience. The following day, the press was unanimous, and I was suddenly the toast of the town. But we had to be on our way; city after city, we brought the house down all the way to Los Angeles. Just around the corner from the legendary Hollywood studios, I played a venue that was used for the Oscar Award ceremony in those days; I got my Oscar when I saw a galaxy of stars sitting in the front row, many of whom had inspired Aïda and myself when we were still kids.

Before I went on, Gina Lollobrigida, with Glenn Ford on her arm, came backstage to say hello. Our conversation in French irritated her companion, who gruffly remarked: "Can't you speak English?" After the show, he behaved in a friendlier manner, as if he had been soothed by the music, and he even ventured a few words in French. For the first time, the press echoed the audience's sentiments and, to my amazement, reacted enthusiastically to the tour. One newspaper headline even ran: "Charles Aznavour makes friends faster than de Gaulle makes enemies."

Back in New York, we had a summit meeting in my hotel suite to decide what tactics to employ on our next visit. I came up with the idea of performing in university concert halls, as this was common practice then; the normal procedure was for a committee to decide which artists would be booked.

"Can we hire the halls?"

"Yes, if you put up the money, you can, but none of these students know who you are. They need a big name."

"How much are the tickets?"

"Five dollars, on average."

"OK, I'm your big name. We'll sell the tickets for one dollar."

"But you won't make a penny!"

"If I cover my expenses and we pull it off, then it's a good invest-ment."

The following season, I set out again along the same route with a few additional dates: Dallas, New Orleans, and a good dozen or so universities. We had come a long way since the day I played the Pacra! I was rather proud of the way the tour turned out; I managed to break even without trying to cut costs. I had brought Richard Balducci, my press agent, my secretary Jacques Vernon, my French impresario, Jean-Louis Marquet, my stage manager, lighting and sound man, Dany Brunet, and five French musicians over with me, the latter having managed – a rare thing at the time – to get work permits from the all powerful American Musicians Union.

CHAPTER 41

Speechless

W hen I woke up that morning I had lost my voice. I was not just slightly hoarse, I was completely aphonic. Although I had worn an eye mask and earplugs, I had lain awake for most of the night. For a singer, sleeplessness is the worst of curses. And so I awoke in a dreadful state, bags under my eyes, or more like trunks, I was in a foul mood, my skin had the pallor of an old rag. I was coughing fit to burst and spill my lungs all over the floor. Grumpily, I glanced in the mirror. A nightmare! I looked about a hundred and fifty! I was a mess, a real mess.

I did my best to try and remedy things: Glotyl, Solupred, Fluimucil[1], steam inhalations; nothing worked. Wrapped up as if I were about to leave for Siberia, I made my way to the theatre: the dressing room was beautifully festooned with flowers, a basket of fruit, three bottles of a famous grand cru Bordeaux, and a thick wad of telegrams. The promoter informed me that all the seats had been snapped up and sold out in just one morning. This was nothing short of a disaster! Now what? This bloody throat of mine was incapable of producing a single wretched sound. Someone called a doctor; he would not be able to come by until he had finished his round of golf. I was like a caged

---

[1] Anti-inflammatory and bronchitis medication.

lion. Finally, he turned up in his golfing garb, as snobbish as they come and terribly sure of himself. His first remark was:

"I don't normally come out on Sundays." Are you kidding, at the price he was charging! While opening his bag, he asked me: "So, what is wrong with you?"

"I've lost my voice and I have to sing in an hour's time.

"Oh, so you're a singer are you?" Schmuck! Just where did he think he was and why exactly did he think he's been called out? He gave me a routine inspection, took my blood pressure – why not an electrocardiogram! – and inspected my ears – as if that had something to do with my vocal cords! "So, you're a singer are you?" The idiot, he was in my dressing room, the town was plastered with posters, in fact there was on the wall staring him right in the face: "You're singing this evening?" I had just told him that, I tried to keep my cool.

"In one hour. When this happens to me, my doctor gives me a camphor injection or something like that, and I'm usually able to sing."

"Why didn't you have someone call him?"

"Because I'm three hundred miles from home!"

As he wasn't listening to me, apparently searching for something in his bag, he repeated mumbling: "You should have called your general practitioner." I could have strangled him! I repeated:

"If you could just give me an injection ..."

"Out of the question, I never give injections, I'm going to prescribe you some tablets. In an hour's time, you'll have a voice like a tenor."

Just my normal voice would do. Then he fretted about his fee. Well, rounds of golf don't come cheap, do they ... "My manager who is in the dressing room next door will settle up with you."

He left me a few pills and a prescription, packed up his things, and repeated once again: "So, you're a singer, are you?"

And satisfied, he turned on his heel and left. An hour later, I went on stage with a hoarse voice and made the best of a bad job. It is true, that the audience had first known me with a voice that sounded like it was coming from the horn of an old gramophone, back when I started out – some people even sent back the record they had just bought, believing that they been sold a secondhand one – so it was hard to tell the difference.

CHAPTER 42

Special Treatment

She came into the room where I lay on the bed, immobile with pain; she was not unattractive, a little plump, her blouse betrayed the contour of heavy breasts that would have fit comfortably into a man's hand; her short, tight skirt stopped just below the arch of her thighs. She spoke only her mother tongue, and Russian, the mandatory language under the communist regime. Employing the few words of Pushkin's tongue that I knew, and borrowing a little from Marceau's international language of mime, I managed to convey to her why she had been summoned to my bedside: I had a "beethovian" problem, as I called the pain caused by my compressed vertebrae, between the fourth and fifth.

I thought it strange, however, that she had not brought a folding massage table with her. I stripped off down to my underpants, which I kept on in spite of her insistence that I remove them. She indicated that I should lie flat on my stomach. Once she was ready, applying an oily fluid, she began caressing my lower back, occasionally administering small slaps close to my buttocks. After fifteen minutes of this relaxing but rather ineffective massage, she indicated that I should turn over. I felt like a fish in a frying pan. Having smothered my chest and my stomach in oil, she straddled me to complete her task with greater ease, smiling broadly. Her breasts were bobbing up and down right in front of my face, and I was could see the tiny, immaculate white triangle of her small panties. She seemed completely unaffected by the situation and was chattering away, without bothering to find out if I understood or not.

When she had finished her work, if you could call it work, she asked me if there was anything else I wanted. Anything else? The only thing I wanted was some relief from the pain, for heaven's sake! At my reply of *niet* and in the face of what she felt was an outrageous lack of enthusiasm, she gave a small pout and went and washed her hands. To the customary enquiry of "*skolke*," she named an exorbitant sum, which I paid in spite of everything and then asked her for a receipt. She had forgotten her counterfoil book, but she promised to drop one off at the hotel the very next day – I'm still waiting . . .

Then she left as she had come, lightly dressed and short-skirted, abandoning me to my pain and the feeling that this had been no physiotherapist, but more of a 'physio-hostess", my money being the only thing she had managed to relieve me of. The following day, I had a visit from a genuine physiotherapist, who made no attempt to give me any pleasure, but who, on the other hand and for a far more reasonable price, did me an infinite amount of good.

CHAPTER 43

My Little Sister

Don't think for one minute that I have forgotten about Aïda, my little big sister. No, she is still with me, tucked away in a corner of my heart, silently present, of invaluable help to me musically. We share the same memories; she has a greater ability than I to recall events and people that I often forget. My sister and I were born sixteen months apart, and basically grew up like twins, playing the same games, enjoying the same things. If I had a sailor suit, Aïda wanted one just like it. She was very protective towards me, especially when we were very young. She was convinced that it was her duty to keep an eye on me and took this self-appointed role very seriously. We could be left alone at home even as very small children; there was no danger of anything happening to me. Except one thing. My sister liked to make sure that I never went hungry, she would feed me with anything she could get her hands on, sugar, pieces of meat – and I was still toothless! – but also coins and buttons. Full of trust, I would swallow whatever my sister gave me as if I had a cast-iron stomach. To please her, I even took her medicine, and without any song and dance as I enjoyed being looked after by her. She used to call me *arhparik,* which means little brother in Armenian, I reciprocated and called her *arhparik,* believing that this was how we were supposed to address one another.

Aïda had piano lessons while I had to learn to play the violin. I didn't like the violin. I would have preferred to play piano, like my sister. After several months of sawing away at the strings of my instrument with the bow, I decided that I would never grow up to be a violinist. On the day that we bought the violin – I was a very small boy indeed – I remember standing in the Rue Champollion near our grandfather's restaurant and torturing the strings in the street. The passers-by must have taken me for a poor little Gypsy boy, trying to earn a few pennies. But I do not remember receiving a single contribution – who knows it might have encouraged me to continue my lessons! So blame the people in the street for my failure to become a great violinist! In any case, Yehudi Menuhin would have had nothing to fear from me.

In 1957, when I returned from Canada, Aïda introduced me to a young composer of Armenian origin, who had adopted the strange pseudonym of Dyran Web. Fortunately, he dropped this soon thereafter to go back to using his real name. As far as I knew, for I did not know him personally, Georges Garvarentz was a rock and roll songwriter. I had only heard the song that he had written for Eddy Mitchell, *Daniela,* an excellent song as it happens, but not the genre of composition that I had in my repertoire. So when Aïda urged me to give him some lyrics to put to music, I didn't say anything, but decided to audition him in my own way by sending him a some mediocre lyrics that I had no faith in. When he returned with a melody that was far better than my words deserved, I resolved to give him some lyrics that were worthy of his talent. Punctilious to the extreme, he was continually questioning his work. Whenever I wrote any lyrics and could not find the right music for them, I passed them over to Georges. He wrote a number of classic compositions for me, such as *Paris Au Mois D'Août, Non Je N'ai Rien Oublié, Et Pourtant, Les Plaisirs Démodés, Ave Maria*[1] and many more. Besides being a gifted composer, Georges was blessed with a priceless sense of humour and real knack for doing impressions.

Aïda was a pianist, and when I set about tinkling the ivories she

---

[1] *Paris In The Month Of May, No, I could never forget, The Old Fashioned Way, Yet… I Know, Ave Maria.*

sometimes found my playing below par — to be honest, it was appalling. From day one, she has always been in the studio with me, correcting any notes that sound off key to her or picking me up on my diction. There are certain songs that I would not have attempted if it had not been for her encouragement and insistence. Heaven knows why, but *La Mamma, Il Faut Savoir, Que C'est Triste Venise*[2] were among the songs that I had rejected for my live set. This was back when I had decided to give up trying to score hits in the charts and stop recording singles so that I could concentrate on making albums. Although she was talented and had a promising career — her records sold reasonably well — Aïda decided to drop it all and follow Georges Garvarentz whom she had just married, in order to devote herself to her husband's career. Georges never used to compose unless Aïda was there; she sat and did crossword puzzles, never far from the piano. If he ever happened to forget a melody while composing, he knew that he could count on Aïda, who has extraordinary musical recall, to come over and play it for him on the piano, before returning to her crossword puzzles.

[2] *For Mama, You've Got To Learn, How Sad Venice Can Be.*

CHAPTER 44

The Press

Accolades and laudatory press notices have been few and far between. To be frank, when I started out, there were none. The demolition job on the Aznavourian edifice has been in full swing for several decades. Strikes and unemployment are unknown in this sector! Oh, yes, I was not handsome, worse, I was unwatchable, and my voice was unbearable. To top it all, I wrote unpopular songs about far-fetched and totally uninteresting subjects. With so little going for me, I should have hit a brick wall. The public were starting to take to me all the same, my records were selling reasonably well, and I was often able to draw a full house, particularly south of Lyon.

The Critics (La Critique)[1]

They sit back and wait
Theirs is not to sweat and fret
When you lose your nerve
Stricken by stage fright

---

[1] From *La Critique / The Critics* by Charles Azanvour.

And shaking like a leaf
In the spotlight
In stony silence
They watch from the shadows
Pens poised to strike
No matter what you say or do
They will find the chink
In your armour
Broadsheet or tabloid
Pundits left or right
I somehow doubt
That those ordained to write
Have filled their pens
At the font of goodwill
What can you do
Up there alone
Brittle as a clay pigeon
When they shoot you down
Kiss your dreams goodbye
And shut your mouth

Yet the press, and radio, in particular, were giving me the cold shoulder, worse than that, they tore me apart. I didn't flinch, but it cut to the bone. I have never put pen to paper nor picked up the phone to complain to the editorial staff of a newspaper, or even to a journalist. I remained unresponsive, going so far as to pretend that I never used to read any of my press. Opportunistic photos, the work of French and Italian paparazzi, have never driven me to instruct my lawyers to intervene on my behalf and claim damages for invasion of privacy.

No, I have taken refuge in silence; it occurred to me that the authors of those destructive reviews must have been tearing their hair out in frustrated handfuls when they saw that that they could not sway the public or hold back my career with their words. I never reacted: the controversy that would have ensued from any intervention on my part would have simply disrupted my life even further. I thought: "All said and done, each to his own trade!"

Blows below the belt, like kicks in the teeth, ultimately build strength of character; and, at the end of the day, what do people remember more? The article disappears with the next new issue; the song, immortalised on record and relayed by radio, can still be heard day after day, year after year, carried by the singer's voice. I would be putting on a brave face if I were to pretend that none of this affected me. But I took a deep breath and threw myself headlong into my work, with the firm conviction that nothing can beat fifteen to eighteen hours of effort a day. Wallowing in bitterness and rancor would have given me an ulcer or, worse, a heart attack. And I certainly wasn't going to file a suit for media harassment by the press as a whole! In any case, there was a good chance that I'd have lost anyway. Such is the lot of an entertainer.

And so? And so I preferred to devote my energies to learning and understanding; to continue putting my all into my profession. I have written close to seven hundred songs, and not bad ones either, even if I say so myself; I've more or less mastered five languages, which has allowed me to record and perform in some ninety different countries. To say nothing of the films that I have made that have been well-received by the critics. But as a singer-songwriter, now there was the rub, I was only fit for the rubbish tip. As it turned out I wasn't biodegradable. I refused to give up, and for someone who had no voice, who was physically unattractive, talentless, and had no future as an artist, I didn't make such a bad job of it. The new generation of critics seem to understand me better than those who have since faded into retirement.

I can admit now that it hasn't been easy. Doubt, anxiety, stage fright before a performance, and the awful feeling that every member of the audience must be carrying one of those crushing reviews, have all kept me company for many a sleepless night. But these days, thank goodness, I feel fine, and if I don't sleep so much, it's my age, I suspect, and nothing to do with persecution by the press. What can my detractors say today? That I have changed? Even back then, Raoul Breton had an answer for that: "He hasn't changed, you have."

It looks as if I'm settling old scores here, and why not? I am not ashamed to admit it. I'm not bitter and I'm certainly not looking for revenge. I believe that, in spite of everything, I have managed to lead an honest, dignified and, to a certain extent, exemplary career. Of the two us, the press and I, who has egg on their face now?

I know that journalists have a difficult role to play; consequently it behooves them to temper their words when dealing with a new-comer; to remain constructive, disposed to help the artist correct his or her mistakes, and progress in life, with each article; like other spe-cialists they contribute to the fulfillment and the success of the artist. Journalists have these responsibilities, not only to the artist, but also to their readers, even themselves and the beauty of their profession.

I went back and looked at my lyrics to try and see where the fault lay: *Sa Jeunesse, Parce Que, Pour Faire Un Jam, Je Me Voyais Déjà, Je Hais Les Dimanches*[2], which had just been awarded the Society of Dramatic Authors' prize at the Deauville Song festival. Rhymes, caesura, and hemistiches have all been respected, and the subject matter was orig-inal for the time. To my credit, my songs were not derivative. Other singers made my songs their own and even asked for more. So what was it that the press held against me? My appearance? I had no choice in the matter; we can't all be born looking like matinee idols. My voice? Ah, my voice! My voice has launched a thousand pens. Husky, broken, sure it was; but it was the voice of the street, the voice next door, and the audience seemed to like it. Why is it acceptable for an American singer to have a husky voice but not a French singer? Should I have honed my voice to make it softer like Tino Rossi's? Should I have invested in a brow like Jean Marais, a nose like Marlon Brando or a mouth like Maurice Chevalier? Or revived the practices of the Middle Ages to gain a few inches on the rack? No way! I did-n't give a damn what they thought; I carried on writing love songs of everyday life.

After Love (Après L'Amour)[3]

After love
Our two bodies are one
After love
When our breath is short

[2] *His Youth, Because, Swing, It Will Be My Day, Sunday's Not My Day*
[3] From *Après L'Amou r/ Don't Say A Word* by Charles Aznavour.

We lie in bed
You and I almost naked
Happy without talk
Illuminated by our smiles

For over fifteen years I waited for my detractors to soften their tone, to change their stance, in the face of my international popularity. Nothing, niente, rien, nada. So I carried on in my own sweet way, performing mostly overseas where the press had been on my side from the start and made me their darling. In Poland I had even been dubbed "The Napoleon of Song"; not bad for someone whose only ambition was to get up on stage and bring the house down!

One member of the demolition gang, because it was fashionable or out of sheer bloody-mindedness, an administrator of the Comédie Française – who was also a journalist and had written several scathing articles about me – needed a big name for a charity gala to pull in the crowds and ensure the success of the event. I am told that the Academie members were unanimous in their choice: "Aznavour". So our friend was left with a serious dilemma on his hands; what would I say? Not daring to face me himself, he sent an emissary to tell me the news, to whom I listened calmly and politely. After he had submitted his request, which was larded with grand expressions such as "an exceptional evening that will be attended by leading figures from the artistic community and top politicians, and held in one of the world's most prestigious venues and blah blah blah, and blah blah blah", I looked him straight in the eye without giving anything away. Then he laid it on thicker, convinced that he was impressing me.

Just imagine, they were handing me a royal opportunity on a plate. To think that Molière himself was going to roll out the red carpet for a poor little common or garden variety singer like me! They were probably expecting me to fall on my knees, overcome with emotion and moved to tears, before mumbling, "Thank you, oh, thank you," in an even more broken voice than usual. I know my profession and the power of a protracted silence: he must have thought that I was so consumed with emotion that I was lost for words.

Then suddenly, calmly, taking my time and pausing between each sentence, I replied in an excessively restrained manner, smiling naively: "And why did the honourable administrator not come in person? After all, you are not offering me a contract, but asking me to perform at a charity event for nothing." The man lost something of his high and mighty tone and stammered a few pathetic, empty excuses. To cut him short, I stood up, adding courteously: "I would be delighted to give my answer to the honourable administrator, and to him alone."

And that was that, exit stage right, a small, satisfied grin on my face! Forty-eight hours later, I was lunching with the honourable administrator, and, on the night of the gala, Molière rolled out that red carpet for me. I gave my one and only performance of "No Trifling With Azanavour[4]" at the illustrious Comédie Française theatre.

The following year, I returned to the stage with another show at the Olympia, I had completely forgotten about the charity gala episode when Raoul Breton came into my dressing room, brandishing the entertainment page of *L'Intransigeant*[5]*,* in which a headline in bold print that stretched across two columns bore the legend: "MEA CULPA". It was signed by the administrator of the Comédie Française, Marcel Iskovski. As far as I know, he is the only critic who has had the guts to publicly express his remorse, as he did with this Latin confession. I felt no sense of vindication when I read his wonderful piece, which deeply moved me. He had finally listened to me sing, he had heard my voice and my songs. Today, I would like to thank him for that gesture. I didn't at the time, because of my decision to appear indifferent to everything that was written about me.

The Critics (La Critique)[6]

Critics, critics
However much you tell yourself
That you couldn't give a damn
Critics, critics
They bring you down
And lay you low

[4] Ref. to *On Ne Badine Pas Avec L'Amour(No Trifling with Love)* by Alfred de Musset.
[5] Evening paper.
[6] From *La Critique / The Critics* by Charles Azanvour.

My records were already selling well, and were being played on the radio; people also heard my name when other artists covered my songs – this practice of announcing the names of the songwriter and lyricist later disappeared. I was reasonably well known in the French provinces. Jean Renzulli, the most Southern of French promoters, decided to book me on Léo Marjane's tour as the main support act. Jean-Louis, who had not worked with Renzulli in the past, insisted that he pay for all the shows up front. And Renzulli, who wasn't entirely what kind of artist I was, came to see me perform at the Olympia. Upon hearing the first song, he was appalled by the sound of my voice and said in his local accent: "This'll never work in Marseilles! My wife warned me to be careful what you get yourself into." By the time the song was over, and when he saw that the crowd were bringing the roof down, he added: "They're plumb loco, these Parisians." The longer the concert lasted, the more our man began to panic: "To think I've paid for the whole thing in advance!" Seeing how delighted the audience were when the curtain came down, he got to his feet, saying: "After all, who knows, maybe it *will* work."

As it turned out, the South, particularly Marseilles, was my first bastion of success. At Édith's, I had got to know Tony Reynaud, the owner of Les Variétés and Le Gymnase in Marseilles. The latter venue didn't have a stage entrance and stood in a very narrow street. On the way in, it was fine, as I arrived before the audience, but when I came to leave, generations of OM[7] fans would be waiting for me. You can just imagine what a corrida it was. To spare me from the crush of the crowd, security arranged a police van, more commonly known as a Black Maria,[8] which allowed me to leave the establishment without incident and brought me back to my hotel, where I promptly put myself under lock and key. Witnessing this spectacle, my father wryly remarked: "To think that my son is driven away like a common criminal every night!"

---

[7] Olympique Marseille, Marseilles' football team is commonly referred to as the OM.

[8] *Panier à salade* (Salad basket)

CHAPTER 45

California Here I Come

I had a two-week contract to sing at Huntingdon Hardford theatre, in Hollywood. It was the first time that I had been booked to play more than one consecutive date in this town. The first night was looking good; the venue was going to be packed, a rare feat for a little known artist. I couldn't help but be delighted as I was only getting paid a small guaranteed fee plus a percentage of the door. Before curtain up, I was terribly nervous. I watched the fateful hour draw closer, my legs had turned to jelly and my forehead was damp. Maurice Chevalier offered to introduce me, before I came on. Maurice was an idol in this country; you couldn't wish for a better introduction. He made his entrance, slowly, full of confidence; this was a man who knew his audience. The audience responded with a resounding ovation, then he launched into the little speech that he had meticulously prepared. In flawless English, tinged of course with that Parisian accent that was an integral part of his success on this side of the Atlantic, he began thus: "I'm going to introduce you to young man, a great French talent. Actor, songwriter, composer, singer, he can do it all and does all brilliantly." He paused, then continued: "I confess, I would have liked him for a son." Another pause. "Though, I would have been happy to have him for a brother."

Finally, he added: "But to be perfectly honest, I would have rather had him for a father."

The audience laughed heartily and applauded. There was then a kind of ripple in the room as Marlene Dietrich rose from her seat, majestically, to make her way to the foot of the centre stage where Maurice bent forward, almost kneeling, and planted a light kiss on Marlene's lips. Greeted by thunderous applause, Marlene slowly returned to her seat. Maurice returned backstage.

By this time, my stage fright had given way to full blown panic; I was in a sweat. How was I ever going to manage to acquit myself respectably after that? But a man's got to do, what a man's got to do; I made my entrance as if I were about to confront a dragon. The musicians started playing. I couldn't tell you if I was met with any applause or not as I came on. I launched into my first song, upping the tempo to increase the intensity of my performance. My hands were shaking, my legs, too, but the audience thought this was all part of the act. I was reassured by the enthusiastic response. The rounds of applause had something of a calming effect on me, but I kept on singing as if a pack of rabid dogs were after me.

I sang with a vengeance, a burning passion. By the end of the show I was spent, strung out, and bathed in sweat, oblivious to what was happening around me. I was rewarded with a resounding round of applause, which was immediately followed by a standing ovation, a phenomenon that had not yet made its way to France. This was not the kind of orchestrated standing ovation that you now see on French television shows, but a sincere, spontaneous one, and it was followed by a series of curtain calls of the kind that are usually reserved for classical musicians at the end of a concert.

After the show, I was fortunate enough to have the stars who had been in the audience line up to come and say a kind, friendly word to me: Marlene and Maurice, of course, but also Nathalie Wood, Loretta Young, Norma Shearer, Gene Kelly and Mike Connors, to name but a few. When they had left, and the lights had dimmed, the limousine drove me back to my luxurious bungalow. I felt like a robot, my head was still full of the applause and the congratulatory words. I thought of my parents, of Piaf; they would have been so proud of me that evening. "Nahé ourh éïnk ourh éguank", as we say in Armenian. "Look were we came from, look how far we have come." Me, that son of stateless parents, who had run the gauntlet of the critics, who had nothing to offer, the one who should have given up a hundred times over; today, I had reaped the fruits of my labours, all the days and all the nights. And this, in the country that haunted every artist's dream, the land where show business is king. That night, sleep evaded me. A thousand things went through my mind; only in the early hours did I finally fall asleep, with a strange desire to laugh and cry at the same time.

CHAPTER 46

Ulla Ingegerd Thorssell

.

She will definitely not appreciate me talking about her and us, how she hates to draw attention to herself, but never mind, I'm going to risk it! After all, I can hardly write about my life without mentioning the person who has been living at my side for more than thirty-nine years now. Thirty-nine years already, yet she has only been seen with me in public on rare occasions. When I have a opening night, she asks to be seated so that she can slip away quickly during the interval and at the end of the show, preferring to be poorly seated rather than seen. She likes to be incognito when she comes to a venue and never attends the receptions that are held after gala evenings.

In the course of my adventures, I have never known if people befriended me out of genuine feeling or whether, like moths flocking to an acetylene lamp, they were drawn by the glare of the spotlight. In Saint Tropez, where I was living the life of Riley, you'd find me gyrating to the latest rhythms every night in some discotheque until late. It was always the same sketch: I would have a drink with a friend, then someone would come and muscle in on our conversation and invite his or her own friends to join us and, gradually, the gadflies would gather in droves around our table. As the evening wore on, this charming crowd would disperse without so much as a word of thanks, leaving me, naturally, with the honour of footing the bill. My champagne was beginning to leave a sour taste in my mouth.

One night, I stopped a playboy friend of mine, whose company I enjoyed, from paying for a round of drinks. I asked for the bill myself, and when the waiter asked me: "Everything on the same bill?" I replied: "No, just for me and my friend." A wave of panic swept through the hangers-on, freeloaders of all sorts, who had invited themselves to join us; they were dismayed, outraged even, at having to pay for their own drinks. From that day on, the news having doubtless spread like wildfire, this strange menagerie never deigned to honour us with its cumbersome presence ever again.

On one of those legendary nights when I had invited a few friends from the business – none of those freeloaders – to join me in Saint Tropez, I confessed to Régine, a close friend, that this footloose and fancy-free existence of mine was beginning to really get me down. Living a bachelor's life that was periodically interrupted by a series of furtive, charming and short-lived affairs, forced me to wonder: was it the glare of the spotlight that made me attractive to these young women?

It was June, 1964, and the previous month I had reached an age at which – in theory – you owe it to yourself to start taking life seriously: forty. I was in a Saint Tropez nightclub with a handful of friends including Régine and Sacha Distel, when Régine motioned with her chin to draw my attention to a pretty blonde girl, and said to me: "That's the type of woman you ought to be meeting." I turned round and recognized the young Swedish woman that Essy, a Finnish girlfriend, had introduced to Ted Lapidus and I, one night when we were dining at Don Camillo's in the Rue des Saints Pères. I got up and asked her to join us. But the beautiful creature was wary. A new arrival in France, she did not recognize any of the faces at the table, although all rather well-known if not downright famous. Like the good citizen of a socialist, protestant land, that she was, she tended to be on alert. In the end, she stayed a short while, visibly ill at ease, but accepted all the same to have lunch with me on a beach the following day. I had just met someone, at last, who had no idea who I was, and, moreover, who took me for one of those rich kids living it up on the Côte d'Azur.

I had to make do with a couple of lunch dates. Then, a few days later, she left for Paris to resume her job at a Swedish bank. I later learned that she had done some modelling, but since she would refuse to comply with the photographer's ideas, the work gradually dried up. I knew where she was staying; I sent Dany to find her and, if possible, bring her back, imagining that if the Swedish army were made of the same stuff, the country would be impregnable.

If I had to describe Ulla in a few words, I would say that she has something of a Greta Garbo about her. We did meet up again, but as far as that's concerned, my lips are sealed! If I say another word, I'll get my knuckles rapped, and since we haven't fallen out a single time in thirty-nine years of shared existence, I am not going to start rocking the boat now!

A Ring On Her Finger

We had been living together since Saint Tropez, I was quite happy with the arrangement, but my protestant companion had principles: she wanted to start a family, she wanted to have *children*. I was already a father and I had my fingers burned by two less than convincing experiences; I considered the case closed until she left one day, to go to her family in Sweden.

I called, but no one picked up the phone. Day after day, my countless calls remained unanswered. I was worried, I was due to leave shortly, to go and sing in San Francisco. I had grown accustomed to her silences, but this was a deeper silence than before, and seemed to have swallowed her up. I decided to leave for the States without her, and continued calling in vain from there. She had left suddenly in the wake of my unhappy words on the subject of marriage; after two negative experiences I had absolutely no desire to tie the knot again. I was sorry now for what I said; my words were surely the cause of her silence.

By dint of calling and calling and calling again and again, I got her to pick up the phone. I gave her no time to speak, but suggested she go over to Lapidus' and get a dress made before coming out to join me so that we could be married. And so we were married at City Hall, in Las Vegas, on January 11, 1967, by the city mayor; the civil ceremony was followed by a reception attended by our witnesses, Sammy Davis Junior, Petula Clark, Aïda, Georges Garvarentz, as well as friends who travelled from France, Kirk Douglas and his wife, and a large number of artists who were performing at that time in Vegas.

When we returned to France, I wanted to have a traditional marriage, in the presence of our families. So I went to see the archbishop of the Armenian church in the rue Jean-Goujon to set a date for the ceremony. When he pointed out that I had already received a blessing in that same church a couple of decades earlier, and that the Christian church did not sanction divorce or remarriage, I presented my infallible argument that this marriage would be an excellent promotional exercise for the church, that it would encourage young couples like us to return to their beginnings. After hesitating for a short while, the good man agreed, but warned me: "This is the last time, my son." And it was. Ulla's refusal to convert was not a problem, and so, one year and a day after the civil wedding in Vegas, the Armenian archbishop united us on January 12, 1968, for better, and not for worse.

Ulla, always and forever. Ulla loves her children, her family, her childhood friends, her dogs and me – at least I hope she does! – more than anything else. She is always ready to laugh that delightful laugh of hers, especially with the children who, in this respect, take after their mother a great deal. Small, everyday things make her laugh, rather than the usual elaborate jokes and funny stories that you hear. When she is seized by uncontrollable fits of laughter, tears form in the corners of her eyes and she cannot stop. At moments like this I can see her as a child, in the snows of her Swedish homeland, surrounded by her friends and siblings – she comes from a family of six children, perfectly programmed: boy, girl, boy, girl, boy, girl – in an atmosphere which I, naturally incorrectly, imagine to be totally Bergmanesque, a series of silences punctuated by whispered words, and gentle, chaste, measured gestures.

When we met, our friends gave our relationship two or three months at most. What could these still waters possibly want with a turbulent torrent like me. I never put the question to her. And what could my interest be in a woman who was so far removed from the preoccupations of my profession? Yet no concessions had to be made. We accepted each other for what we were, with our strengths and weaknesses. More than anything, she loves to go for long walks in the woods, which is not my cup of tea at all, particularly since she walks too fast for me. So, for this activity, the dogs take my place. I like going out in the evenings, she does not; so for this our children take her place. We've been together for thirty-nine years already – or for only thirty-nine years! I have livened her up a little, she has mellowed me greatly. Who could ask for more?

CHAPTER 47

And They Lived Happily Ever After

October 10, 1970; Ulla knew that this was the day. She had already packed her bag a few days previously and had prepared herself, calmly, for the big day. I got dressed quickly, helped the expectant mother into the car and, using the emergency lanes, sped to the Sainte-Isabelle Clinic in Neuilly. "All the same," I thought, "how can she be so sure of the date?" But Madame is like that, she's punctual, precise and certain. Having entered the clinic through the casualty entrance, I accompanied my wife to her room: "Right, there's no point in you hanging around here, why don't you go for a drive and come back in an hour or two," she suggested. We are both too reserved, she and I, for me to stay and watch a birth. So I didn't wait to be asked twice and made myself scarce; besides, you shouldn't upset a pregnant woman, especially the day of the birth of her first child. It is hers and hers alone. I left and drove aimlessly around Paris. When I arrived back at the clinic, two nurses emerged from the lift, wheeling a hospital trolley containing a still dazed Ulla and a pink, chubby Katia in her arms, the long-awaited child, Ulla's child, her baby that no one could touch, so to speak. The child belonged to her, was her creation, and I alone was allowed to approach her.

When Mischa was born, everything was more relaxed. Nicolas, the youngest, who is twenty-six years old now, was born in the middle of August, when I was supposed to be on tour in Italy. Ulla advised me to go, taking the other two children with me, insisting that she could manage perfectly well on her own. In fact, she called us a few days later, to tell us that it was a boy while Katia and Mischa were splashing about happily in the pool of a San Remo hotel. And when we returned home to the house in Geneva, the whole family was swimming in joy.

CHAPTER 48

The Tree of Life

I have never written any songs about my own life, with the exception, of course, of the one that I called *Autobiography*. But today, looking back through some of my compositions, I am surprised to discover a considerable number of maxims and ideas that are just like me or that reveal something about me, hidden in some of the phrases and lines that have flowed from my pen. As if I had unconsciously anticipated the future, and, indeed, from a very young age. This has nothing to do with instinct, intelligence or culture, no, it's something which cannot be defined, something amazing; I wonder about it but I have no answers. *Sarah*, for example, for which I wrote the music, a text that was floating around in Jacques Plante's papers and that he had no plans for, struck a nerve with me a soon as I read it. It was the story of a Jewish tailor's daughter, who marries and leaves for America, far away from her family. I am neither a tailor, nor Jewish, but my daughter Seda left to be married there. I selfishly like to have my family around me, or at least nearby, and I was devastated by her departure, just like the Jewish family. Once she had settled there, Seda became an American and presented me with two beautiful grand-children, Lyra and Jacob, whom I see too infrequently for my own liking. Fortunately, my concerts sometimes take me to California where they live; then I can visit these grandchildren who don't speak Armenian but who make the effort to speak with me in French, with a hint of that American accent that is so popular on this side of the Atlantic.

My dream of founding a large family, after the tragedy that had deprived my kin of their own, finally came true. Four children, three grandchildren already, new branches are constantly being added to our family tree. The most recent is Leïla, born to our daughter Katia. And so I have reconciled myself with what we call fate. After all the pain that fate inflicted upon my people, it has smiled upon me. But many still wait for fate to give them a small chance.

CHAPTER 49

Women's Intuition

I first met Lévon Sayan one night when I was singing at Carnegie Hall, a few weeks before the wedding in Las Vegas. We were supposed to be leaving on a tour of Maine, but it turned out that we would need a car to transport the little equipment that we had. Henri Byrs, my piano player from Marseilles, turned up one day with a young man with a strong southern French accent whom he introduced by saying:

"He's Armenian and he has a big car."

"Let's take a look at the car, first," I replied, "because the fact that he's Armenian is irrelevant." The car was a strawberry-and-cream-coloured convertible, it was perfect; as for my Armenian, he was lively, likeable, witty, sharp and savvy, and I adopted him on the spot, especially since he was a man of broad experience who got things done fast and properly without making a song and dance about it, and without angling for money. We have been working together now for thirty years. This man who had been living in the States for fifteen years followed me back to France and Switzerland, fulfilling multiple roles: stage manager, soundman, secretary, driver; the mechanics of the show business industry no longer held any secrets for him, in France or in the States. I should add that he also attended my marriage in Las Vegas.

Subsequently, Ulla and Aïda both advised me to hire him to look after business for me. Women have instincts which we men lack, and I have never regretted taking their advice. This was the first time, too, that I had worked with an Armenian; but again, the fact that someone is Armenian or a childhood friend is not a justification in itself, talent and expertise are what count.

CHAPTER 50

Orphaned

In 1966, in New York, where I was going to be performing, I had rented a small fourth floor apartment, without a lift, just a stone's throw from Washington Square, in the Village on Waverly Place. I had furnished it with the essentials; the piano gave the removal men quite a head-ache. It was delightful, it was "La Bohème", but instead of Verdi's score there were plenty of bags to carry up and down the stairs whenever I was touring. It's at times like these that you appreciate hotels, the porters and, most of all, the lifts. I soon missed the comfort that I was accustomed to. After a few months, with a sense of relief, Ulla and I moved back into a good hotel. Farewell Mimi and Rodolphe, and bohemian nonchalance! Hello Charles and Ulla, in American-style comfort! "Leave the New Yorkers to play at living the Montmartre life. We'll be chameleons and live the American life," I said to myself.

Henry Coldgran, my agent in the States, always managed to make sure that things cost me as little as possible, if anything at all. He had located a Jewish cabaret in upper New York and knew the artistic director there. I didn't have to shell out a penny to hire a rehearsal room and could go ahead and rehearse there for free with my musicians.

It was in New York that I learned of my mother's death. She was in Moscow and had been about to board the plane back to Paris when it happened. An Armenian woman who was waiting to take the same flight, had had time to arrange for the body to be taken care of and contact my sister, who, in turn, called Coldgran; it was he who broke the news to me, with great sensitivity. This man, whose respect for tradition was immense, who would not let me work at Yom Kippur, even though *Fiddler On The Roof* was playing non-stop in town on the very same day, who stayed at home praying and didn't leave the house for any reason, well, this wonderful man, Henry, came over to offer me his support, and managed to find me a return ticket to Paris.

I was devastated. I felt remorse. I began to wonder: had I not failed to give a little more time to my mother so that I could put my career first? I was lost. I was so far away! After hiring an Air France Caravelle jet, Aïda and Georges had flown to Moscow to organise the repatriation of the body. A coffin could not be found for love nor money; no one wanted to help them. A distant cousin, of whom Aïda and I had never heard, then ran the risk of prison in order to find one, and worse than that, a cross. Finally, after countless problems, they were back by the time I arrived. "*The show must go on.*" I told myself during the flight. I recalled that the day after my grandfather's funeral, my mother had sent Aïda and I to the pictures. "But we're in mourning," we told her.

"Going to the pictures is part of your profession!" she retorted.

In New York, Ulla was there, silent but steady, to support me. I had come alone and I arrived in time for the mass and the burial. I left again the very next day in order to fulfil my engagements. That first night, it was very hard for me to sing *La Mamma;* everyone advised me: "Forget it, you can put it back into the set once you feel stronger." But, "*the show must go on.*" Whether you fall off a horse, or a bicycle or you take a bad tumble while skiing, you have to pick yourself up and get back on right away, or you never will. So I sang *La Mamma,* with tears in my eyes and a lump in my throat. As it was the last song of the set, I was able to leave the stage and regain my composure before going back out to greet my audience.

A few years later, it was my father's turn. He had undergone an operation for cancer of the vocal chords, and hadn't the patience to go through proper rehabilitation. He left us the morning after my final show at the Olympia. With his passing, Aïda and I had lost our final link to our Armenian past, we were suddenly both orphans. You're never too old to be an orphan.

CHAPTER 51

Japan

In the land of the miniature, the average-sized man is king. Here was a country that was just my size. Here the "tall ones" are the ones who have trouble fitting in. There are no outsized departments in Japan, only Sumo wrestlers have their clothes made to order. Elsewhere in the world, oh the humiliation; someone of my stature visits the childrens' department, shamefaced, story prepared, to try on clothing for a kid brother, of course, who luckily just happens to be more or less the same size as his older brother ... Oh, how we dread the shop assistants' smiles, their condescending, understanding looks, which seem to say: "Right, your kid brother, we've heard that one before." How painful they are. But in Japan there is justice: there, the small Nipponese men and women get to snicker at the sight of gargantuan frames. The kimonos that the hotels provide for their guests, the windows, the washbasins, are all just right. No sooner do I leave Japan than I feel as if I am suddenly shrinking, falling back into this oversized world, which seems like a huge bowl in the bottom of which I struggle like an insect, slipping down the smooth sides. When you are Nippon-sized, you ought to be Nipponese. Life's not fair.

CHAPTER 52

Thumbs Up

I noticed the insidious signs once the bath water had drained away. My hair. There it was, lying there in the plural, useless, disconnected, and pathetic at the bottom of the bath. The first time, I didn't pay too much attention to it, but after two or three baths, seeing that the phenomenon was repeating itself, I began to panic, I scrutinized the teeth of my comb, and meticulously inspected the crown of head from all sides in the mirror. The naked evidence was glaring me in the face. I was going bald; it was enough to make me pull my hair out!

Being of an optimistic nature, my first thoughts were: don't panic, there has to be a remedy. Hell, this is the twentieth century, there must be a procedure or a miracle product, if not in France, then at least in the States, or Germany or Switzerland, or somewhere or other. I tracked down all the newspaper and magazine articles I could find on the subject. Alas! Nothing but false advertising claims: "Results guaranteed in just three months," with the obligatory blurry black and white before and after photos, showing the kind of hair that drag queens would die for.

I tried everything: scalp massages, lotions and shampoos of all description, dry products, oily ones, liquid ones, concentrated ones, pills, a shaman and the oily stuff that you coat your head in and leave in a sticky mess all night long. Here's to progress! Nothing made any difference, the hair loss was irreversible, little by little the thinning gained ground; the only option left was a hairpiece. But a man of seduction cannot bring himself to take such extreme measures. The risk of the ridiculous fluffy coiffure fluttering to the floor to expose the glabrous dome to the wide-eyed gaze of one's companion was simply too great to bear.

My decision was final. To hell with false hope and miracle cures, I would get a transplant. Having checked my head, the doctor reassured me: since the acreage was still fertile, there was every reason to believe that we would see a bountiful crop after a few sessions. And indeed, my mirror and I are more than happy with the final outcome of this hair-raising adventure.

CHAPTER 53

On the Steps of the Palace

I had not set foot on a Parisian stage for seven years. Negotiations with Jean-Michel Brois, who had succeeded Bruno Coquatrix as the artistic director of the Olympia, had come to nothing, so Lévon Sayan and I chose the Palais des Congrès for my return performance. I found the stage too large and decided to have a staircase placed in the centre so that I would not have to walk too far to reach centre-stage when I appeared. I had a nagging doubt: what if the applause were to cease before I could make it that far. But the opening night reassured me, I had never received such an ovation in Paris for a return to the stage. The whole venue was on its feet, artists and audience alike. They had come, they were all there; inside I saw all the years of struggling, of being misunderstood flash by in a fraction of a second. I felt the spiritual presence of all those who were no longer with us, but who had loved me from the start and believed in me, they were all behind me, with the orchestra, MY PARENTS, Édith Piaf, Raoul Breton, Henri Deutschmeister, Patrick, and so many others ...

CHAPTER 54

Young and Troubled Days

Success is something that is shunned in France. Unlike Anglo-Saxon countries where no secret is made of it, in France we conceal it, we look for excuses to avoid being tagged a fat cat. For example, when someone says to you: "You make a good living," you feel obliged to reply, reluctantly, in the affirmative, before adding:

"But I have so many expenses, and then, the government takes such a chunk that, at the end of the day, I don't make as much as you might think."

Similarly, some artists keep their tours abroad quiet. French audiences are very possessive; only artists whom they have ceased to care about may perform abroad. As for the Anglo-Saxons, they take pride in the success of their artists.

I am not a political animal, I have never really become involved in any movement. There are good and bad people everywhere, and, as far as I am concerned, my audience is not defined by religion, or social status, or any specific political stance. When I sing, I see only lovers of the arts, and song lovers in particular, out there in the room. I sang prior to a speech by François Mitterand, in Marseilles, when he was still just a party leader; in Bologna, at a L'Unità meeting[1]; in Paris,

[1] Italian newspaper, formerly the mouthpiece of the Italian Communist Party, now defunct.

at the *Fête de L'Humanité*[2]*;* and on the occasion of a speech by Valéry Giscard D'Estaing. They each thanked me in their own way: François Mitterand presented me with my first Legion Of Honour, while Giscard's election earned me nothing but headaches. Hounded under the fallacious pretext of making the rich pay up, I had no choice but to spend a fortune to defend my good name out of my own pocket. Let's not deceive ourselves; in France, in this kind of profession, it is absolutely impossible to amass a sizeable fortune in the same way that you could in Italy, Germany, or Britain, not to mention the United States. The published figures are purely for show. How many artists disappear, fade from limelight and end up eking out an existence on a meagre pension . . .

But let's get back to the story. After I had toured the USSR, my tax man, failing to find any earnings from this tour on my tax declaration, issued me with a tax adjustment including added interest for late payment, which resulted in a fine of six or seven times the amount in question. Try as I might to explain that artists performing behind the so-called Iron Curtain were forbidden from taking a single ruble out of the country, and that I had been obliged to spend every penny there and then, my protests fell on deaf ears, the sum was due and that was that. I bit the bullet and paid up, but I had learned my lesson; my future tours in Eastern Europe were on an all expenses paid basis and I took no fee.

On another occasion, the authorities did me the distinguished honour of taking me to court in spectacular fashion, just to make an example of me and prove that I was one of the great fortunes of France. A charming anecdote springs to mind. A man of rather advanced years was waiting for me with a warm smile as I left the Versailles court; he spoke to me in Armenian, placing one hand on my shoulder: "You see, my son, this too is an honour for you."

As far as he was concerned, I ought to feel gratified at the lengths that the authorities of a powerful country like France would go, to do battle with a small foreigner like myself. I had a good laugh about

---

[2] The annual post-Summer vacation three-day music event organised by *La Humanité* newspaper and the French Communist Party.

that; René Hayot, my lawyer, did not laugh so loud: in the crush at the Palais de Justice, a pickpocket had lifted his wallet.

"You see, René, you can't even feel safe in secured areas these days..." I said.

CHAPTER 55

Books

Although I can express myself relatively correctly in Armenian and have no accent, because of the way my life turned out I never learned to read and write the language that should have been my native tongue. Hence my poor knowledge of Armenian literature, which, I am told, is a rich body of work. In my younger days I never felt the urge to delve deeper into it and I sometimes regret this, but time passes and there is no going back. It's only later in life that you say to yourself: "If only I had known!"

I am neither an intellectual nor a scholar – or someone would have noticed by now – but I read voraciously; books by authors from Russia, America, Italy, Spain, South America, Britain, Germany, and, of course, France. Yet there are still many authors whose work I have never found time to embrace, not least the ancient Greeks, whose lands I have seen but whose literature remains a closed book to me, much to my regret and shame.

As a child, I would often borrow books from the small library on the Rue Saint-Séverin, close by the church where used to served early morning mass before attending school – the sectarian school on the Rue Gît-Le-Coeur. However genial and friendly these places were, there would be no introductions to classical literature here.

Later, when Micheline and I were newlyweds and living at 8 Rue de la Louvois, in the small sixth floor room that had been lent to us by cousins, with no lift, and whose only window looked out onto a corridor, I would often walk past that Fort Knox of literature, the French National Library. To avoid the trauma of being surrounded by so many works without knowing where to begin my education, I never ventured inside. There were too many authors collected there who were unknown to me. It would have been like attending one of those receptions to which I was often invited and where I never knew who to speak to.

Although I delight in reading and avidly devour some seventy or seventy-five books each year – or about four thousand works in sixty years of steady reading – I always considered myself to be uncultured. Aware of the gaps in my knowledge of literature I feared that I might lose my appetite for reading if I were suddenly confronted with so many works. It's true, it would have been too painful! Dreams and illusions must be allowed to take root and flourish, not nipped in the bud. Racine, La Fontaine, Molière, Corneille, Victor Hugo … I, who wanted to be an actor, read them all, it was the simplest and best way to learn; I later added Aristophanes, Sophocles, and Terence. But perhaps I was too young, for I found the company of the latter three rather dull. Yet I read them stoically to the end, to learn and understand, and, primarily, for the sake of appearances! Subsequently, in my professional life, the only authors who have been of use to me are French writers such as Jean La Fontaine. With the exception of Victor Hugo whom we read at school, it was only later that I discovered the French writers. I grew up hearing my parents recite verse by the Armenian poets, Sharantz, Grigor Narekatsi, especially Sayat Nova, the poet, songwriter and troubadour whose works my father sang with great sensivity.

Books, books, books, yes but which ones? Where to begin? Students have professors to guide them, stimulate them and show them the way. But when you are left to your own devices, when you are timid and self-conscious, you feel your way forward and you are left wanting. Honoré de Balzac, Émile Zola, Anatole France, Voltaire and Rabelais are all names which stand proudly on street name signs in France, but there is no mention of the authors' works, only their birth and death dates.

Fortunately, in life, you meet people who open new windows of thought, who shed light on new areas of understanding. It was Jean Cocteau, no less, who gave me my first such gift. I had, miraculously, received a handwritten note from him, in his delicate, elegant, distinguished hand. The short note – brief missives were the best kind in his opinion – which he had delivered to me, as people used to do back in the Age of Enlightenment, advised me of the visit of a friend of his whom he said appreciated my songs. She would come and see me at the end of my show at Beaulieu Casino. The lady in question, Madame Francine Weissveller, invited me to lunch at her home in Cap-Ferrat, together with Jean, who was a regular visitor to the house.

It was a wonderful experience. I was immediately captivated by this extraordinary and timeless personality. He was unassuming and charming, as he always was, and I taught me something of fundamental importance that stayed with me all my life. After lunch, it was Jean's wont to retire, not to rest, but to write. One day I enquired whether he was working on a new play or book. He replied: "No, I'm not. I write every day because it is important to write a little every day." Writing is a muscle that needs regular exercise. Since that day, I never let a day go by without putting pen to paper. It's often nothing of great interest, some texts I tear up, some I keep, just in case. The only important thing is the act of writing itself.

CHAPTER 56

I Love or Hate

I passionately love the professions that I have chosen. I dedicate most of my time to pursuing them. I live surrounded by keyboards, pens and computers; I take particular pleasure in trying to find the perfect word, the rhyme that fits, the perspective, the note, and in waiting anxiously for the public's approval.

As an actor, I like to feel new, empty, open, in the hands of the director; my sole concern is my desire to give the best of myself and reinvent myself. I don't perform a role, I become that character.

As a singer, I enjoy performing the same song a hundred times over, improvising some small change with every rendition to surprise both of us, myself and the audience. Curiously, I am seldom convinced by comments such as: "Oh, you were on better form than usual, this evening." I rely little on the judgment of others and believe that I alone can truly know if I was at the height of my powers during any performance. I am at a complete loss when people pay me compliments, and my clumsy efforts to deflect them with humour rarely save me.

As a writer, I am the happiest of men. I am in love with the French language, though I do not claim to have mastered it perfectly. In spite of all my hard work, my language is still laced with lacunae. I love words, the evocative sound of words: for example, the word "round" really does feel round in your mouth, while "sliver" is sharp on the tongue ... When writing, I do not always choose a word because of its meaning, but because of the way it sounds. A word such as "tornade" (tornado), whose r's can be deliciously rolled in French, is far more powerful than "typhon" (typhoon) or "tempête" (tempest). The only word I loathe is "triumph." "I triumphed, he triumphed, we all triumphed the other night." It is meaningless.

By force of circumstance and fate, I have ended up with four professions, one leading to another, one fueling another, and sometimes overlapping; four different disciplines which nonetheless compliment each other, when all is said and done: actor, singer, songwriter, composer. I have been a little impulsive in my approach at times, something of a vagabond, but never amateurish, although perhaps not completely professional. The key was always a feeling of a job well done, "a fine piece of work", as we used to say in a certain epoch. Today, as far as one of my crafts is concerned – that of singer – after sixty-nine years of performance, I think, in all honesty, that I have fulfilled the contract that bound me to my audience, my employer.

CHAPTER 57

England

She[1]

She may be the face I can't forget
A trace of pleasure or regret
May be my treasure
Or the price I have to pay

She may be the song that summer sings
May be the chill that autumn brings
May be a hundred different things
Within the measure of the day

She may be the beauty or the beast
Maybe the famine or the feast
May turn each day
Into a heaven or a hell

[1] By Herbert Kretzmer/Charles Aznavour © 1974 Editions Musicales Djanik for France and Territoires SACEM – Standard Music Ltd for the rest of the world.

She may be the mirror of my dream
A smile reflected in a stream
She may not be what she may seem
Inside her shell

She who always seems so happy in a crowd
Whose eyes can be so private and so proud
No one's allowed to see them when they cry

She maybe the love that cannot hope to last
May come to me from shadows of the past
That I'll remember till the day i die

She maybe the reason I survive
The why, and wherefor I'm alive
The one I care for
Through the rough and ready years

Me, I'll take her laughter and her tears
And make them all my souvenirs
For where she goes I've got to be
The meaning of my life is − she

England, so close to France and yet so far away, no one can say why. There is between Paris and London a sort of love-suspicion relationship that has always been difficult for me to understand. We have so many things in common! I had never agreed to perform there. Before singing on a London stage I wanted to perform in the US first as I knew that country and thought the English audience would be much colder. Therefore, after my debut in the US I finally agreed to perform in England in any theatres or venues.

I walked around London and I fell in love with the Royal Albert Hall − 7,000 seats! I was told it was too big for a singer who was almost unknown. But as I am stubborn, I decided it would be there. However, the producer who had given up fighting, accepted, persuaded he would lose money. Forty hours after the box offices were opened he phoned me and was utterly surprised. All the tickets were sold. "Sold Out". Therefore, I thought I became the "Unknown Sold-out".

After the first show everything went perfectly well. I had songs that could be perfectly adapted in Shakespeare's language by the marvellous Herbert Kretzmer and on top of it, *She*, for which I composed the music went number one in the charts, twenty years after its first release.[2]

---

[2] 'She' topped the UK charts for four weeks in July 1974, and a cover version by Elvis Costello reached number 19 in August 1999 when it was used on the soundtrack of the movie *Notting Hill*, starring Hugh Grant and Julia Roberts.

CHAPTER 58

Autumn

When I was fourteen or fifteen years old, the mere idea of having to face death some day made the hair stand up on the back of my neck. After that, I was too preoccupied with pleasure, girls, success, and the thought faded into the background, only resurfacing with the loss of a family member or friend. Then I reached the time of life when, with the coming of autumn, you find yourself looking tenderly at the leaves on the trees as they turn from green to yellow to purple before they fall to be swept away by the wind. It is a time in life when you start to count the years you have left! The thought of death becomes the constant companion of your days, or rather your nights. You envisage it, you question yourself. Believers and non-believers alike, we all have our doubts. The past comes back to you more clearly and you begin to change your way of life. I went many long years before I learned to enjoy nature, became interested in trees and flowers, yet I have always wanted to live in the country. Today I would like to know the name of every plant, every insect, everything that the earth produces; now I would like to know how to paint. Is this an attempt to suspend the inevitable? Is it a feeling of having passed beauty by?

We have entered the third millennium. People may be happy to have left the second millennium behind them, but I look back nos-talgically to the one that has just drawn to a close, that has seen the most amazing inventions, the most incredible discoveries. I believe that we have just entered the era of every man for himself, of non-conviviality, immodesty and vulgarity. There are no more taboos, time is big money, while a human life seems to be worth less than a Magnum .357 bullet.

Time races on, as if the wheel of my existence were spinning out of control, as if I, in my ripe old age, were trying to hold it back. The further my childhood is carried away by the rapids of time, the more I feel the need to be with those who are close to me, my family, my friends. I constantly want to say to them, "See you soon!" as a day will come when one of us will regretfully say, "It's a crying shame that we didn't see more of each other."

Today, I think of all the people I knew, with whom I spent time, and loved in my younger years; I feel a mixture of regret and remorse in spite of myself. Too busy bringing home the bacon and living my lost youth to the full, I forgot to return to my childhood pastures, to see what Mina and Pierrot Prior were up to. I have since wondered what became of them, I wonder how they died. I think about the troupe again: Bruno, Jackie, Tony Guiguiche and so many others … Half a century later, I was anxious to go back and see the village of Quinson, in Alpes-de-Haute-Provence, where nothing seemed to have changed. I ran into Palmyre there, she was married to the mayor and first lady of the region for a while.

With the arrival of the Liberation troops, I saw Harry Scanlon return from England; the Englishman's son had managed to make his way to London and join the Free French Army in whose ranks he contributed to an exemplary war. The others, all the others who could have looked me up, considering my name, had the discretion never to do so. What a pity! I still think about all those friends; we shared a childhood that was full of emotion and tenderness. I can see us now, driving down to the south, uncle Prior behind the wheel of his "right-hand drive" Renault, Mina to the left of him, and the whole gang squashed in the back seat. I can still hear Mina's near hys-terical cries every time her husband, a maniac in his day, threatened to exceed thirty miles an hour: "Pierrot, you'll get us all killed!

Pierrot, slow down ... Pierrot, my heart ..." Did she really have a heart problem or was she just putting on a performance every time?

Georges Garvarentz, my brother-in-law, the most exceptional song-writing partner I ever had, and my friend, underwent a quadruple bypass operation: he was too passionate about his work, burning the midnight oil for nights on end, glued to his piano and his orchestration scores to ensure that no film release or studio recording were ever delayed; and drank too much coffee, and smoked too hard. Having endured a great deal of suffering in rehabilitation centres in Garches and Hyères, having written me a melody as beautiful as the one for *Ton Doux Visage,*[1] he left us, like Édith, Amalia, Dalida, Thierry Le Luron and so many others, creating a void that can never be filled. On the last two occasions that I have returned to the stage for a new season, it has been without him; the rehearsals and the shows have been deprived of his reassuring and incredibly entertaining presence. Then it was Madame Breton's turn. According to her wishes, my friend, Gérard Davoust, and I bought Raoul Breton's publishing company – which is a treasure trove of so many great French chanson classics, mostly written by Jean Nohain, Charles Trénet and Mireille – much to the delight of Charles Trénet, before he, too, left us, just a short while before Pierre Roche. Day after day, the pang of nostalgia grows a little stronger.

My Birthday

May 22, 2001, I was lucky enough to see this side of the new millennium. Seventy-seven years old, all the sevens, Sunset Strip. What's the point in celebrating when another year lived means another year less to live? My life is ticking away hour by hour, day by day, irredeemably, bringing me closer to the other side of existence. I look at my hands, they have recently become freckled with liver spots; my hair – what's left of it – has lost its colour. Many of my friends have turned to the skillful science and sorcery of plastic surgery; I could do the same, but what would be the point? Behind this slightly sagging weather-beaten facade, nothing can really change; the seventy-seven bells have tolled and nothing can give me back the litheness and

---

[1] *Your Sweet Face*

vivacity of my twenties. So what would be the point? To kid myself or kid the public that I am eternally youthful? After staying with me for decades, they have seen how time has shaped me, carved my brow, and have become accustomed to me as I am, as I have myself. As for having an operation, heaven knows what I might end up looking like: a sort of old young man, smooth as a Peking duck, with a bluish tint to my dyed black hair. No thanks, I'll pass.

I Didn't See The Time Go By (Je N'Ai Pas Vu Le Temps Passer)[2]

The more I live my life
The more I realise
In the light wind of my madness
I didn't see the time go by

Between the bed covers of my youth
When I slept without a care
In the time of my weakness
I didn't see the time go by

I didn't see the running of time
I didn't hear the ringing
Of the hours of my evolution
As I charged straight ahead
To what I thought was my future But which was already my past

The thousand questions that arose
In my troubled mind
Only one answer comes to me
I didn't see the time go by

I'm sure someone must have robbed me of twenty years without me noticing. I didn't see the time go by, I feel twenty or thirty years younger when I'm on stage. Dear, oh dear, my fingers, which are beginning to look like gnarled vines, bring me back down to earth,

---

[2] From *Je N'ai Pas Vu Le Temps Passer / I Didn't See The Time* Go by Charles Aznavour.

like my eyes, which have needed glasses for twenty years now. So it's my birthday, and, as on every birthday, people ask me how it feels. Well, I don't feel anything in particular. I must be a little odd. Most of my friends experience what seems to be a small bout of depression every time they hit a new decade. It probably has something to do with my Eastern origins. Life, that's life; and death is part of it, you just have to live with it! Today, I have a wife, children, and grandchildren, so I want to stay around to see them born and watch them grow. But death no longer frightens me, it has become something natural, about which I can talk and joke frequently; because when I look back over my shoulder, assessing the journey so far and taking stock of the luck that I have enjoyed in spite of everything in life, I say to myself, miracles do happen, and then I disarm death with a smile.

Why have I become who I am? My own personal conviction is that a voice was needed to remind the world of the continuing existence of the Armenian people, in spite of everything that they had lived through and suffered: the genocide, the treachery of the Western states who chose petrol over the blood of a people, the trampling of the Geneva convention and others like it, the (so-called) reasons of State, the Soviet subjugation of tiny Armenia when the country was on its knees, the earthquake, the Karabakh affair, the Turkish blockade. I firmly believe that I am that voice. Why me, why not someone else? God alone knows the answer to that question.

For You, Armenia

The earth shook in Armenia, this small, landlocked country, with no natural resources to speak of, where the life is hard and difficult, a country which has had its fill of Stalinism, persecution, and troubles of all kinds. The earth shook and felt the reverberations, too, of the conflicts with its neighbours which destroyed towns and villages, killing and injuring tens of thousands of men, women and children. The earth shook and the already bleak horizon grew darker still. I had never felt particularly concerned by what was going on over there, on the far side of our memories, I had always been more preoccupied with my work, when, suddenly, I became aware of my roots, aware that it had all begun centuries before, for my kin, on that soil where the earth had just opened up, an immense grave for many Armenians, a new abyss of misery and grief. I immediately asked Lévon what could be done to help the victims; we set up the "Aznavour For Armenia" association and I wrote:

For You, Armenia (Pour Toi, Arménie)[3]

The springtime will bloom again
The bright sun will rise again
After the winter
After hell
The tree of life will grow again
For you, Armenia
The seasons will sing again
The children will build a stronger world
After the terror
After the fear
God will treat your wounded soil
For you, Armenia

The following day, Georges wrote the music. Then, together, we called upon all our friends to make a record that reached number one in the charts and stayed there for several weeks, and which allowed us to help the disaster victims. Lévon, I and the others members of the association went over there, thanks to the kindness of Monsieur Dassault who graciously put one of his aircraft at our disposal. And there I was, I who had never been involved in anything political; I was even invited to the Kremlin to discuss the freeing of the thirteen imprisoned Karabakh Committee members, including Levon Ter-Petrossian who would go on to become the first President of the young Republic of Armenia. Since that time, I often visit this wounded, sullied, starving, bruised country, this land of orphans that has suffered invasion after invasion since its beginnings; this abandoned, forgotten, rocky country, where everything is in short supply, that is struggling to survive but continues to dream, as it has for countless centuries, of a brighter future for its sons and daughters.

[3] From *Pour Toi Arménie / For You, Armenia* by Charles Aznavour.

CHAPTER 59

A Few Regrets

No, I regret nothing, except the loss of my parents and friends who have left us. Except perhaps that I was not born in one of those small French villages, the kind you find in Alsace, the South-West or Provence, one of those villages where you belong forever and to which you return in the autumn days of your life.

I was born in Paris, in the 6th arrondissement. We often moved home, so I never succeeded in making childhood friends, I was never part of a local gang of kids. In this sense, I am nostalgic for a past that was never mine, for memories that I never experienced: the first day at the village nursery school and later the primary school, the youth club, fishing in the small local stream, the mad bike races, bumps and bruises that were quickly forgotten, the regional patois, doing our military service together, furtive first loves and "rolls in the hay", lovers trysts behind the church, stolen kisses in the spring moonlight, leaving Paris to make our fortune. "When I was eighteen, I left for the city." My songs are not autobiographical, but there is something of me in all of them. I would have returned to the village crowned in glory, longing for the calm of a country home where I could rest up for the holidays or between tours, always up for an epic game of petanque or a darts match in the back room of the village café with my friends; a regular face at weddings and christenings, or, sadly, to give one of those friends a final send off in the small cemetery, where I, too, and my family would one day find what they call eternal rest, though I still much prefer the daily grind of life.

My roots run deep in a country that escapes me. And where exactly should I look for this country? In the desert on the Turkish border where my people's bones have turned to dust and are scattered by the winds blowing in from the Asian continent? Is it in Georgia, the family's native soil on my father's side? Or is it in Armenia where we originated? I remain a nomad, an emigrant, a son of stateless parents who adopted a new country, a new culture, and a new language, but whose past still eludes him. Afterall, we can't all be called Dupont, Martin or Durand. My name is Aznavour and my name has served me well. But, all the same, I would have liked ...

Limousines, planes, hotels, restaurants, theatres, hotels, limousines, planes, day after day, week after week, packing your bags, finding someone to iron your suit, or wash your shirts on a Saturday, Sunday or national holiday. After sixty-nine years of it, I've had my fill. I've had it with hotels, and I'm done with delayed flights that have me fretting about missing shows. I love my audience and my profession, but the logistics wear me down: all the comings and goings, the trains, planes, hotels, packing, unpacking, and packing again *ad infinitum*.

On The Road (Je Fais Ma Valise)[4]

I pack my bag
I unpack my bag
I pack my bag again
My days are without surprise
My nights are all the same
Hotel d'Angleterre
Hotel du Belvèdére
Hotel des Mousquetaires
I'm traveling France from coast to coast
Hoping to sell my wares

[4] From *Je Fais Ma Valise / I'm Leaving* by Charles Aznavour

I would love to be like Pablo Casals, in Prades, and give concerts in the village where I live, without pomp or ceremony. I would just sing what I felt like singing, all the songs that went unnoticed, overshadowed by the hit on the A-side that monopolised the air waves, all the songs that were sacrificed for the sake of an album. Forgetting that it's a profession and singing purely for the listener's pleasure and my own; forgetting that I am Aznavour and going back to being just Charles. What a luxury, to be able to welcome your audience as you would welcome friends to your home, in your village ...

There comes a time in life when you attend more funerals than christenings. With the passing of the years, your memory begins to resemble a slice of swiss cheese; every hole harbours a name, a smell, or the reflection of a face that claws at you with melancholy as you turn a street corner, sit down at a restaurant table, or gaze upon a familiar landscape. What really hits us hardest? Is it the loss of a friend, a family member, or the sudden feeling that time is slipping away and that our days are numbered. We do not always shed as many tears for others as we do for ourselves.

It hurts me to think of my parents, my friends, it hurts me to think of a thousand things, yet I carry on drinking, eating and living my life. Those who are with us take the place of those who are absent, and life goes on, breached now and then by memories of the past.

Whenever I escort a relative, friend, or colleague to their final resting place, I wonder if I am next on the Grim Reaper's list. Besides this fear, many thoughts race through my mind. Too many, I'm sure. I think of my family first and foremost, and all the trouble that my passing will cause them, the expense, the administrative nightmares. Then I am filled with silent anger at the thought of the state helping itself to a disgraceful cut of the money that I have earned and saved, although I have already paid my taxes. Perhaps we would be better off squandering the lot in our own lifetimes. I wonder too, how I will be remembered by my children, I don't know how they see me now ...

Religion proclaims
Science disclaims
Believer and atheist
Both live in doubt

On opposite sides
A mirror image

Little by little I let go of things that used to seem important. I give things away, I destroy things and throw them out. I no longer read newspapers or magazines, I make do with headlines and photos. Except for one or two programmes, television bores me; I prefer listening to the radio. Just like the old days when I used to build my own radio sets. Talk shows are my favourites.

It exasperates me that one or two radio programmers have the power to decide which ten or twenty songs we should be listening to every day. I cannot bear to see the same song performed *ad nauseum* – such are the dictates of promotion – on every show, and mimed to a backing track, no less, for the sake of sound quality! I prefer to go and see live shows where artists are free to unleash their talent.

CHAPTER 60

From Hunger to Harvest

Between the hunger of the early days and the heights of success at the end lies hard work, and all the misadventures and setbacks that I have known along the way. Was success due to chance, destiny, a lucky star, an all powerful being who watched over me, or something else beyond my imagination? The bottom line is that I have managed to sidestep pitfalls and outrun failure. Success? I have never been comfortable speaking about it; in an unjust world it seems indecent to make a show of my travels and the advantages that my "celebrity status" as a singer has earned me. I'm not saying that I didn't flatter my ego and ambition somewhat with a Rolls-Royce in the early days, when everything that was happening to me went to my head, but I soon measured the vanity of it all.

After sixty-nine years of long and faithful artistic service, I feel it is not unreasonable to think about hanging up my stage suit, consigning it to memory's vault and taking a step back. I don't intend to say goodbye, but simply appear less often in public. The audience took time to accept me, and I will take my leave slowly, very slowly – I would not want them to think that, fortune made, I am about to disappear without so much as a look back. In truth, it's not easy to make my exit; there is nowhere I would rather be than on stage, and the

281

audience feels like family to me. They have given me everything, and I, too, have made many sacrifices for them, but there are no regrets for we have both remained faithful.

However, I have no wish to die on stage, unlike many of my confreres. I fail to understand their motivation. I do not see myself emitting an ear-splitting note and collapsing on stage with my face contorted into a ridiculous grimace – leaving the spectators with a less than flattering final image of myself – looking foolish, as foolish as death. If I could be sure that I would fall in one fell swoop, handsome to the last; not after shrieking one last note into the microphone, but after softly murmuring some classic phrase, my last breath magnified by the echo chamber as the spotlight on me faded ingeniously to black, well, then fine! But, without that assurance, I prefer to shuffle off this mortal coil, if God insists I must, at home, in my Napoleon III style bedroom, surrounded by my children, their children, their children's children, and why not, their children's children's children, well, all right . . .

I have no wish to be the most famous resident of the Montfort-L'Amaury cemetery where I have acquired a charming family tomb for twelve people. If we squeeze up a bit, we might be able to fit fourteen of us in there. No, I have already written my epitaph: "Here lies the oldest man in the cemetery." And when I say old, I mean old, really old, wrinkled, silver-haired, hollow-faced but sound of mind, with my humour intact and nails at the ready to hang onto this bloody existence for dear life. For I have yet to find anything better.

I have experienced my greatest joys performing for the audience; the best moments of my life belong to my family, my friends, and the stage. The stage has given me the chance to meet nearly all those that I admired as a child, when Aïda and I used to play truant and go to the pictures: Charles Chaplin, Michel Simon, Harry Baur, Victor Boucher, Danielle Darrieux, Charles Boyer, Louis Armstrong, Sugar Ray Robinson, Arletty, Danny Kaye, Damia, Bette Davis, Claudette Colbert, Loretta Young, Norma Shearer, Marcel Pagnol, Jacques Prévert, Jean and Cocteau, not to mention the actors, singers, lyricists, composers, writers, painters, and sculptors of my own generation. I am aware that the people we admire play an important role in our personal development, whether we meet them in person or know them from the silver screen. I see myself as the sum of all those who have, unknowingly, contributed to my development. I am eternally grateful to these influences and would not renounce a single one of them.

Whenever fate brings me back to a country, town, or village through which I have already passed on the long journey of my life; names, faces, and situations come flooding back to me; there are happy ones and sad ones, but they are all suddenly tinged with melancholy. It is not the past that is painful to me, but the altered appearance of places. I catch myself telling the person I am with: "Here there was …", "Here I met …", "There I saw …", thinking all the while to myself: "Stop forcing your past on everyone." Yet I carry on regardless, for in truth, I am telling these tales to myself. You want everything you have known and seen to stay the same, for people to stay young and never change; you want the impossible.

The past is a rich reservoir for the pen and anyone who gives themselves over to writing.

Armenia has long been a crossroads; it has witnessed the passage of many armies, the journeys of caravans along the Silk Road; it has been a crossroads of ethnic diversity, religion, language and culture. The country has gradually become more westernised, beginning with the adoption of Christianity as the state religion in the 3rd century AD, and later putting a French prince on the throne. The country became torn between two ways of life: that of its neighbours and that born of the alliances that it forged at the time of the Crusades. I am the son of two cultures. Like this country, I was overcome, inhabited and conquered by different ways of life at a very young age; I was shaped by every aspect of my native soil, in music, in poetry, both classic and popular, Russian, Jewish, Gypsy, Arab, and Armenian, and then French, Spanish, American … If I am asked whether I feel more Armenian or more French, I only have one reply: one hundred percent French and one hundred percent Armenian. I'm like a white coffee: once the two ingredients have been mixed, they can never again be separated. These two influences in conjunction with all the others have enriched me and have fashioned a style of my own in spite of myself. While others had to give themselves over to study, I already had these two cultures in my blood. I may have encountered many setbacks and stumbling blocks in life, but this cosmopolitan knowledge was a lucky gift. Speaking two languages from birth and being exposed to two or three others every day is probably the key to being able to absorb new languages quickly and plunge into other cultures.

Two Guitars (Deux Guitares)[1]

Two guitars in my mind
Allow me with great trouble
To sing of the futility
Of our existence
What are we living
Why are we living
What is the reason for being
You are alive today
You'll be dead tomorrow
And even more the day after

From Moscow to New York, from Rio de Janeiro to Singapore, from Paris to Sydney; I have travelled the length and breadth of the globe, journeying around the world several times, without ever losing my appetite for discovering, learning, and getting to know new peoples, languages, religions, ways of life, for tolerance and understanding. I have learned never to be judgmental and, above all, never to pontificate. I have seen so many things, yet I feel that I have seen nothing, and my thirst for discovery is insatiable.

The More I Do (Plus J'En Fais)[2]

The more I do
The more remains to be done
The more I drink
The emptier my glass
The more I say

---

[1] From *Deux Guitares / Two Guitars* by Charles Aznavour.
[2] From ?

The less I have left to say
The longer I live
The less I have left to live

Everything comes to an end, but I cannot resign myself to inscribe that word at the bottom of the page. I will leave that to life itself.

APPENDICES

ALBUMS DISCOGRAPHY

Jezebel
Le Feutre taupé
Sur ma vie
Bravos du music-hall
C'est ça
Je m'voyais déjà
Il faut savoir
Qui
La Mamma
Hier encore
65
La Bohème
De t'avoir aimé
Entre deux rêves
Désormais
Idiote je t'aime
Visages de l'amour
Voilà que tu reviens
Je n'ai pas vu le temps passer

Autobiographie
Une première danse
Charles chante Aznavour & Dimey
Toi et moi
Aznavour 92
Je bois
Embrasse-moi
Aznavour 2000
L'Essentiel
Eˆtre
Mes amours
Pierre Roche / Charles Aznavour
Plus Bleu
Jazznavour
20 Chansons d'or
40 Chansons d'or
Récital au palais des Congrès 87 (extraits)
Récital au palais des Congrès 87 (intégral)
Olympia 1978
Palais des Congrès 97/98
Palais des Congrès 2000
Live à l'Olympia
Aznavour/Minnelli

VIDEOS

Charles Aznavour 2000
Aznavour Live à l'Olympia
Aznavour Live 97/98
Aznavour pour toi Arménie
Aznavour au Carnegie Hall
Aznavour-Minnelli
Aznavour au palais des Congrès 1987
Aznavour au palais des Congrès 1994

DVDs

Aznavour/Minnelli au palais des Congrès 1991
Aznavour au palais des Congrès 1994

Aznavour au palais des Congrès 2000
Charles Aznavour au Carnegie Hall
Pour toi Arménie
Live au palais des Congrès (1997/1998)
Olympia (1968, 1972, 1978, 1980)

APPEARNCES IN FILM, TV AND ON STAGE
(Directors in parenthesis)

Feature Films
1936 *La Guerre des gosses* (Jacques Daroy)
1938 *Les Disparus de Saint-Agil* (Christian-Jaque)
1945 *Adieu, chérie* (Raymond Bernard)
1949 *Dans la vie, tout s'arrange* (Marcel Cravenne)
1956 *Un gosse sensass* (Robert Bibal)
1957 *C'est arrivé à trente-six chandelles* (Henri Diamant-Berger)
1957 *Paris Music-Hall* (Stany Cordier)
1958 *Pourquoi viens-tu si tard?* (Henri Decoin)
1959 *La Tête contre les murs* (Georges Franju)
1959 *Le Testament d'Orphée* (Jean Cocteau)
1959 *Les Dragueurs* (Jean-Pierre Mocquy)
1960 *Le Passage du Rhin* (André Cayatte)
1960 *Tirez sur le pianiste* (François Truffaut)
1961 *Horace 62* (André Versini)
1961 *Les lions sont lâchés* (Henri Verneuil)
1961 *Les Petits Matins* (Jacqueline Audry)
1961 *Un taxi pour Tobrouk* (Denys de La Patellière)
1962 *Le Diable et les dix commandements Sketch "Tu ne tueras point"* (Julien Duvivier)
1962 *Les Quatre Vérités Sketch "Les Deux Pigeons"* (René Clair)
1962 *Le Rat d'Amérique* (Jean-Gabriel Albicocco)
1962 *Pourquoi Paris* (Denys de La Patellière)
1962 *Tempo di Roma* (Denys de La Patellière)
1963 *Les Vierges* (Jean-Pierre Mocky)
1964 *Cherchez l'idole* (Michel Boisrond)
1964 *Alta Infedelta Sketch "Péché dans l'après-midi"* (Elio Pétri)
1965 *La Métamorphose des cloportes* (Pierre Granier-Deferre)

1965 *Paris au mois d'août* (Pierre Granier-Deferre)

1965 *Thomas l'imposteur* Georges Franju

1966 *Le facteur s'en va-t-en guerre* (Claude Bernard–Aubert)

1968 *Candy* (Christian Marquand)

1968 *Caroline chérie* (Denys de La Patellière)

1968 *L'Amour* (Richard Balducci)

1969 *Le Temps des loups* (Sergio Gobbi)

1969 *The Adventurers* (Lewis Gilbert)

1969 *The Games* (Michael Winner)

1970 *Un beau monstre* (Sergio Gobbi)

1971 *La Part des lions* (Jean Larriaga)

1971 *Les Intrus* (Sergio Gobbi)

1972 *The Blockhouse* (Clive Rees)

1974 *Dix Petits Nègres* (Peter Collinson)

1976 *Folies bourgeoises* (Claude Chabrol)

1976 *Intervention Delta* (Douglas Hickox)

1978 *Ciao, les mecs!* (Sergio Gobbi)

1979 *Claude François, le film de sa vie* (S. Pavel)

1979 *Le Tambour* (Volker Schlöndorff)

1981 *Qu'est-ce qui fait courir David?* (Élie Chouraqui)

1982 *Édith et Marcel* (Claude Lelouch)

1982 *La Montagne magique* (Hans W. Geissendörfer)

1982 *Les Fantômes du chapelier* (Claude Chabrol)

1982 *Une jeunesse* (Moshé Mizrahi)

1983 *Viva la vie!* (Claude Lelouch)

1986 *Yiddish Connection* (Paul Boujenah)

1988 *Mangeclous* (Moshé Mizrahi)

1991 *Les Années campagne* (Philippe Leriche)

1992 *Il Maestro* (Marion Hansel)

1997 *Pondichery, le dernier comptoir des Indes* (Bernard Favre)

1997 *Le Comédien* (Christian de Chalonge)

1998 *Laguna* (Denis Bezrry)

2001 *Ararat* Atom (Egoyan)

Short Films

1959 *Gosse de Paris* (M. Martin)

1968 *Bambuck* (Adolphe Drey/Jean Kargayan)

Television

1985 Paolino, la juste cause et une bonne raison (François Reichenbach)

1985 *Le Paria* (Denys de La Patellière)

1989 *Laura* (Jeannot Szwarc)

1991 *Il ritorno di Robot* (Pino Passalacqua)

1991 *Le Chinois* (A series in episodes: "La Lumière noire", "L'Héritage", "Le Pachyderme", "Les Somnambules", "Un tour de passepasse") (G. Marx/R. Bodegas- Rojo)

1991 *Le Jockey de l'Arc de Triomphe* (Pino Passalacqua)

1993 *Un alibi en or* (Michèle Ferrand)

1994 *Baldipata* (Michel Lang)

1996 *Baldipata et la voleuse d'amour* (Claude d'Anna)

1996 *Baldipata et les petits riches* (Claude d'Anna)

1997 *Sans cérémonie* (Michel Lang)

1997 *Le Serment de Baldipata* (Claude d'Anna)

1998 *Baldipata et radio-trottoir* (Claude d'Anna)

1999 *Baldipata et Tini* (Michel Mess)

1999 *Les mômes* (Patrick Volson)

2001 *Le Passage du bac* (Olivier Langlois)

Theatre

1933 *Émile et les détectives* (Studio des Champs-Élysées)

1935 *Margot* (Pierre Fresnay Marigny)

1935 *Beaucoup de bruit pour rien* (La Madeleine)

1936 *L'Enfant* (L'Odéon)

With the New Season Company

1939 *Les Fâcheux* (Jean Dasté En tournée)

1939 *Arlequin magicien* (Jean Dasté En tournée)

Revues

1935 *Ça c'est Marseille* (Henri Varna Alcazar – Paris)

1936 *Vive Marseille* (Henri Varna Alcazar – Paris)

1938 *Son excellence (*Théâtre des Variétés)